plagued

Australia's two years of hell
– the inside story

plagued

SIMON BENSON
and Geoff Chambers

PANTERA
PRESS

PANTERA
PRESS

First published in 2022 by Pantera Press Pty Limited
www. PanteraPress.com

A Cataloguing-in-Publication entry for this work is available from the National Library of
Australia.

ISBN 978-0-6454767-5-0 (Paperback)
ISBN 978-0-6454767-6-7 (eBook)

Cover Design: Luke Causby, Blue Cork
Cover Photos: Adam Taylor, Sam Mooy/Stringer Getty Images #1279749177, Quinn Rooney/Staff
Getty Images 1346984770, Jono Searle/Stringer Getty Images #1279730625
Publisher: John M. Green
Author Photos: Courtesy *The Australian*
Printed and bound in Australia by McPherson's Printing Group

The paper this book is printed on is certified against the Forest
Stewardship Council' Standards. McPherson's Printing Group holds
FSC' chain of custody certification SA-COC-005379. FSC' promotes
environmentally responsible, socially beneficial and economically viable
management of the world's forests.

To Harry, Elsie and Molly

CONTENTS

PROLOGUE

*P*LAGUED ATTEMPTS TO document the two and half years of the Covid-19 pandemic and the Morrison government's response to it, viewing it through the prism of what went on inside the cabinet room as the government grappled with the greatest geopolitical challenge in generations.

This was a period, and these were events, that changed Australia forever.

The pandemic delivered an economic, health and social shock to the world, the likes of which had not been experienced since the Spanish flu and the Great Depression.

And then, on 21 May 2022, Australia underwent another great upheaval. This time it was political. And just like the pandemic, the 2022 federal election will enter the history books as an event that comprehensively reshapes the nation's future.

A wave of discontent swept through the nation's political architecture, shaking the foundations of the two-party system. Never had Australians so conclusively rejected both the major parties that, between them, had provided the country with an unprecedented period of postwar political stability.

Despite the unquestionable success of the Morrison government in steering the country through the worst of a one-in-100-year crisis, when the voters finally had their say, they inflicted on the Liberal Party a crushing defeat.

Some inside the Liberal and Labor camps compared the outcome to Winston Churchill's postwar loss to Labour's Clement Attlee in the 1945 UK general election, which proved that incumbency during a crisis accounted for little once it had passed.

The scale of the Coalition's electoral losses on 21 May was so great that it stole from the Liberal Party a potential future leader, Treasurer Josh Frydenberg, as a generation of moderate Liberal Party MPs were swept from office by a franchised 'teal' brand of independents campaigning on climate action, women's rights and integrity in politics.

While the swing against the government was profound, it showed no great love for Labor. While Labor won enough seats to narrowly form government, it was elected on a record low primary vote of under 33 per cent. Two in three voters had rejected Labor.

Regardless, the election result was seen as a categorical revolt against Prime Minister Morrison. By the time of the campaign, he had become deeply unpopular, a lightning rod for the frustration, fatigue and anger felt by so many Australians.

Voters appeared intent on erasing their memories of the past two and half years by embracing Labor's promise of 'safe change' under a government led by Anthony Albanese.

The virus had taken a back seat to other domestic issues.

Morrison, Frydenberg and the retiring Health minister Greg Hunt, the principal architects of the pandemic response, believed they had saved the country.

And on any comparative assessment, they would be right to think so. The economic, social and health outcomes for Australia were among the most impressive of all the nations of the OECD.

The macro-economic picture reflected the success of the government's pandemic policy settings, which set the country up for its lowest unemployment rate in 48 years. Jobs and lives had undeniably been saved.

Morrison's concern about the rise of an arc of autocracy with China and Russia, and his strong pushback against China's coercion and aggressive stance in the Asia-Pacific, had also alerted the West to the new strategic challenge.

His signing of the AUKUS nuclear submarine agreement with

the US and the UK was one of the most significant defence decisions an Australian government had made in decades.

Recognition for the accomplishments of the administration – preventing 40,000 deaths, saving thousands of businesses from closure, returning the country to full employment amid an economic crisis, encouraging one of the highest vaccination rates in the world and securing a strategically important new defence partnership – was not shared by the electorate.

Rising cost-of-living pressures, fuelled by runaway inflation and low wages growth, had quickly become the new post-pandemic economic discussion.

But there was more that drove voters from the government: mistakes, gaffes and scandals.

On one side were those arguing that the Liberal Party had lost the wealthy inner-city enclaves that once defined its base by failing women voters and not doing enough to address climate change. This stood in contrast to another view that the party had abandoned its Menzian base – the suburban family – and that by failing to properly articulate conservative values it could no longer define what it stood for.

Morrison also lost the politics.

Early on, he had made a strategic decision that as prime minister during a crisis, he needed to vacate the field of day-to-day combat. The ordinary stuff of politics.

His colleagues accused Morrison of not doing enough to take on state premiers who, unsurprisingly, used the stature and prominence that his novel national cabinet afforded them to also campaign against him.

The irony was not lost on the prime minister. But what was the alternative?

Nor did Morrison do enough to challenge Labor's campaign to define him as electorally aloof, out of touch and absent.

Labor had prosecuted a relentless case against the government's every misstep, portraying it as slow-moving and reactive. Such as with the vaccine rollout.

When that perception spread to the dire, albeit transitory shortage of rapid antigen tests over the summer of 2021/2022, Labor's narrative began to write itself.

There wasn't a single issue that would explain the Coalition's comprehensive defeat but crucial to it were the loss of Morrison's personal appeal, the mistakes he felt he had apologised for and his mishandling and misreading of an issue such as the treatment of women.

He may have been the first prime minister to serve a full term since John Howard, but the Coalition was seeking a fourth term in office weighed down by the political baggage that a government accumulates from being in power for almost a decade.

While the pandemic was fading in the voters' rear-view mirror as the election approached and passed, the outcome did nothing to alter Australia's other great challenge, one that persisted throughout the pandemic and which will endure well into this century: China.

The period 2020 to 2022 saw Australia's leaders forced to deal with crisis after crisis like almost never before. *Plagued* tells that story.

CHAPTER 1

We've been here before

*What has been will be again, what has been done will be done
again, there is nothing new under the sun ...*

Ecclesiastes 1:9

MORE THAN 100 years before the first wave of Covid-19
arrived by plane and by ship, Australia's ports were the
gateway to another global cataclysm. Rising from the mud, butchery
and horror of the trench warfare that had raged across Western
Europe for four years spread a pandemic that would eventually kill
between 50 and 100 million people globally, at least fivefold the
death toll of the Great War. More than a third of the world's citizens
would be infected with what came to be called the Spanish flu.

Geographically remote and, in 1918, culturally adolescent,
Australia had a population of less than 5 million. Its leaders knew
that distance would not protect it from the virus or its unknowable
consequences.

The Spanish flu would not only test the political structures
of a fledgling federation but challenge the youthful notions of a
germinal national identity.

It would also inflict a misery with profound implications.

Australia would ultimately bounce back from it significantly
less scarred than many other nations, as it would more than a
century later when tested again, having found its own unique
yet imperfect road through adversity. The rich parallels between
then and now raise the central question of whether the world, and
indeed Australia, had learned the lessons of history.

While there is no consensus on where the Spanish flu originated, that history, or at least one version of it, was believed to have begun in late January 1918 in the remote, rural and sparsely populated US county of Haskell, Kansas, where a local doctor, Loring Miner, noticed something strange about his patients.

'Miner had seen influenza often,' wrote American historian John M. Barry in *The Great Influenza*, discerning that the likely origins of the Spanish flu could be traced back to this obscure region on the semi-arid high plains of the US Midwest, an hour's drive from Dodge City.[1] '[Dr Miner] diagnosed the disease as influenza but he had never seen influenza like this,' wrote Barry. 'This was violent, rapid in its progress through the body and sometimes lethal. This influenza killed.'

It was rapid in its spread through Haskell County but then it seemed to peter out. The first official health notification, prompted by Dr Miner's warnings, wasn't published until 5 April, two months later, when the weekly US Public Health Reports impassively noted severe illness in 18 people and the death of three civilians.[2]

The affected area was isolated. It was felt unlikely that with such a small and dispersed population, especially in that pre-globalised era, the disease would spread beyond its geographical limits. What officials didn't count on was the war.

While Haskell County is documented as having the first official outbreak of the Spanish flu, the question as to where it started remains unanswered. 'We don't know and will probably never know,' Barry said in 2020, sixteen years after publication of his book. 'The best evidence points to China. Other theories suggest France or Vietnam.'[3]

Mystery still surrounds the precise biological ancestry of Spanish flu, an H1N1 influenza virus of avian origin, as well as the moment in history that it most likely passed from a domestic or wild bird population to humans.

What is now acknowledged, though, is that the overcrowded, unsanitary conditions of the land war in Europe and the movement of troops helped spread the disease swiftly and silently to all corners of the planet.

It wasn't long before it had taken hold in South Africa, South America and Asia. India, where it was referred to as the Bombay Fever, would become the most savagely afflicted country, registering up to 18 million deaths.

Its popular name – Spanish flu – is owed to censorship. The warring nations, worried about morale, refused to disclose how viciously the disease was spreading through their military ranks. Spain, a neutral country in the raging war, had no such hesitancy. Its media was issuing daily reports of how the virus was decimating the population.

*

The accidental prime minister

The virus was only just beginning its voyage across the Atlantic aboard American troop carriers when Australia's prime minister Billy Hughes departed by ship on 26 April 1918 to attend a meeting of the Imperial War Cabinet convened by British prime minister David Lloyd George. Hughes sailed to Canada and the US before arriving in London just over three months later.

News of plague-like outbreaks in other parts of the world took its time to reach Australia. It wasn't until July 1918, according to an account by Australian socialist historian Humphrey McQueen, that commonwealth quarantine officials were alerted to 'the existence of a new influenza type'.[4]

Unlike other influenzas, the 'Spanish' variety came on rapidly with fits of fever, violent bouts of expulsion, an unproductive cough, severe headache and in most cases a disturbing shift in the colour of the skin to a blueish purple. It often led to fatal complications through pneumonia.

In almost an historical prequel to US president Donald Trump's alleged joke about injecting disinfectant to counter Covid-19, the best medical advice Australian health authorities could provide in 1919 was to use a mouthwash of boric acid, borax, a teaspoon of salt and a teaspoon of baking soda regularly gargled in a mixture of near-to-boiling water.

The NSW Department of Public Health also advised that patients should consider a daily evacuation of the bowels – as if it were needed, considering the symptoms – by ingesting Epsom salts, citrate of magnesia 'or some such purgative'. In the case of collapse, a hot compress was to be applied over the region of the heart while the patient was to be provided with sips of brandy until they were revived.[5]

By September, official reports were filtering through to the NSW government of 'devastating outbreaks' of influenza in South Africa and America.[6] And by October, it had arrived in New Zealand. Australian ports were bound to be next.

Hughes – now in Britain – contemplated returning home immediately. Like most of the rest of the world, Australia was war weary and barely prepared for what was to come. However, the end of war was in sight. He believed that the prudent course was to stay on in Europe to ensure Australia had a seat at the table during the Paris Peace Conference.

Hughes had left the running of the country to his Treasurer, William Alexander Watt, an almost accidental acting prime minister, and a man few Australians have ever heard of, yet one who turned out to be eminently capable.

The 47-year-old Watt had no misgivings about his abilities to lead the country against a great scourge. Historical accounts of the time depict Watt, the 11th and youngest child of Scottish immigrants, as precocious but highly astute with youthful dreams of becoming a top-flight orator. Indeed, he became a powerful force in Victorian state politics, as premier and thereafter a leading federal figure of the Nationalist Party under Hughes, for whom he had little if any personal affection.

'With deep-set eyes, Watt had a broad, pugnacious face and was clean-shaven,' according to the *Australian Dictionary of Biography*.[7] Portrayed as a complex but brilliant character, a champion debater and a man with little tolerance for pomp and ceremony, he would show even less patience for the states when it came to fighting the flu.

'Known in middle age as William, Will or Willy (never as Bill [or Billy like his prime minister]), he began to compensate for his early teetotalism and remained a pipe-smoker. His manner was breezy, his humour witty though mordant, his aplomb marred by fits of temper.'[8]

After Hughes' departure, Watt continued to address the nation's financial dilemma, due to its ballooning war debt. He also used the time to prepare for the arrival of the pandemic.

As a first line of defence against this new but unseen enemy, Watt decided that Australia's international borders had to be closed. And that is precisely what the federal government did, on 17 October 1918. With news of outbreaks in New Zealand, and ships known to be en route, the Australian Quarantine Service enacted a maritime quarantine.

There had been reports in the media of local Spanish flu outbreaks from as early as July but these were dismissed by authorities as cases of ordinary seasonal illness.

The first infected ship, the *Mataram*, arrived in Darwin a day later, on 18 October, via Singapore. It was immediately interned.[9] A week later, on 25 October, a vessel from New Zealand landed in Sydney. The infected passengers were taken off and incarcerated at North Head quarantine station, the natural gateway to Sydney Harbour.

Over 26 and 27 November 1918 – in the shade of the Armistice signed just two weeks earlier – the Commonwealth and state governments held a crisis meeting in Melbourne to discuss contingencies for a 'threatened invasion' by the disease. At this Melbourne Special Conference, Watt and the state health ministers, along with the British Medical Association representatives from each state and the Minister for Quarantine of the Commonwealth, resolved to adopt a national approach to deal with the potential domestic outbreak of disease, which was given the name of 'Pneumonic Influenza'.[10]

In a telegram to the premiers on the conclusion of the summit, Watt summarised the outcome and recommendations, urging them all to sign the communiqué.

In view of the heavy mortality attendant on epidemics of pneumonic influenza in other countries and the evidence that its spread coincides with the rate of human travel, this conference is of the opinion that it is desirable in the public interest to take any measures to check public travel that are at all likely to lessen the spread of the disease.

It is recognised that such restriction does not afford an absolute safeguard and is liable to prove ineffective at some stage in the course of the epidemic but the conference, while recognizing this, nevertheless considers that the attempt to limit the original epidemic by this means should be made and should be continued until proven unsuccessful, in order to give neighbouring states time to complete their organization and also to afford some delay which may remit in some diminution of the virulence of this epidemic.[11]

From a nascent federation, less than two decades old, Watt had just fashioned a template for what and what not to do when, a century later, the world and Australia would once again be plunged into a viral darkness.

He outlined the thirteen conditions, which all the parties agreed to, based largely around the division of quarantine powers and internal border controls.

The federal government was to take responsibility for maritime and land quarantine facilities, as per the powers vested to the Commonwealth under the constitution. The states would be responsible for building emergency hospitals, vaccination centres and providing the necessary medical and nursing staff as well as police. They would also take responsibility for the public awareness campaigns required to keep the populace informed.[12]

The quarantine system worked for a time and the agreement for national cooperation effectively stopped the virus entering the community. Between October 1918 and the beginning of January 1919, Australia remained free of Spanish flu as far as anyone knew. More than 320 ships were intercepted. Over half carried the infection. Many of those infected died in quarantine stations built almost a century earlier to protect the island nation from scourges such as measles, scarlet fever, typhus fever and even syphilis. Fuelled by the grim characterisations in the media of another 'black death', there was a constant and palpable fear that at any time, there could be an outbreak.

This honeymoon phase had a tangible and lasting outcome. It also allowed Australia to play what the government believed was an ace: the Commonwealth Serum Laboratories. Conscious of Australia's vulnerability to supply chains for medicines – exposed during previous pandemics, of which there had been several, including the Russian flu of 1889 – the government had established the CSL facility in 1916 for the sole purpose of locally manufacturing vaccines. CSL was among the first institutions in the world to begin work on an experimental vaccine for the Spanish flu, and it produced 3 million doses by June 1919.

Coming a decade before the discovery of penicillin, and unknown to science at the time, the Spanish flu was a virus and not bacterial as had been assumed. As a consequence, the CSL inoculation didn't work against the virus itself. It had no hope of doing that. But it's believed the therapy might have lessened the severity of the secondary bacterial pneumonia infections that proved so lethal elsewhere.

The Spanish flu affected young, presumably healthier adults more than the groups normally at risk, such as children and the elderly. Men were more likely to be struck down than women.

Such were the early successes prior to the first wave that the NSW government prematurely hailed its achievements, claiming its 'precautionary measures' – including a free inoculation of questionable efficacy – had kept the virus at bay.

But it was quarantining of vessels, isolation of the sick and the mandatory use of face masks that would prove most effective at first.

*

Recalcitrant premiers: Shoot the returning soldiers?

Watt's prediction that the precautions were merely buying time was realised when on 24 January 1919, a 'suspicious case of illness' appeared at the No. 4 Randwick Military Hospital in Sydney's eastern suburbs.

In a 1920 report to the NSW Parliament, the Director General of Public Health, Robert Paton, detailed the event. 'This patient had arrived overland from Melbourne on the previous day; within a few days several other cases were reported, in each instance the patient being a recent arrival from the southern capital. When the State was first known to be invaded, every precaution possible was taken to limit the spread of the infection but without avail.'

Victoria's failure to report the case, apparently an act of deliberate obfuscation, shattered the national agreement and triggered indignant responses from the other states.

The NSW government considered Victoria's delay in notifying the national director of quarantine of a known Melbourne case was an egregious breach. It withdrew from the federal agreement and slammed the border between New South Wales and Victoria shut. With the November plan effectively shelved, every state went its own way.

Watt's troubles with the premiers had begun.

This was the pivotal moment that, through a haphazard series of events set Australia's federation on a new and uncharted course – one which would be repeated a century later. It was also the beginning of a great social upheaval.

The virus would come in three waves in Australia between March and the end of 1919. The first wave was mild and the death rate low. The following two waves saw some people dying within hours of developing symptoms, suffocating from the fluid filling their lungs.

'The public was stunned by the ferocity of the pandemic and newspapers fanned public unease with regular reports of cases and deaths and lurid descriptions of former plagues,' wrote Macquarie University researchers Peter Curson and Kevin McCracken in a paper for the NSW Public Health Bulletin in 2006.[13]

'There were reports of people waking fine in the morning and being dead from influenza by nightfall. With so many people off work due to illness, normal social services and activities were severely disrupted. Thousands sought popular cures and medicines ... People shunned outsiders and interstate visitors fearing they were a potential source of infection ... Over 5000 children lost one or both parents.'

Over the course of the next 12 months, Australians would experience death, social deprivation and harrowing tragedy. Schools would be closed, pubs shut, public gatherings banned, and internal hard borders imposed.

Families would wake to witness the city streets sprayed with disinfectant before queuing up to get inoculated.

Society would be divided into the rebellious and the compliant.

Once the virus crossed the quarantine threshold, the complexities of dealing with a pandemic, and more importantly the difficulty of containing outbreaks within a nation of sovereign-minded states, quickly became apparent. As did the difficulties for Watt in navigating the often haughty positions taken by the provincial leaders.

The National Museum of Australia notes that 'tensions in the new Federation surfaced as the other states viewed Victoria's delay in confirming the outbreak as a breach of the November agreement made with the Commonwealth. Soon each state made their own arrangements for handling and containing outbreaks, including organising their own border controls'.[14]

These internal border measures, unsurprisingly, inspired the first point of conflict among the states, and between the states and the commonwealth. The chief argument was over which jurisdiction would provide the patrols to guard the state boundaries. Watt was forced to clarify it a month later when, on Christmas Eve, he sent a telegram to the premiers to remind them of what they had agreed to in November with the 13-point plan:

> In order that traffic may be restricted as contemplated in the resolution of the Conference it will be necessary that the various roads across the border be strictly guarded.
>
> With a view of being in readiness to take immediate action should the necessity arise, it is suggested that the police department of your State be requested to be in a position to reinforce the police at the border roads in order to maintain a night and day control ... and to allow no person to cross the border unless he produces satisfactory evidence that he is a bona-fide resident living within 10 miles [16 kilometres] of the border.[15]

Watt had put the states on notice about what he expected of them.

All the states replied, agreeing to use their own police to patrol the borders, except for Tasmania, which felt that because it had no land border with the mainland, there was no reason to patrol something that didn't exist.[16]

And while New South Wales agreed, it subsequently protested. On 26 January, NSW premier William Holman, with his state about to be shut down, cabled Watt, a fellow Nationalist. Due to a lack of policing resources, he asked for 75 military personnel to patrol the NSW-Victoria border. With Watt refusing the request point blank, Holman put Sydney – a city of just under 500,000 – into a virtual lockdown, a move that helped to slow the spread.[17]

But it didn't contain it.

On 28 January the Consultative Medical Council issued advice which prompted the NSW government to take first steps in containing the spread of the disease, beginning with the closure of all libraries, schools, churches, theatres, public halls, and 'places of indoor resort for public entertainment'.[18]

'This was followed on 30 January by a trifecta of proclamations: people were required to wear masks covering the mouth and nose; the congregation of people in public spaces was disallowed; and restrictions were placed on crossing from Victoria into NSW,' according to an historical summary of the pandemic contained in the NSW State Archives and Records.[19]

'The requirements applied firstly to metropolitan Sydney, but soon spread to cover the entire State. The Consultative Medical Council also made a general recommendation that the best "natural resistance" to the disease was fresh air.'

A decree issued by Holman and published in the *Sydney Morning Herald* on 3 February mandated the wearing of masks for the entire NSW population, effective immediately:

A danger greater than war faces the State of NSW and threatens the lives of all.

Each day the progress of the battle is published in the press. Watch out for it. Follow the advice and the fight can be won.

Already the efforts made by the government have had the effect of keeping New South Wales figures down. But everybody is not yet working so from TO-DAY on the government insists that the many shall not be placed in danger for the few and that EVERYONE SHALL WEAR A MASK.

Those who are not doing so are not showing their independence – they are showing their indifference for the lives of others – for the lives of the women and the helpless little children who cannot help themselves.[20]

While different restrictions were imposed in various states, with some states doing very little, further impositions were placed on Sydneysiders and across New South Wales throughout February as the initial strategies failed to stem the spread throughout the state. Racecourses were closed and public meetings banned.

Fines of £20 were introduced and doctors given the power to place restrictions on people who might have come in contact with the infected.

Frictions between the Commonwealth and the states meant that with the November agreement in disarray, there was no uniform approach to checking the spread of the virus. Watt would become so frustrated that he would eventually withdraw from the national agreement as well.

As McQueen wrote, it was not a 'universal unpreparedness' that caused the ensuing chaos but the inherent tensions within the federation, which faced two fundamental challenges, aside from preventing deaths.[21]

The first was how to manage the return of Australian troops from Europe, many of whom could have been exposed to the virus. The second was how to maintain a uniform cooperation between six former British colonies.

Watt was constantly dealing with competing demands, inspired less by political partisanship than a fierce parochialism among the state leaders. For instance, Watt had come under pressure from several states to establish quarantine stations along the internal borders.

In a 6 February telegram to Victorian premier Harry Lawson, also a Nationalist Party member, Watt refused what he deemed a state responsibility:

> The Commonwealth Government ... is not prepared to establish land quarantine stations at the various State borders.
>
> Effective quarantine administration is so impracticable in the circumstances and the risks involved in the event of an outbreak of the epidemic in a hastily established and ill-equipped quarantine station at border presents such possibilities of tragic results that the Commonwealth government does not in any circumstance feel justified in running the risk of establishing border stations, which would necessarily have no proper sanitary or hospital convenience.[22]

Watt had similar exchanges when the country's transcontinental train was seized by the West Australian government near Kalgoorlie and incoming passengers quarantined. South Australia, meanwhile, begged for federal funding to pay for the use of its own police force.

Tasmania, which enjoyed the lowest infection rate in the world, was particularly recalcitrant and went as far as petitioning the king for a suspension of the constitution in what McQueen described as prayer 'for deliverance from federal control'.[23]

Watt's clashes with the Queensland Labor government were among the fiercest. While Queensland had agreed to the terms of the November Conference, by the end of January 1919 it was still refusing to formally sign.

With Queensland's premier T.J. Ryan, also away in London, only to be later struck down by influenza, Watt sent a blunt telegram on 30 January to then acting Labor premier, Teddy Theodore, demanding a reply as to why the state had not yet signed:

> Re quarantine agreement arrived at by conference Commonwealth and State authorities November twenty seventh have not yet received formal acceptance by your government ... as emergency may arise any day please give matter your attention otherwise proclamation and operation of agreement would be difficult if not impossible.[24]

Watt and the Queensland government didn't have to wait long for that emergency to arise. It came when several troop ships sailed into Queensland waters.

Two days later, John Hunter, a minister without portfolio in the Ryan government who appeared to be acting on Ryan's behalf, sent an urgent telegram back to Watt threatening to stop the troop vessels landing in Brisbane's port:

> There seems to be grounds for supposing 1300 soldiers are about to be returned to Queensland. Extremely difficult to prevent them breaking quarantine if landed and detained at Lytton (quarantine facility). I strongly recommend quarantining them in ship that brings them into Brisbane waters.[25]

On 3 February, Watt shot back a response demanding that Queensland stick to its agreement and allow the soldiers off the boat at a recently constructed quarantine station on the mouth of the Brisbane River:

> Quarantining soldiers at Lytton is necessary if effect is to be given to agreements between the States and Commonwealth. Similar numbers of soldiers have been quarantined frequently on other quarantine stations in Australia during past three months without incident. See no reason for trouble at Lytton.[26]

Watt refrained from sending the full contents of advice he had received from the naval secretary, George Lionel Macandie, that same day. Macandie had asked Watt to send Hunter a far more colourful telegram:

> Referring to your telegram 2nd February regarding disembarkation of troops and handling of troops destined for Queensland. Unless the government is prepared to resort to the most extreme measures (which may and probably will result in firearms being used and men shot) it is thought that the men will not submit to being retained on board ship in more than one State in quarantine.[27]

Watt toned it down, simply saying that it would be unwise to keep the troops afloat and strongly urging Hunter to comply.

Hunter eventually relented, but he was particularly concerned about the *Karoola* – a ship due to dock at first light the following day – and for good reason.

Within 12 hours of being interned at Lytton, four troops jumped camp and ran amok through Brisbane.

Hunter alerted Watt by telegram on 5 February. In his curt reminder that Watt had ignored his concerns, Hunter wrote:

> Police officers who are acting under federal authority report last evening four soldiers who arrived from overseas during the

afternoon by steamer Karoola broke out of quarantine camp at Lytton and came to Brisbane by train.

They visited friends in various parts of suburbs and were taken in custody while on their way back to Lytton at 5.30 this morning. The houses visited have been isolated.

I wired you protesting against your decision to land soldiers at Lytton pointing out that landing anybody of soldiers coming from infected State was a direct menace and danger to citizens of Queensland ...

That protest though supported by medical men of military experience and also by competent military experts was ignored with the result that there is no certainty but that this criminal disregard of advice tendered may lead to the gravest of consequences.

I again assure you of the desire of the Queensland government to cooperate with federal authorities in every way in preventing the spread of disease to Queensland.

I am given to understand that it is the intention of the military authorities to land two thousand five hundred soldiers in Queensland during the present month and I venture to hope that the failure of the experiment of attempting quarantine soldier on the mainland will prevent a repetition of the mistake of yesterday.[28]

It didn't. Watt continued with his policy despite similar incidents occurring in other ports in other states. He refused further requests for military guards to be posted at the quarantine stations.

On land just as at sea, tensions also grew over the treatment of citizens used to travelling freely within Australia, without regard to internal borders, fuelled by the inconsistencies between state jurisdictions.

Queensland had already broken its pledge to the November agreement by closing its border on 29 January, two days after New South Wales and 24 hours after Victoria, a foreshadowing of scenes that would be repeated without shame more than 100 years later.

The closure was so swift and draconian that Queenslanders on the southern side of the twin cities of Coolangatta and Tweed Heads, having gone to work that morning, couldn't get home for almost two weeks.

The quarantine camps established along the border were so abysmal that they required daily disinfection. The story was similar on the NSW-Victorian border.

The situation became dire and the intractability of the states so entrenched that by the end of April, Watt had threatened economic sanctions if the quarantine measures weren't lifted.

*

Anti-vaxxers revolt

Ironically, it was only after the virus eventually spread across the country, making border restrictions meaningless, that some stability was restored to the federation.

Watt's dilemma hadn't been confined to recalcitrant premiers. The Commonwealth public service was resistant to an important measure designed to stop the spread of the virus. Vaccination.

Cables between the Postmaster-General's Department and Watt reveal how frustrated he got trying to compel those who worked for the government to do their part.

As early as 29 January, the Director of Quarantine, John Cumpston, advised Watt that while it was 'desirable' if not necessary for the public service to be inoculated, he knew of no regulation by which it could be mandated. [29]

In an 18 February cable, the secretary of the Postmaster-General's department, Justinian Oxenham, told Watt of increasing incidences of public servants objecting to vaccinations:

Several officials this department [Brisbane] have refused in writing to submit to inoculation.

Shall be glad of advice as to how they are to be dealt with.

They have been definitely warned inoculation is compulsory

16

in accordance with the direction [of the] acting prime minister. [30]

A dispatch from the department's Hobart office reported similar rebellion.

> I shall be glad of advice as to what action if any is to be taken against those officers who object to inoculation. There are some 10 to 12 who have refused inoculation on the grounds that they do not believe it has any efficacy ...[31]

An estimated 50 per cent of Sydney's population had queued up to have the vaccine administered voluntarily in the belief that it would work, despite the absence of any clinical trials. By the end of February, Watt was forced to concede that the government had no legal power to force inoculation among the public service.

This wasn't Watt's only problem. There was also the question of how to classify an infection no one knew much about.

On 15 February 1919, Percy Sheaffe, the acting secretary of Home and Territories, sent a memo to the Attorney General's Department asking it to 'kindly prepare a proclamation declaring Pneumonic Influenza to be an infectious disease under the Public Health Ordinance, No. 4 of 1912 for the Territory for the seat of Government'.

He was acting on the advice of Quarantine Director Cumpston, who had three days earlier told him the disease 'may well be made notifiable'.[32] A declaration would give the authorities the means to track the spread and contain it where possible.

But on 24 February the Attorney General's Department's acting secretary responded that there was no simple mechanism available to make the flu a notifiable disease:

> I understand that it is desired to make pneumonic influenza notifiable disease. I know of no way in which this can be done by proclamation but it might be done by an amendment of

the infectious disease regulations 1914 and I am accordingly forwarding a draft amendment for your consideration.

Eventually, the regulations were amended by adding 'pneumonic influenza' after the entry for 'membranous croup'. Yet within five months, New South Wales rescinded its own proclamation that the Spanish flu was a notifiable disease, claiming it had become a pointless exercise.

The official records show that between January and August 1918 there were 21,700 cases notified in New South Wales. But the actual numbers were something like 13 times greater, according to a 1919 report from the Director-General of Public Health:[33]

> The notified cases do not, however, indicate the number of persons who have suffered from the disease. The Deputy Director General in his extremely able and exhaustive report estimates that in the metropolitan area alone 290,000 people or over 36 per cent of the population contracted the disease in a more or less virulent form.[34]

The economic impacts of the Spanish flu were significant but not well documented. By April, the NSW government had established a compensation board to deal with enterprises suffering material loss by being forced into economic hibernation. This led to the Influenza Epidemic Relief Act that allowed for businesses to claim rent, rates, taxes and other expenses.

'The Act resulted in a bewildering number and variety of claims being made most of which were not covered by the terms of the Act,' according to the NSW State Archives.[35] 'The claimants consisted mainly of private schools, wine and billiard saloons, hotels, picture theatres and play theatres.'

Fewer than 20 per cent of the claims were found to be valid and were paid.

*

Island fortress

Over 1918-19, the Spanish flu ran its course, globally, and pitilessly, after four waves which had by 1921 infected up to a third of the planet's population. The total number of deaths can only be guessed at, considering the lack of any reliable method of calculating the human toll at the time. Some estimates suggest as many as 100 million people may have lost their lives to it.

While the first wave was considered to be mild, which explained Cumpston's initial impressions that it was simply another seasonal flu of no particular significance, with each subsequent wave, it grew in its lethality until herd immunity eventually snuffed it out.

In Australia the swift actions to close international borders and delay its onset meant that by the time it took hold, its virulency was not as great as it could have been.

Nonetheless, it heaped tragedy upon tragedy in a country still mourning the war dead, and exposed the substandard living conditions in many parts of the continent at that time.

By December 1919, more than 4000 Sydneysiders had died from Spanish flu and 2 million Australians had contracted the disease. In today's terms, that would equate to more than 25,000 dead in Sydney alone.

Curson and McCracken[36] described the Spanish flu as 'among the greatest natural disasters of recorded history rivalling the Black Death of the 14th century in mortality and social and economic effects ... While the death rate was lower [in Australia] than many other countries the pandemic was a major demographic and social tragedy affecting the lives of millions of Australians.'

Anywhere between 12,000 and 15,000 Australians lost their lives, less than a quarter of the number of Australian soldiers killed during the Great War.

Yet at 2.7 deaths per 1000 infections, Australia's mortality rate was among the lowest in the world.

Australians had risen to the challenge. And despite the political posturing and argy-bargy, the newly formed federation withstood forces that could have easily seen it crumble.

CHAPTER 2

A day from hell

THURSDAY 23 JANUARY 2020 had an 'end of days' feel about it for the tight crew of Scott Morrison's senior staff and advisers, a team of around 10, some of whom had cancelled leave and returned to Canberra.

For most of January, the rich western slopes of the nearby Great Dividing Range were either charred by fires or browned by drought and the Canberra air thick with a choking carbon haze.

Today, it was a blistering 34.9°C, though not as bad as the scorching start to the year when the bush capital recorded its highest ever temperature, 44°C, with pollution levels the worst of any city in the world, beyond even Delhi, due to smoke from the bushfires up and down the NSW coast.

The tinge of the sky and acrid whiff in the air added a physical dimension to the sense of doom within the Prime Minister's Office (PMO), with Morrison politically damaged over the Hawaiian family holiday he had to cut short in December because of the fires and the human tragedy they had inflicted.

But another potential crisis appeared on the radar inside the PMO that Thursday morning, after a briefing – the third in as many days – from Australia's chief medical officer, Dr Brendan Murphy, a kidney specialist who most Australians had never heard of but who would soon emerge as a man of unflappable calm behind his serious, bushy brows.

Murphy had been in Rome with his family for Christmas, having arrived back in mid-January to learn of reports out of China about a mystery respiratory illness.

Initially, he had not been overly worried. But that quickly changed as more information came to light about a novel animal coronavirus that had crossed the infection barrier to a human host – most likely from a bat.

He was now bringing Morrison his concerns that Chinese authorities may have been withholding data about what was actually going on.

Overnight, he told Morrison, China's government had locked down three cities, including the suspected source city of Wuhan, whose population was 11 million, almost half of Australia's.

Canberra was acting swiftly. The Department of Foreign Affairs and Trade (DFAT) had already escalated its travel advisory to level 3, explicitly warning Australians against travelling to Wuhan and Hubei province: 'reconsider your need to travel'. A day later DFAT raised it to level 4, 'Do not travel'.[1]

On Murphy's recommendation, the precautionary principle was applied and preparations were underway for a potential global-scale crisis. And this was almost three weeks before the World Health Organization even had a name for the virus (SARS-CoV-2) and the illness it caused (Covid-19).

That 23 January morning, Morrison was informed that China Eastern Airlines flight MU749 from Wuhan was landing in Sydney, and that Australian biosecurity and health officials were scrambling to make sure they could assess disembarking passengers for any signs of illness.

MU749 would be the last flight allowed in from Hubei, the Chinese province where Wuhan is the capital.

That same day, but half a world away in pristine, sub-zero Geneva, Switzerland, the WHO was also discussing the outbreak, their second meeting in 24 hours. In retrospect, their delay in declaring the new virus a Public Health Emergency of International Concern would make the WHO look like it had been asleep at the wheel.

The sense of uncertainty in the face of an unfolding crisis was palpable inside the PMO. Only the day before, Morrison had issued a press release announcing Murphy's appointment as the new secretary of the Department of Health – a public servant's highest possible departmental position. But the CMO – in this case Murphy, a man Morrison had high trust in – is the one inside the department who coordinates the national response to any threats to public health. That morning, one day later, Morrison was telling Murphy his promotion was being delayed in the national interest. Even as the outlines of the looming threat were still coming into focus, Morrison knew he needed to keep the highly experienced Murphy in his current role.

*

'Dad's gone'

The potential national and international health crisis was not the only thing weighing on Morrison's mind. Unknown to almost everybody, he was consumed by deep personal sorrow.

At 9pm the previous night, he'd taken a call during a dinner he was hosting at The Lodge for Treasurer Josh Frydenberg and Deputy Prime Minister Michael McCormack, the Nationals leader.

The trio had met to discuss another headache consuming his government; what to do about the deputy Nationals leader, Agriculture and Sports minister Bridget McKenzie and what the media had labelled the 'sports rorts affair'. McKenzie was facing calls for her resignation over a controversial $100 million government grants program and an audit office report suggesting it had been used by the government to fund sporting projects in marginal seats prior to the 2019 election.

The phone call was from the prime minister's elder brother, Alan. Morrison could sense the dread in his brother's voice even before he heard the fateful words, 'Dad's gone.'

Morrison's father John, an 84-year-old former policeman and local mayor, had been in poor health and was living in an aged care home in Sydney's eastern suburbs.

So while Alan's call wasn't a complete shock to Morrison, the news was devastating. And to those around Morrison, it showed.

When close friend and assistant minister Ben Morton stepped into Morrison's commodious office early that Thursday morning, he found the PM sitting at his desk in a pensive mood. Four others were already there: chief of staff John Kunkel, principal private secretary Yaron Finkelstein, director of communications Andrew Carswell and Morrison's executive officer Nico Louw.

Morton and the other four formed the core of the PM's inner circle when it came to day-to-day strategic planning and political counsel.

All were well aware of Morrison's strong connection with his dad, and how much family meant to him. Once Morton heard the news, he assumed Morrison would clear his diary and head back to Sydney to grieve with his loved ones.

The summer bushfires still dominated the PM's thinking. He was badly bruised by the fierce criticism of his family's Hawaiian holiday. The political noise from that was still bellowing out of social media. The bushfire and post-bushfire crisis was also dictating the cabinet's tactical thinking. At an unscheduled strategic cabinet meeting on 6 January – just two weeks after he returned from Hawaii – Morrison led a discussion on plans for a bushfire recovery agency, telling his ministers that Australians had high expectations of the Commonwealth's role in combating the fires and driving the recovery.

Today, and more immediately the key event in the schedule, one that was months in the planning, was an historic meeting with Indigenous leaders.

Morrison and Indigenous Affairs minister Ken Wyatt were due to meet with 50 community leaders, representing the peak Indigenous bodies. They'd travelled from all over Australia for a roundtable on Closing the Gap. This would be the first time any prime minister had sat at a table with all those leaders. For some of them, it would be the first time they'd been inside the cabinet room.

Despite the significance of the meeting, Morton wasn't convinced the PM needed to attend in person. Given Morrison had just lost his dad, Morton argued, it would be entirely appropriate if he cancelled his schedule for the entire day and flew back to Sydney.

With an eye to the historical importance of the roundtable, Morrison gave him a flat 'No!'

A press conference was planned for noon. Surely, Morton argued, at least Morrison should cancel that. 'I advised him not to do the press conference; a number of the others did as well,' Morton says in his recollections of that extraordinarily fraught day. 'I said, "Mate, you don't need to go out there today. Your dad has just died." He really didn't want to cancel the meeting with the peaks, and we accepted that. But we didn't see the need to do a press conference.'

Morrison was insistent on doing both.

*

China's mystery virus

Weeks later, when casting his mind back to his meeting with Brendan Murphy that Thursday morning, Morrison registered how much the chief medical officer's tone had shifted since their first face-to-face SARS-CoV-2 briefing of only 48 hours earlier.

Murphy's demeanour had changed over those few days from mild concern to a darkening cloud of unease. And it wasn't just Murphy. Morrison observed a similar change in many other advisers and colleagues, especially with his Health minister, Greg Hunt. The pace and gravity of their discussions over the mysterious pathogen from China were intensifying.

Other than the little China was willing to reveal, not much was known about the new virus. The first reported case is believed to have been on 1 December 2019. But it could have been circulating as far back as October or November.[2]

The first cluster was identified by Chinese physicians on 26 December. It was linked to a local wet market in Wuhan, the Huanan Seafood Wholesale Market, where live animals were sold and butchered. Despite China's denials that this was the source, local authorities closed it down on 1 January.[3]

Outside of China, the wet market theory quickly became the dominant narrative for the origin of the virus.

Suspicion about its source, however, also fell on a Chinese facility, the Wuhan Institute of Virology, widely known to be conducting research into a range of viruses, SARS (severe acute respiratory syndrome), influenza H5N1, Japanese encephalitis and anthrax. The research lab was located in the industrial outskirts of Wuhan's metropolis, on the southern side of the Yangtze River that divided the city.

WHO officials based in China were first alerted to a potential outbreak after spotting a 31 December 2019 media statement on the Wuhan Municipal Health Commission's website, warning about cases of 'viral pneumonia'. From there they began piecing together an emerging health crisis.

Despite speculation and rumours swirling on social media that the virus had been engineered or had spawn from a lab accident, the broad consensus of the scientific community supported the theory of a natural leap from a wild or domestic animal species to humans and that the market was the likely source.

The Chinese government, in an act of deliberate mystification, began peddling the idea that it was imported from the US or through frozen produce.

On New Year's Day, the WHO requested information from Chinese authorities on the reported cluster of 'atypical pneumonia cases in Wuhan'. It also activated its Incident Management Support Team coordinating responses at local, regional and global levels. On 3 January, the WHO's China office received information there were cases in Wuhan of a 'viral pneumonia of an unknown cause'. It took Chinese health officials a further eight days to provide the WHO with a genetic sequence for the new virus – the same day state-owned media reported the country's first death.

This time gap would prove pivotal in the virus's spread and the pandemic's severity as health authorities across the globe, including in Australia, desperately sought answers from the WHO about what was happening on the ground in China.

By mid to late January all countries were at risk, although few realised it.

Thailand had reported its first case on 13 January. Two days later, a person who unknowingly carried the virus left Wuhan for America and before a week had passed, the Atlanta-based Centers for Disease Control and Prevention (CDC) would be confirming that the virus had appeared in the United States.[4] By 16 January, it had spread to Japan, and within days it had shown up in South Korea, Taiwan and Hong Kong.

By mid-January, Australia's health officials, even though they didn't yet fully understand the scale of the threat, were flagging with Morrison that two-way travel with China was potentially risky. Morrison knew he had to address the Australian public even though the medical community were still working out what they were dealing with. The question for the PM was how to elevate the level of public awareness while maintaining a sense of calm. The tone of the messaging was critical.

The way Murphy was reading the situation, the virus could have entered Australia without anyone realising. If not, it was bound to turn up soon.

Gradually, a fuller picture began to emerge. It was the health equivalent of astronomers trying to deduce the Big Bang by looking at shards from ancient stars.

*

'Pandemic of catastrophic proportions'

Despite the developments in China and elsewhere, the government's focus in Australia was still on the deadly bushfires and their aftermath. It was the dominating topic for the first scheduled cabinet meeting of the year, on Monday 20 January.

Morrison urged his colleagues not to forget about the drought and reminded them that, in addition to dealing with these crises, the government had a country to run. He emphasised that by Australia Day, in less than a week's time, the country needed to feel that the government was 'back to business'. He also outlined the next phase of the government's foreign policy agenda for the Indo-Pacific and provided an update on the geopolitical situation with China.

At that stage, the PM was not inclined to make too much of the virus in the cabinet discussion until more was known about it. He kept the details of a phone call he had that morning with Hunt between the two of them.

'The medical advice we are getting on this is really quite serious,' Hunt told Morrison. 'Every fibre of my being says we are going to have to follow that advice.'

Hunt was regarded as having a forensic eye for data and detail. The word 'pandemic' was firmly lodged in his mind long before 'Covid' entered his lexicon. For one thing, his wife, Paula Lindsey, who once worked as an infection control nurse in operating theatres, kept on a bedside table at home a copy of *The Coming Plague*, a 1994 book by award-winning health journalist Laurie Garrett.[5]

When Hunt was made Health minister in January 2017, Paula quipped, 'You better make sure we are prepared.'

Her message was powerfully reinforced when Australia's pandemic planning was one of the first items covered in his three days of incoming departmental briefings, a stark reminder of what epidemiologists believed was an inescapable reality. 'One day this will happen,' an official told him three years before it did happen. 'We don't know how big or small, but it will happen.'

Hunt relayed to the PM a conversation he had just had with Murphy. The CMO, in his typical fashion of cutting to the chase, informed the minister that human-to-human transmission of the virus had been confirmed. No one yet knew if it would spread beyond China to the rest of the world.

Murphy then gave Hunt a warning no Health minister would want to hear: the next day he was going to declare this a disease of pandemic potential under the Biosecurity Act.

The information coming through to Australian Health officials was sufficiently worrying that Murphy brought all state and territory chief health officers into the loop and listed the outbreak on the agenda for that day's meeting of the Australian Health Protection Principal Committee (AHPPC). As the peak health emergency management committee with responsibility for disease control, it was the AHPPC's role to provide advice directly to the prime minister.

Murphy also activated the National Critical Care and Trauma Response Centre, the National Medical Stockpile and the National Incident Room. Its focus was on the logistical health response that might be needed, including ensuring supply chains of medical supplies, and personal protective equipment (PPE) such as face masks, were maintained.

The National Incident Room is run out of the Health Department's complex at Scarborough House in Woden, South Canberra. It was already up and running after the bushfire crisis had triggered a rolling air pollution emergency in Sydney and Canberra. As well, it had only just finished repatriating victims of the White Island volcano disaster in New Zealand, which had claimed 14 Australian lives.

The following morning, Tuesday 21 January, journalists caught a glimpse of Murphy's deepening concern at his media address.

A 'human coronavirus with pandemic potential' was added to the Biosecurity (Listed Human Diseases) Determination 2016.

There would now be daily meetings of the AHPPC and state, territory and Commonwealth health ministers to begin planning work to ensure the state and territory health systems were ready to cope.[6]

Describing the situation as 'rapidly evolving' and admitting that concern was heightened over the past three or four days, Murphy reassured the public, 'We are updating our advice and analysis on a daily basis in partnership with the World Health Organization and very importantly in the Commonwealth in partnership with our state and territory health officials, who have the primary health response in the public health arena.'

Murphy's message was there was no need for panic. 'The risk to the Australian public from this novel virus remains relatively low, although we do need to keep a precautionary and active surveillance of the situation.'

He had reached out to health counterparts among Australia's Five Eyes security and intelligence partners, the US, UK, New Zealand and Canada. In his briefing to the PM that day, Murphy passed on a piece of good news he'd got from them about the virus, chiefly that it wasn't in the same league as SARS in terms of severity of disease.

But events were moving swiftly and by Wednesday 22 January, alarm bells were ringing in the PMO.

Hunt, who was in Melbourne, had received some troubling data-based projections from top departmental staffers, and, recognising their sensitivity, called the PM straightaway.

It was only the day before they had agreed in a private conversation they could never again get caught behind politically during a crisis, like they had with the bushfires. Above all, they would follow the medical advice. 'I want to do this through consensus decision-making,' Morrison told Hunt. 'I want to use all the instruments of state, cabinet, NSC [National Security Committee of Cabinet], the ERC [Expenditure Review Committee].'

What Hunt told Morrison was that early epidemiological modelling was predicting not only a possible pandemic but one of potentially catastrophic proportions.

'We don't know how big this will be,' Hunt admitted, then fell silent while at the other end of the line Morrison considered the stark consequences.

The stakes had just been raised. As had the complexity of the problems the government faced, including ensuring transparency while maintaining public calm. Morrison and his team became singularly focused on staying ahead of the game.

The PM's chief of staff, John Kunkel, was also about to become a central figure as the government moved to a war footing against a microbe it still knew very little about. Kunkel, an economist and former member of John Howard's Cabinet Policy Unit, was taking the view that Canberra should move early, for reasons both political and in the national interest.

'We were still at that point trying to understand the virus. It was still a China, Hubei province issue,' Kunkel recalls. 'There was no sense of the mortality of it. There seemed to be a one-to three-per cent death rate. We just didn't know. The WHO still didn't regard it as a health emergency. We disagreed.'

*

On 23 January, Morrison went ahead with his media conference scheduled for 1pm. It was in the Blue Room at Parliament House, on the ground floor and across the hall from the entrance to his office. The original dual purpose of the conference was to speak to the ongoing bushfire crisis and the Indigenous leaders' roundtable. The chief of the Australian Defence Force, General Angus Campbell, was to stand with Morrison and announce the scaling back of the ADF's bushfire reservist units who were deployed in recovery operations. Given the unfolding health crisis, Morrison added Dr Brendan Murphy to the run sheet.

Morrison chose his words carefully so as not to provoke panic. 'This is a rapidly evolving matter, and we're obviously taking advice from the World Health Organization,' he told the journalists.

The journalists' focus turned to Murphy. China had now recorded 571 cases and 17 deaths, he told them. 'The other developments are that the Chinese authorities have now stopped transport out of Wuhan city, including after the flight today to Sydney. There'll be no more flights from Wuhan city, we're being advised, nor will there be other transport out of Wuhan to other parts of China.

'There have been no reported confirmed cases of the coronavirus in Australia as yet.'

Morrison ended the press conference with some good news on the economic front: a footnote on labour force data released that day showed the unemployment rate had dropped to 5.1 per cent.

He had no sense that day of how central to the nation's economic future and the government's political narrative these data sets would become over the coming two years.[7]

More frustration was in store for the prime minister before the day was out.

While he was talking to the journalists a bushfire had broken out on the perimeter of Canberra's airport.

When Morrison returned to his office, finally focused on getting back to Sydney, Ben Morton drew him aside and explained the fraught logistics. With plumes of smoke obscuring the flight paths of inbound aircraft, the main access roads to the airport cut off, the airport had shut down landings for commercial air traffic. The close personal protection unit of the Australian Federal Police (AFP) was now liaising with the RAAF's 34 Squadron about getting the PM safely out of Canberra.

'If we're unable to get you to the airport,' said Morton, 'you may have to be driven back to Sydney.'

The hint of a shadow crossed Morrison's face. The fallout from his Hawaiian vacation during one of the country's worst bushfire seasons was still dogging him. The criticism was something he'd struggled to fathom at first: he'd made a big effort to visit bushfire-affected areas prior to his Hawaiian trip and hadn't anticipated any backlash. Not for the last time, he would question his political judgement. The political pain had not yet ended; nor had the fires.

News came through that the AFP found a way to get Morrison into the airport via a security access gate to the adjoining military firing range. Before long, he was in the back seat of the PM's BMW X5 tearing through a paddock on his way to the RAAF base on the opposite side of the airport where his plane was ready to depart. Sitting next to him in the car was his senior media adviser Nick Creevey, who had just received a text from Nico Louw, a cool-headed confidant of Morrison who acted as his eyes and ears.

There was even more bad news.

The bushfire crisis wasn't over. Creevey leaned over and relayed the update from Louw. He told the PM that a Hercules C-130 water bomber fighting a fire just south of Canberra had gone down and crashed into an active fire zone in the Snowy Mountains. What they didn't know at the time was that three American air crew piloting the plane were believed dead.

When Morrison finally made it to the tarmac he would be confronted with soldiers preparing to deploy as part of a recovery mission for the downed plane. He addressed them personally and thanked them for their service.

Reflecting later on the events of 23 January, Morrison said, without hesitation, that it was the hardest day of his life.

But things did not ease up. On 25 January, Australia confirmed its first case of Covid-19. A man who'd flown in from Wuhan on 19 January tested positive in Melbourne.[8] Three more returned travellers from Wuhan – who had disembarked in Sydney – would test positive that same afternoon.

Everything was about to change.

CHAPTER 3

The twilight zone

ON SATURDAY 1 February, two days after laying his father to rest in a private ceremony, Scott Morrison sat in his study at Kirribilli House, the Gothic twin-gabled prime ministerial residence on the shores of Sydney Harbour. He was facing a decision no prime minister before him had been forced to contemplate outside of wartime.

Morrison had made up his mind that Australia would have to close its borders to China. It was only a question of when.

Morrison was by then acutely aware of the potential for an escalation of Covid-19 cases coming into the country, which in turn would cause an explosion of local infections. Up until that morning, closing the border to China would have been unthinkable, the consequences too far-reaching, economically and politically. But overnight, US president Donald Trump had announced that his administration was doing just that.

Australia's diplomatic relationship with China was already strained. The decision in 2018 to ban Chinese tech company Huawei from the 5G network, and the urging by Australia for its Five Eyes partners to do the same, had enraged Beijing.

It was the beginning of an accumulation of unjustified grievances the Chinese Communist Party levelled against Australia.

Morrison was acutely aware that closing the border to two-way traffic with China would prompt an even fiercer reaction. But there could be no compromising on public health.

Morrison reached for his phone. It was time to speak with his health minister. When Hunt picked up, Morrison could hear shouts and whoops in the background. Hunt was at a son's cricket match at Balnarring, not far from his home at Mount Martha, a semi-rural coastal township on the Mornington Peninsula, about an hour southeast of Melbourne. A committed exerciser, Hunt was walking laps of the oval in the rain. He's on record as saying that he can tackle anything provided he has his family and running.[1]

'We're going to have to call a National Security Committee meeting today,' Morrison told Hunt. 'I think we need to close the borders [with China].'

'I was about to call you,' said Hunt. He'd only just finished a conversation with Murphy who was also in Melbourne. 'Brendan and I have spoken, and we said the same thing.'

A three-way call was then set up between them. Murphy repeated to Morrison what he had told Hunt, that he had reviewed the epidemiology from overseas counterparts overnight. The virus had spread to every province in China.

'If we want to stop this happening here, we need to shut the borders to China,' Murphy told them.

Morrison said he wanted Murphy to get the AHPPC ready to meet by midday, ahead of a top-secret meeting of the NSC that he was going to call for 2pm. Hunt and Murphy both hot-footed it to the Commonwealth Parliamentary Offices (CPO) at Treasury Place in Melbourne where they met to dial in to the NSC meeting remotely.

Morrison headed to the CPO building on Bligh Street at Circular Quay in Sydney where he had access to a small, highly secure room, one level up from his office. From there he could take command in front of three video screens.

*

One of the first calls Murphy made that morning was to Home Affairs secretary Mike Pezzullo, who was pushing a trolley full of groceries in his local Coles store in Canberra.

Other shoppers would have had no idea that the tall, stern, balding man on the phone, walking through the aisles with his phone to his ear, was being told about a development that would have enormous consequences for them, not least regarding their own shopping habits. When Murphy told him Morrison was closing the border to mainland China, Pezzullo didn't bat an eyelid.

'The initial closure will be for 14 days,' said Murphy, adding that Morrison doubted the measure was going to be as short-term as that.

Since late January, Pezzullo and the relevant agencies had been putting plans in place for a worst-case scenario.

He left Coles immediately, wasting no time setting the wheels in motion. The border-closure decision was made, so the only question was how quickly he could get it done.

At the 2pm NSC meeting, Pezzullo told Morrison and the committee that the border closure to China could be in place that night. Australian Border Force (ABF) commissioner Michael Outram was well prepared.

'Outram and I had a couple of discussions and we thought – at the outside – 12 hours to get all the planes [headed to Australia from China] down. But in the end we were able to execute it in about eight hours,' recalls Pezzullo.

Murphy outlined the latest evidence – that cases of the virus were growing outside the Hubei province – with significant human-to-human transmission.

What he was hearing had changed his view of the situation. He now believed China was under-reporting cases and mortality and he recommended that Australia go immediately to a level-4 'do not travel' alert for the People's Republic of China, not just Hubei province.

This was DFAT's highest category of advisories for travellers. It was reserved for threats of terrorist attacks, violent social unrest or widespread disease.

Murphy also told the NSC that while there was some discussion in the scientific and medical community about whether the virus may have escaped from a laboratory, the wet market theory still seemed the most plausible.

But the main focus of the meeting was operational, on what to do and how to get it all done. Morrison predicted some of the state premiers would be opposed to the border closure so he said he would call them, reminding them that this was a Commonwealth decision, and that he would not be swayed.

The meeting broke up by 3pm.

Morrison stayed back to phone New Zealand's prime minister, Jacinda Ardern. At that point, New Zealand was taking its cues from Australia. The two leaders discussed the need for such a drastic step as shutting off travel to and from China. Ardern agreed and informed Morrison that New Zealand would shut its border to China as well.

Later that evening, Murphy and Hunt flew from Melbourne to Canberra aboard the VIP – shorthand for the RAAF's fleet of Boeing business jets. They arrived at the National Incident Room just before midnight and worked into the early hours of the morning with deputy chief medical officer Paul Kelly on solving the logistical challenges they knew were coming. Supply chain issues for medical equipment were chief among them.

Morrison knew the impact of the actions he was about to take.

'Closing the Australian border [with China] was a big deal. We knew it was shutting down tourism and international students,' Morrison later recalled. 'It was a huge decision.

'Even at that time, we were thinking, "How do we get back to normal? Is it temporary? How quickly can we open it up again?"

'It became apparent that it was just the beginning. In the initial phase we were thinking of letting international students in, but by that afternoon the AHPPC said no.

'I was terribly worried about the economics: I knew it was going to hurt.'

*

When Australia announced that foreign visitors who'd recently been in China would be denied entry, the response from Chinese embassy officials in Canberra was immediate and fierce but not unanticipated.

Though Russia, Japan, Italy, Singapore and Pakistan had announced similar measures, Beijing reserved its ire for the US and Australia, accusing Canberra of a xenophobic overreaction.

China was not the only party vocal in its opposition to border closures; so was the WHO, which suggested that travel restrictions might cause more harm than good by triggering economic impacts and disrupting medical supply chains. The global health organisation even suggested that closing borders could accelerate the spread of the virus because people would simply enter countries illegally.

The WHO's reaction was confusing because, only days earlier, on 30 January, it had moved to declare Covid a 'public health emergency of international concern'.[2]

The Geneva-based WHO is governed by a 16-member committee whose decisions on matters like this – classifying a disease outbreak – need to be unanimous. China sat on that committee. Also, it appeared that the WHO didn't want to repeat the mistake it made a decade earlier when it was accused of acting too hastily by declaring the 2009 swine flu a pandemic.

None of this sat well with Australia's government. The SARS outbreak in 2002–2004 had been in our part of the world, so Canberra had a heightened sensitivity to the pandemic potential compared with the European nations.

*

In just over a week since Morrison's first press conference on coronavirus and then the border closure to China, the pressure to get Australians back home was mounting.

Morrison and Foreign Affairs minister Marise Payne were making efforts to bring people back but the road to repatriation was paved with political and logistical challenges.

Australian consular staff based in several missions across China had driven by road to Wuhan to help organise on-the-ground operations. When they got there, local officials informed them that Australia would have to supply its own PPE, for any Australians wanting to leave. Morrison was also being pressured from some sections of the media about why Wuhan repatriations were taking so long when the US had already flown in its own aircraft to retrieve its citizens.

On 29 January, Qantas CEO Alan Joyce texted Morrison, who was at home at Kirribilli House with his family and still processing the loss of his father. Joyce was offering to fly a Boeing 747 into Wuhan to bring back any Australians who wanted to leave.

Morrison called Kunkel and asked him to speak to Joyce. They decided to bring the passengers to Western Australia – to the RAAF base Learmonth in Exmouth – then fly them, on smaller aircraft, to Christmas Island.

Joyce told Kunkel it would take 24 hours to get a crew from Hong Kong in position. In addition, the airline was getting pushback from the unions over the health risks posed to pilots and flight attendants. Meanwhile, Payne was trying to obtain confirmation from Beijing that the Qantas jet would be even allowed to land in Wuhan.

The federal government had also begun building the logistical infrastructure to quarantine travellers entering the country. The AHPPC commenced daily meetings to determine the measures needed and to provide ongoing advice to the government. It was quickly established that incoming arrivals would require 14 days of isolation based on medical advice that this would be the upper limits of the incubation period.

Up until then, the advice for people developing symptoms after arriving in Australia had been to see a doctor, or if gravely ill, attend hospital where they would be treated under strict isolation protocols.

Murphy had concerns, however, about the repatriation flights from Wuhan. He told Morrison that it wasn't safe.

An early move by the government was the repurposing of Christmas Island's immigration detention centre as a quarantine facility for returning Australians. The federal Labor opposition and the Australian Medical Association opposed this on the grounds that a mandatory 14-day quarantine period there would put additional stress on Australians returning from the virus epicentre.

A week later, the government announced it would reactivate a mothballed mining camp at Howard Springs on the perimeter of Darwin, which Murphy had identified as a potential short-term solution to repatriate Australians. He and Hunt had flown up to inspect it and, within 48 hours, the army had got it up and running.

It wasn't built for quarantine but in Murphy's view, it would do. It would be managed by the AUSMAT (Australian Medical Assistance Teams). Staffed by doctors, nurses, paramedics, fire-fighters, logisticians and other health workers, including radiographers and pharmacists, AUSMAT was a world-leading rapid response unit established under the National Critical Care and Trauma Response Centre set up by Prime Minister John Howard and then Health minister Tony Abbott in the wake of the 2002 Bali terrorist bombings.

By then, handheld thermometers were being supplied to airport and port personnel, and more than 800,000 face masks had been distributed to primary health networks for the use of health care workers. A new acronym was becoming common around Australia: PPE, for personal protective equipment.

The first mercy flight – with 72 passengers aboard – touched down in Australia on 4 February. In total, Qantas flew four of these flights, bringing back more than 240 people.

As the passengers were stepping back onto Australian soil, TV news reports were featuring disturbing scenes from Wuhan: people collapsing in the streets from Covid, residents locked inside their apartment blocks to contain the spread.

Australian health officials were seeing hard evidence of how quickly a second-world health system could buckle under the pressure of a local 'epidemic'. At that stage the WHO was still unconvinced of a need to declare a 'pandemic'. The big question was how Australia would cope if it spread to our shores.

*

No escape: the virus spreads

If January was Australia's wake-up call, February became our Covid twilight zone. The focus for federal, state and territory health officials had shifted to preparing hospitals, intensive care units, PPE, ventilators and working out what medicines could be used to support Covid-19 patients, if and when they started coming.

Much was still unknown about the virus, other than that it was spreading. Like the influenza virus, Covid-19 was an RNA virus, which meant that it mutated rapidly to adapt to humans. Crucially, its infection and lethality rates were poorly understood.

At that time, it was believed to be less transmissible than the seasonal flu and significantly less lethal than SARS or MERS.

Yet the range of symptoms was extremely broad, and could be so mild that some people wouldn't realise they had the virus.

The consequences, however, were still grim for some. Those dying from it experienced great trauma – effectively death by suffocation.

This raised yet another headache for authorities: infected individuals could spread the virus far and wide without knowing they carried it, or well before they showed any symptoms. This became a hallmark of Covid-19 and set it apart from SARS and MERS, which were transmissible usually only after people had become demonstrably ill.

By early February, the CSIRO's high-security biocontainment facility at Geelong – formerly known as the Animal Health Laboratories and later rebadged as the Australian Centre for Disease Preparedness (ACDP) – had set itself a 16-week timeline to engineer a vaccine.

The ACDP was one of four biosafety level-4 labs in Australia and hosted the most sophisticated physical containment laboratory anywhere in the world, the PC4 Zoonosis Suite. It housed the planet's most lethal known pathogens, including Ebola and Zika viruses. It was in here that scientists were the first outside China to start examining a lab-grown copy of the coronavirus, in a bid to identify it more thoroughly and understand its behaviour.

The virus was still without a workable name. It was 12 February 2020 when the World Health Organization announced Covid-19 as the common name of the disease it caused.

By then, the death toll in China had already ticked over 1100 and had surpassed that of the SARS outbreak of 2002–03. The virus was beginning its march across Asia, to Europe and the UK and to the Americas and the Pacific.

This had prompted Morrison to tell his cabinet in the Monday 3 February meeting that the government needed to demonstrate that it was taking preventative action.

'We need to be stoic, calm and reliable,' he told his ministers.

A week later at the Monday 10 February cabinet meeting, Brendan Murphy gave another update on the global coronavirus situation and the Australian context. While there were still gaps in the data, he said, the trend was steady, meaning the case numbers were not rising exponentially. But he cautioned the government against 'under-estimating or over-reacting' in public statements. The good news, he told the cabinet, was that Australia's containment protocols were working: there appeared to be no spread of the virus beyond cases of those who had re-entered the country and were being effectively isolated.

In other words, there was not yet any community transmission – the term used to describe spread into the general population. And no one in Australia had yet died from the infection.

The border closures to China were due to expire in five days and following probing from Morrison and another meeting of the NSC, three days later the restrictions were extended for another week on the AHPPC's advice that while there were only 15 cases in Australia, there was 'concerning growth' in cases and deaths in China.

Through February, the number of people entering Australia who had been in mainland China had been cut by 70 per cent and the stringent border controls, including 14-day self-isolation protocols for returning travellers, appeared to be working. Of the 546 people returned from Wuhan or the 29,000 mostly Australian citizens or permanent residents given an exemption to return from mainland China, not one tested positive.

But events abroad were moving rapidly; flow-on effects were starting to become apparent.

The Chinese stock market had plunged on Monday 3 February – the first day of trading after the Lunar New Year – as the country began shutting down cities. One of the domino effects was a steep drop in Chinese energy demand. With China's transportation systems effectively grinding to a halt, a dispute flared between Russia and the Saudi-led OPEC, which was seeking to cut oil production to stabilise the global market. The virus even featured in Trump's State of the Union address: 'My administration will take all necessary steps to safeguard our citizens from this threat.'

Even though Morrison was developing a sense that the world was about to change dramatically, it was still largely politics as usual – if usual meant continuing to grapple with the human tragedy and the political crisis of the bushfire season and a Nationals' leadership spill. For most Australians there wasn't any sense of anxiety or urgency about the virus. No one was wearing face masks.

But by the end of February, the picture of the emerging virus was coming much more sharply into focus and, on 25 February, the WHO gave startling news: for the first time, more cases had been recorded in a single day outside of China than within it and the global death toll from coronavirus was growing, doubling in the space of a week.

*

'Thousands will die'

These were days of demonstrable uncertainty and growing disquiet within government.

Morrison's top public servants were crunching the numbers, poring over data for infection rates and mortality rates from all over the world.

Some of the predictions the bureaucrats were seeing were deeply worrying. One scenario, based on an unconstrained outbreak, with no intervention, forecast a death toll of up to 150,000.

For Morrison and Hunt, this was clearly an intolerable outcome and one that had to be avoided at all costs.

Concerns were also already being raised about the potential economic impacts from the virus. The aftermath of the bushfires had seen growth forecasts and budget expectations being written down by the Reserve Bank and Treasury. The latest discussions within Treasury were primarily focused on the impacts the slowdown in China would have on Australia's economy. As the virus progressed this became a day-to-day proposition.

On 18 February, at a meeting of cabinet's ERC – an early planning session for the May budget – Morrison reminded attendees that the budget had to be practical and deliver real benefit to people while staying true to what he claimed were core Liberal principles of economic management – low taxation, prudent spending and fiscal discipline.

'I'm still not giving up on a surplus,' he'd said, even though he was losing confidence that a surplus was achievable.

Frydenberg recalls that the economic threat first hit home for him in Saudi Arabia, where he had flown for a G20 finance ministers' meeting on 22 February.

'The Singaporean and South Korean ministers were both speaking about the impact the Covid was having on their economies,' he said. 'At that stage we were confident of a budget surplus. The Singaporeans, who are well known for budget discipline, were saying how it was driving them into deficit, and so I was thinking about what the impact would be back in Australia.

At that point no one was anticipating what was to play out over the next 12 months, the depth and the extent of the economic shock. At that point everyone thought it was temporary.'

Two days later, on 24 February, Morrison warned cabinet to brace for what may come: the economic impacts on the March quarter were shaping up to be significant. 'We have to socialise the true health nature of the virus,' he told cabinet. 'If it goes pandemic, we are going to have some very difficult decisions to make.'

Morrison had just given the first hint to cabinet colleagues that, eventually, Australia might have to extend its selective border closures and ultimately shut off human traffic to the rest of the world.

On Thursday 27 February, Morrison emerged from a three-hour NSC meeting to warn the public that the threat to Australia had suddenly escalated.

'So while the WHO is yet to declare the nature of the coronavirus – and it's moved towards a pandemic phase – we believe that the risk of a global pandemic is very much upon us. And as a result, as a government, we need to take the steps necessary to prepare for such a pandemic,' Morrison said at the press conference.[3]

After speaking to Murphy, who had come the conclusion that the epidemiology spoke for itself, Morrison made a big call to leap ahead of the World Health Organization.

In the two weeks it then took the WHO to make its official declaration that this was a global contagion – a pandemic – the virus had already begun to cut a deadly path through Europe.

Like many Australians, Morrison was badly shaken by the television footage coming out of northern Italy. He and his wife had been enjoying a rare quiet evening at The Lodge when he'd glanced at the screen.

'It was terrifying. I was looking at that, and if I needed a reminder of what this was about, that was it,' he says. 'I told Jenny, "There are just going to be corpses on the street." I felt the scale of the devastation. I thought, "We are about to see what this thing does."'

A more realistic but no less sobering model was presented to Morrison and Hunt shortly after. This one, based on direct intervention and containment, estimated that the number of deaths from Covid in Australia could be anywhere between 15,000 and 50,000.

Around that time, Australians were seeing TV footage of body bags in the back of trucks on the streets of New York City. If such a disaster could happen in New York, it could happen at home. Which prompted a gruesome question for Morrison and Hunt: what would Australia do with its own dead if the situation got as bad as some of the forecasts were predicting?

What the public did not realise was that this question had already been asked – and addressed – two years before Covid-19 struck, in a review of Australia's crisis management.

In 2017, Pezzullo, who had just been appointed as the secretary for the newly formed Department of Home Affairs, undertook an assessment of the country's crisis management planning. He identified areas that he believed were under-done and he and his team homed in on two of them. 'We picked a massive cyber-attack on Australia's critical infrastructure. The other thing was a global pandemic which resulted in both health and economic impact,' he recalls.

In February 2018, under Peter Dutton as Home Affairs minister, Pezzullo decided to conduct a formal review. He drew in agencies and departments right across government, including Australian Border Force, Australian Federal Police, departments of Health, Defence, Agriculture and Water Resources, Foreign Affairs and Trade, and Prime Minister and Cabinet. They looked at '[the] extant crisis arrangements, including plans, coordination frameworks and communications protocols ... tested through a scenario exercise involving a pandemic outbreak of a zoonotic influenza virus, with escalating severity from ordinary to very significant to catastrophic crisis'.[4]

Pezzullo's war-gaming – he preferred the term 'scenario exercises' – highlighted that outside of bushfires, floods and fires, which came under the auspices of Emergency Management Australia, crisis management theory and planning tended to orbit around the potential of a mass terrorism event. And while that threat was horribly real, Pezzullo recognised that the definition of 'crisis' underpinning those structures was too narrow. So he set about broadening it.

'[Whether] you've lost power or you have a pandemic keeping people at home, the challenge of keeping people sustained and supported is the same,' says Pezzullo. 'The vector might be terrorism, cyber or a pandemic but the sectoral impacts are the same. Basically, people have three essential needs: a livelihood to satisfy their material needs, safety and the ability to live in a community.

'Whether you have kids at home because there is a pandemic or mad terrorists roaming the streets, you have to educate them. For instance, online learning can be used irrespective of the vector of the attack.'

Ultimately, the outcomes Pezzullo achieved included beefing up the capacity of Emergency Management Australia during periods of crisis, strengthening state-territory stakeholder management and identifying what capabilities Australia needed to support recovery from the consequences of a national catastrophic crisis.

He explains, 'This was not about a focus on the Department of Health's preparation; this was all the ancillary and para-health issues that sit around a pandemic, including groceries, supermarkets, public order lockdown arrangements and the rest of it.'

A key finding was the need for early border closures.

Pezzullo says, 'You needed to stand up a coordinating mechanism that brought in states and territories – and the private sector, for groceries, logistics, telcos – basically everyone that you would need to pull together if Australians were in some form of prolonged lockdown or isolation and some form of border closure combined with quarantine or curfews.'

This pre-planning work on the non-health logistics of a pandemic would become critical to a decision by Morrison in the first week of March when it became inevitable the government would have to activate the National Crisis Committee (NCC).

The Howard government established the NCC in response to the 9/11 World Trade Center terrorist attack. Its primary purpose was to take command of ministerial decision-making across all levels of government – including Commonwealth, state and local governments – in the event of a national crisis.

Morrison was concerned, though, that by activating the crisis committee, because of its name, he could enflame public anxiety. Pezzullo had anticipated this too and his department held a fresh name in reserve: the National Coordination Mechanism (NCM).

Explains Pezzullo, 'I suggested to [Morrison] in the room that technically we are activating the NCC, and that brings in the states and territories. I said, "Let's take the word 'crisis' out, and use 'the NCM'. It's the same thing."'

Pezzullo considered that Australia had excellent tactical and operational thinking within each lane but that better 'cross-lane, or cross-portfolio', thinking was required. To his mind, the NCC fulfilled that need. 'Just because it was set up in 2001 by Howard, didn't mean that circumstances don't change and it can't be adapted,' he comments.

Morrison agreed. On 5 March, he announced the commissioning of the deliberately bureaucratic- and innocuous-sounding NCM to manage the non-health response across all jurisdictions and act as a civil logistical command centre for the nation.

The NCM, which effectively took the functions of the NCC out of the Department of the Prime Minister and Cabinet PM&C and nested them in the Department of Home Affairs, set in train a rapid reconnaissance task based on the number of expected deaths and duration of lockdowns and the massive logistical response that would be required to deal with them.

'It focused on things such as how would you get essential food and medicine to the elderly in a lockdown,' explains Pezzullo. Also mortuary services. 'What would happen if our funeral parlours got overwhelmed? We had to do a quick review to determine the capacity of funeral parlours to deal with burials and cremations. That's how graphic the work had to get to in March and into April. In military terms, we were operating under RWC: Reasonable Worst Case.'

For obvious reasons, this level of detailed planning was kept largely out of sight. Fortunately, Australia's Covid situation never got so bad, and by April planning on this aspect stopped. But the other logistical work continued, based on the likelihood that, at some point, millions of Australians might be forced to stay inside their homes.

Of major concern was the capacity of the country's information and telecommunications networks to sustain prolonged periods of lockdown. A telco group convened under the NCM looked at the peak load the system could experience if children were home schooling at the same time as their mums and dads were trying to work from home.

They simulated the potential load, benchmarking it against the so-called 'Netflix peak' at around 9pm. It came close to capacity but not enough to crash the system. However, as things developed, the new peak load would become 9am, not pm.

Similar working groups were set up with other goods and service providers. Peter Dutton was involved in almost every call to private sector CEOs, including the heads of major supermarket chains. He was determined to impress upon each one what the nation needed to achieve so people didn't wither in their own homes.

Pezzullo was given to using direct yet colourful rhetoric. In a meeting of the National Security Committee, in early February, he remarked that Covid-19 was not likely to be the 'zombie apocalypse'.

While the comment earned a rebuke from one of the ministers present, his point was that while Covid-19 was looming serious, cool heads needed to prevail if public order was to be maintained.

CHAPTER 4

'Forget about the surplus'

MORRISON AND FRYDENBERG were in constant dialogue over the updates coming out of Treasury, the slowdown in China and the economic impacts of the border closures. Fiscal measures loomed large in their minds. In the final week of February and into the first week of March 2020, their Treasury briefings began to fully unpack the potential for colossal damage, including mass unemployment, and the economic narrative suddenly flipped. Despite their longstanding commitment to return the budget to surplus, Morrison and Frydenberg knew their government had no alternative to providing a significant stimulus.

On Monday 24 February, Morrison held a scheduled meeting of his leadership group, a tight-knit unit compromising the leaders and deputies of both the Liberal and National parties, selected cabinet ministers including the Treasurer, and those who filled the key roles in the Senate and House of Representatives responsible for the functioning of parliament.

It met every morning of parliamentary sitting weeks to map out the business of the day and once a week on the phone outside of that.

Morrison wasn't mincing his words when he walked into the meeting and made a blunt announcement: 'Well, you can forget about the surplus.'

Uttering those words was an anguished admission. The Coalition had spent the past decade working to restore the damaged balance sheet it inherited on coming to office. The virus was now forcing the government to subordinate the surplus to the need to protect jobs and livelihoods.

Up until then, the focus was on trying to keep the virus at bay and dealing with the impacts of the limited international border closures. Like everyone else, Morrison was observing the global human dimension of the pandemic with horror, but he was acutely aware that the containment measures being put in place would deliver a kick in the guts to tourism, higher education and other sectors, especially those exposed to China.

He was in an ideological bind. He and his party had crucified the Rudd Labor government over its stimulus spending during the Global Financial Crisis (GFC). With what was coming out of Treasury, and what he was seeing globally, he suspected that the pandemic might require stimulus and support measures that dwarfed Rudd's. So he needed to build a narrative – ahead of any stimulus package – that his government was dealing with a global health crisis as distinct from a financial one. The situation was different, which of course it was.

On 2 March, Morrison held a meeting of the Cabinet Office Policy Committee (COPC). It is a strategic group – a cabinet think-tank – that meets on a needs-only basis in the face of significant policy decisions or an unfolding crisis. Morrison was laying the groundwork for the major policy issues he expected he and Frydenberg would be putting to cabinet, the NSC and the ERC, otherwise known as the budget razor gang.

Morrison had tasked Treasury's Steven Kennedy to brief the key ministers on the rapidly deteriorating economic outlook. Kennedy told the COPC that because there had been a radical change in the situation domestically and internationally over the past week, he was becoming increasingly concerned about the disruption to Australia's economy. He foresaw both economic and social turmoil ahead.

Morrison explained that he and Frydenberg were looking at a range of very significant fiscal responses. 'It has to be targeted, scalable, measured and modest,' he told the COPC. 'I don't want fiscal intervention that causes long-term structural problems for the budget.'

He said that business and household balance sheets 'seemed to be okay' but his major concerns were about supply chains and giving top priority to jobs. 'Whatever we do, it must increase investment and productivity on the other side of this,' he told the meeting. 'We need a narrative of hope. And we need to de-risk as much as possible. The priority must be jobs, cash flow and investment. Don't forget it is *us* that will be borrowing the money.'

This was a lightbulb moment, both for the PM and the country: the upcoming May budget would become a fiscal lifeboat.

*

'Tell the banks I'm serious'

That evening of 2 March, Morrison held his first Covid briefing with the governor of the Reserve Bank of Australia (RBA), Philip Lowe, ahead of a rates decision the following day. Frydenberg, Finance minister and Senate leader Mathias Cormann and deputy RBA governor Guy Debelle were also on the call.

It was almost guaranteed the RBA would cut rates. While Lowe, too, was becoming increasingly concerned about the global and domestic outlook, there was little sense of how bad things would get. The biggest decisions were still to come.

The RBA was forecasting Covid would have a similar economic impact to that of the bushfire crisis, with growth to fall by half a percentage point in the March quarter. Yet it was optimistic that travel would return by the second half of the year and the Chinese economy would have largely recovered.

During his conversations with Lowe that Monday night, Morrison formed the impression that the central bank would likely move on monetary policy and lower interest rates the following day. Morrison assured Lowe that if the RBA did move, the government would follow with strong stimulus and he would publicly put pressure on the banks to play ball. To signal how serious he was, and to pressure the major trading banks behind the effort to save the economy, Morrison was happy to float privately, and then in the media, that his government was considering raising the bank levy. The levy was introduced in 2017 when Morrison was Prime Minister Malcolm Turnbull's Treasurer and the relationship between the banks and the government was in acute disrepair.

At a press conference just before Question Time on Tuesday 3 March, ahead of the RBA announcement, Morrison took an aggressive stance.

'Now, there's no doubt if the [Reserve] bank were to take a decision today on cash rates that the Government would absolutely expect the four big banks to come to the table and to do their bit in supporting Australians as we go through the impact of the Coronavirus,' he said. He added that Qantas had done its bit to support Australians, and the banks needed to do likewise.[1]

Frydenberg had called each of the four big bank CEOs the night before to tell them what the government's position would be if they didn't pass on rate cuts in full, should the RBA go down that path. The prospect of a further rise in the bank levy shocked the CEOs. He carried the message well.

Morrison was sitting in the House of Representatives – during Question Time – when the RBA decision came through at 2.30pm.[2] It announced a cut of 25 basis points, dropping the cash rate to a record low of 0.5 per cent. Frydenberg, who was seated beside him, got a text from Matt Comyn, the Commonwealth Bank CEO, who asked the Treasurer whether the PM was serious about increasing the levy, as had been reported in *The Australian* newspaper.

Frydenberg leaned over to Morrison and showed him the text.

'Tell him I'm serious. I'm not mucking around,' said Morrison.

Within minutes of the RBA announcement, most of the banks had dropped their rates, passing on the RBA cut in full.

The goodwill this engendered would become critical to Morrison and Frydenberg's relationship with the banks, which would be called upon again later when economic activity ground to a halt.

Comyn quickly became an integral player in getting the banking sector on the same page as the government in the economic response to the crisis. He and Frydenberg began speaking regularly.

The bank chiefs were not the only corporates Morrison was putting the pressure on.

Panic buying had suddenly gripped the nation as case numbers began to grow amid the threat of school closures and home isolation imposed in some Sydney districts. Toilet paper was fast becoming the most sought-after commodity in the nation as supermarkets started running out of it, as well as more obscure items like baker's yeast, an essential ingredient for the great many Australians who were trying their hands at baking bread. The social contagion was initially sparked by images from Hong Kong and Singapore of shoppers queuing at checkouts. This was despite the fact that Australia's overall caseload was still relatively very low, and nothing indicated an interruption to the supply of household necessities. The CEOs of major supermarket chains Woolworths and Coles assured Morrison that they could keep up supplies of toilet paper and other essentials but, even so, Morrison issued a call for calm.

On Friday 6 March Morrison held another COPC meeting, with Steven Kennedy giving further updates. Hand-picked by Morrison as part of a calculated re-ordering of the top tiers of the bureaucracy, Kennedy had only been in his job for six months. Formally trained as a nurse with a master's degree and a PhD in health economics, Kennedy could not have been more suitably placed to deal with a pandemic. Not that even he could have foreseen what was coming down the pike.

Kennedy briefed the room for the second time that week. He was blunt. Except for 1919, the situation Australia was facing was without precedent, he said. Treasury's modelling was assuming Covid cases would peak by June. His key point was that it was economy-critical that the fiscal response helped the country to avoid unnecessary business closures. He made the point that even if the government 'overshot slightly' on the stimulus, it couldn't lose because interest rates were so low.

Morrison, having already flagged increased support for bushfire victims, expressed his deep concern about potential labour supply shortages in critical sectors such as childcare. Whatever the government did, he added, it couldn't risk affecting the structural integrity of the budget.

He then took COPC through the key messages of a speech he was planning to deliver the following Monday, where he'd be framing the federal government's narrative in response to the looming crisis and its policy principles.

In an early marker of the frustrations Canberra would face throughout the pandemic – a prescient echo of what happened a century earlier – Frydenberg warned the room they could not rely on support from the states.

Morrison's weekend was busy. He visited the Qantas hangar at Sydney Airport on the return of a repatriation flight from Wuhan. He thanked the crew and the government officials for their bravery. He assured them that, 'Our country's story is not going to be written in the aisles of shopping centres having tiffs over toilet paper.'

He did a ring-around of the state premiers and territory chief ministers to take them through the key elements of the stimulus package he would be announcing the following Thursday, ahead of Friday's meeting of the Council of Australian Governments (COAG), the primary intergovernmental forum for the states and the Commonwealth since the early 90s.

Morrison, already full of apprehension, was surprised the state and territory leaders didn't share his concern about how grim the situation could become. Queensland's Labor premier Annastacia Palaszczuk was the exception, worried about a potential Covid cluster on the Gold Coast, Queensland's premier tourist area. Morrison assured her that Kennedy and Murphy would give COAG a full briefing on everything they'd been telling the Commonwealth.

It was becoming evident to Morrison that the economic impacts of fighting Covid-19 could well trump the virus's health effects.

In a speech to an *Australian Financial Review* summit the following day,[3] he signalled the dramatic shift coming in fiscal policy, away from balancing the budget as the chief priority to using the budget as a weapon to defend Australian lives and livelihoods.

What, in a normal year, would have been a headland speech on the government's agenda for the economy became a pledge to rescue it. The speech was pivotal in framing the message that this was no longer going to be just a health response but an economic one as well. Critical to Morrison was laying down the principles on which the government would be basing its economic response.

Morrison, Frydenberg and Kennedy set out seven principles, the first to avoid wasting taxpayer resources. The measures needed to be proportionate to the degree of 'economic shock'.

Measures needed to be targeted, to support the most affected, to be aligned to monetary policy and state contributions and to use existing payment mechanisms – systems that worked – to deliver them.

'That's where it goes pear-shaped,' Morrison recalls, 'if you get that design wrong, as we learned from the last stimulus. We saw those mistakes of trying to rush a range of new programs in response to the GFC.'

Also importantly, given his long commitment to returning a surplus, the measures had to be temporary, accompanied with a fiscal exit strategy. And lastly, the government would favour measures that would lift productivity.

This was not, he stressed, just a government task and he singled out corporate Australia's responsibility to protect its workers.

For the PM, this was a shoulder-to-the-wheel moment for Australia.

*

Extreme measures

For the first few weeks of the crisis – the first phase of January and February, with Treasury focused on the economy's exposure to China, tourism and travel and the knock-on effect – there was an optimism in the PMO that they could hold it off and keep most of the economy functioning.

But by late February, Kennedy was coming to the view that the potential shocks to the supply side of the economy and the consequent loss of confidence meant it could be an economic crisis quite unlike anything before it. Australia was still operating in an unrestricted domestic environment, but some countries in Europe were starting to close down completely.

'When we were working on that first package ... at that stage we were looking for a short-term stimulus,' recalls Morrison.

'We knew we could forget the surplus. It was what had to be done ... and we did it. At the stage in the early phase of developing it, we didn't have social restrictions.

'Our case numbers were less than 100. It was about the impact on tourism and higher education.

'We had to deal with a contraction of activity and we knew that travel and foreign students would have a big impact and we would have to stimulate.

'But it was also getting us fit for the other side.

'We went into that week working out what the principles would be ... we went over the GFC stuff. Steven Kennedy was critically involved in that. He understood the lessons well.

'We knew the principles were critical to how you design things and guide things.

'It has never been argued by me that a surplus was a virtue in itself.

'If you believe that a government has, as its first interest, the wellbeing of the community, the economy is a fixture of that.

'The starting point for us was the integrity of the balance sheet and that would provide a buffer for exigent circumstances.

'Those circumstances arrived far sooner than anyone would have expected.'

After Morrison left the *AFR* summit, confident Australia was well set up to manage whatever may come, he went into a meeting of the ERC – the cabinet sub-committee that decided fiscal strategy and vetted all spending proposals. The core members of the subcommittee, chaired by Morrison, included Frydenberg, Cormann, McCormack and Hunt, with other portfolio ministers joining when needed.

That same morning, Victorian Labor premier Daniel Andrews warned his state was facing potentially 'extreme measures': life as Victorians knew it was soon going to radically change.

Morrison's political thinking and response to the virus would of course evolve over time but in early March and guided by the AHPPC he, like others, was of the view that because of Covid's apparently low mortality rate, at some point it 'could be managed like a bad flu'.

'We have to decatastrophise. We are already into community transmission. But it can't be the end of the world,' he told the ERC. 'We have to stick to our economic principles. Keep it simple and keep it targeted. And we will come out the other side in a stronger position. We can do more in the budget if we have to.'

*

At a meeting of the full cabinet later that day, Frydenberg briefed ministers for the first time on the full stimulus package. The $17.6 billion price tag was eye-watering, especially for a government that had only just brought its budget back into balance.

Most of the cabinet members sat in stunned silence when Frydenberg told them that it was likely to be only the 'opening salvo'. But there was no dissent. The room was seized by a unanimity of purpose.

'We don't know what's next,' he told them.

This $17.6 billion was only part of it. There was also a $2.4 billion health deal struck with the states the day before to provide, among other things, resources to bolster testing and tracing capability, tele-health services, aged care support and replenishment of the national stockpile of PPE.

Morrison then told his cabinet that the pandemic could have a significant economic impact especially because of Australia's exposure to Asia – particularly China, which by then was locked down.

Moreover, he added, the elderly were the most vulnerable and 'we must protect them'.

'These are the most important decisions we will make this term and perhaps in the life of this government, or of any government,' he told the cabinet.

Aside from preventing deaths, the government's focus would be to preserve jobs.

The key political message was that the government was getting ahead of the virus and intended to stay ahead of it. In the meantime, he told them, the ministers had to keep their nerve.

While Morrison was drilling these themes and a sense of urgency into the executive arm of government, the nation's business leaders, as well as the state and territory leaders, seemed to be operating under a willing suspension of disbelief about the magnitude of what was evolving.

*

Morrison and Frydenberg held a dinner at Kirribilli House on Wednesday 11 March, for a select group of CEOs. While it was arranged before the coronavirus was even a consideration, the timing was perfect for a prime minister who saw the need to get business on board.

The mood at the prime minister's official Sydney residence was relatively upbeat. Guests mingled over pre-dinner drinks on the lawns, enjoying the sweeping views across to the city and up Sydney Harbour. It was a who's who of Australia's business community, a corporate cross-section of virtually every crucial industry sector: retail, tourism, manufacturing, resources, food, finance and communications. Among them were Solomon Lew, Qantas CEO Alan Joyce, CSL chairman Brian McNamee, BHP

CEO Mike Henry, Wesfarmers' Rob Scott, Coca-Cola Amatil group managing director Alison Watkins, JB Hi-Fi CEO Richard Murray, Macquarie Group CEO Shemara Wikramanayake and Telstra boss Andy Penn. The big four bank CEOs, including Comyn, were also there.

Notwithstanding the heavyweight attendance, there wasn't a full grasp of Covid's potential long-term impact and where it might be headed. The collective corporate view was that China would bounce back quickly, which would get investment going again.

But as the staff were preparing the 20-seat 1830s era Australian red cedar dining table for dinner, and unbeknown to the attendees, Trump was preparing to close the US border to continental Europe, which would precipitate a collapse in the US stock exchange and the worst day for the bourse since 1987.

Morrison opened up by telling the guests he wanted closer and more regular direct contact with these key leaders, people who were running businesses, rather than information being funnelled through the industry bodies that represented them. His view was that lobbyists often got in the way.

Tax, energy and industrial relations reform were the usual staple of gatherings like this.

The discussion about China and the impact of its shutdown told Morrison there wasn't any measurable disquiet about Covid among these business leaders. BHP was at that stage doing well and CSL, with a large workforce in China, was seeing a lot of activity. Even Qantas's Alan Joyce was relatively cool despite the airline's acute exposure to the border closures and travel restrictions.

To Morrison, this group represented the future of Australian business. They were a new breed of leader, less aloof, less formal than their predecessors and more inclined to build personal relationships. That was particularly so with those now at the helm of the big four banks.

Morrison was impressed with Penn, especially when he assured the gathering that the country's telecommunications systems would hold up.

Lew, a fellow Melbournian and friend of Frydenberg, kept pressing on Morrison that the government needed to connect with the 'man in the street'. He stressed it repeatedly over the evening.

Morrison in turn cautioned his guests that both government and big business had to exercise utmost care with the language they used and the community messaging.

The following day, 12 March, Morrison flew to Canberra to announce the stimulus package. Lowe and Debelle from the RBA, who had been kept in the loop throughout its formation, gave it their public endorsement.

The centrepiece consisted of a $750 individual payment to more than 6 million welfare recipients, wage subsidies for apprentices, cashflow payments for businesses, further asset write-offs and regional assistance.[4]

Unashamedly geared to the demand side of the economy, Morrison said it was designed to support confidence and encourage business investment. He knew that eventually they would have to address the supply side, which would present equally diabolical challenges down the track.

But for now, this was about keeping cash flowing through the economy and maintaining business investment to prevent lay-offs.

*

Having a lark

Morrison flew straight back to Sydney that afternoon and from his study at Kirribilli House he delivered an address to the nation.[5]

'It was really to say we had the settings in place and we were confident that we could get ahead of it by proactively managing it,' Morrison recalls.

'We had gotten our people out of Wuhan, we have the stockpile, we've taken the medical advice and now we have taken economic measures. It was about trying to reinforce to the nation that we got ahead of this early.'

The address over, Morrison walked from his study to the sitting room, where the nation's premiers and chief ministers were mingling. The following day, COAG was meeting, and it was customary for the leaders to dine together the night before.

Morrison had been trying to build a narrative ahead of COAG that would get the states and territories more alert to the economic ramifications. But he still wasn't detecting any sense of urgency among them. Although there was banter about whether people should still be shaking hands, one thing was certain, there was no consensus on a need for greater restrictions.

As the gathering wound up, Victorian Labor premier Daniel Andrews was the last to leave. Morrison had a high regard for Andrews' political skill and the two had built an agreeable relationship since Morrison had become PM. Not all Morrison's colleagues shared his positivity about the fiercely tribal Labor leader.

While the pair enjoyed a glass of whisky from a bottle of single-malt Tasmanian Lark, Andrews fielded text messages from his advisers about the Formula 1 Grand Prix, scheduled to be held in Melbourne the following weekend. Victorian bureaucrats and event organisers were frantically trying to work out how to proceed with an event that typically drew tens of thousands of spectators into the heart of the city.

As Andrews got to his feet to leave, he and Morrison briefly touched on the business of the next day's COAG meeting. While Andrews was deeply concerned about the potential for a health disaster and welcomed the Commonwealth stimulus package, he left Morrison with the impression that there was no need for the states to change their own economic settings.

'Let's see how you feel about that tomorrow,' said Morrison.

CHAPTER 5

Covid kills COAG

NO ONE OTHER than the prime minister knew that Friday 13 March 2020 might be the last meeting of the Council of Australian Governments (COAG).

Health minister Greg Hunt liked to start his day with a walk, time pressures permitting, and this particular overcast Friday he began his six-kilometre ritual along his local beach at Mount Martha and up the Balcombe Estuary, at 6.45am. Half an hour into it, he received a call from the Victorian President of the Australian Medical Association, Julian Rait.

While Rait was an ophthalmologist, what was more relevant to Hunt was an academic thesis he'd once written on the near fracturing of Australia's federation during the Spanish flu crisis.

That morning Rait had called to argue strongly that Hunt and the other political leaders of the day needed to draw some crucial lessons from the 1919 pandemic. Chief among them was how federalism almost collapsed when the politicians let themselves believe they were medical experts. They needed a mechanism that put the expert health advice at the apex of political decision making, along with a unified national approach from all levels of government. Hunt swiftly relayed Rait's observations to Morrison.

The information fell on fertile ground. The idea of creating a new federal structure to bring the two tiers of government together in the battle against Covid had been swirling in the PM's head for several days. A slow-moving, bureaucracy-heavy structure like COAG was, in his view, patently ill-designed to deal with an unfolding national crisis.

One of Morrison's goals for the COAG meeting – due to start in hours – was to get all the state and territory leaders to fall in behind the AHPPC and the difficult decisions that would have to be made, regardless of the differences among the jurisdictions. With what he'd just got from Rait via Hunt, he could point the premiers to history for inspiration about how they should all manage the federation during the current crisis.

COAG's party-political make-up was relatively balanced. On the Coalition side, the Liberal prime minister and three Liberal premiers, Gladys Berejiklian (NSW), Steven Marshall (South Australia) and Peter Gutwein (Tasmania). Three premiers were on the Labor side, Daniel Andrews (Victoria), Annastacia Palaszczuk (Queensland) and Mark McGowan (Western Australia). Also Labor were the two territory chief ministers, Andrew Barr (ACT) and Mick Gunner (NT).

Today's summit was being held 20 kilometres west of Sydney's CBD in the new soundproof conference room at Western Sydney Stadium in Parramatta, which the NSW government had wanted to showcase.

As with all COAG meetings, roughly one every eight months, the agenda was long in its preparation and for 13 March it was packed.

In Morrison's mind, however, and despite all of the bureaucrats' planning, the gravity of the Covid crisis – economically and healthwise – was trumping everything else. The federal government had thrown its surplus out the window, yet most of the states and territories had every intention of hanging on to theirs. So far as Morrison was concerned, he had to convince them to adapt to a new way of thinking, and they needed to do it quickly.

Murphy was upstairs in a separate venue room waiting to chair a meeting of the AHPPC via video link with the state and territory chief medical officers, looking at the pros and cons of staged restrictions over coming weeks to contain community outbreaks. In just four days, case numbers had doubled, Australia-wide, to 199.

He came downstairs to show the COAG leaders the latest round of modelling on the virus with a slide presentation of the infection curve and the incursions and community outbreaks in some states.

'It's looking worrying,' he told them.

'At some stage we will have to look at physical distancing measures and shutdowns. But that's probably a bit of time away yet.'

When he returned upstairs to kick off the AHPPC hook-up, Murphy quickly realised that the state and territory chief health officers, the CHOs as they were called, were moving rapidly in their thinking. They wanted to start shutting down the country that day.

'I've just told the premiers that we might do that in the coming weeks, but not today,' he told them.

Murphy then texted Morrison's health adviser Alex Caroly and told him to send a message to Nico Louw.

'Tell the PM I need to talk to him.'

Kennedy and Lowe by that time had already taken to the floor to brief the premiers and chief ministers on where they saw the economic numbers heading.

Kennedy gave a solemn presentation on how dire things could become. Until now, he had been predicting a sharp V-shaped economic recovery but, as he told them, 'The economic impacts have changed,' and what he was predicting now was a very long and drawn-out U.

Given that, the Commonwealth could not be expected to do all the heavy lifting, he told the group. The states had to open their balance sheets as well.

On one topic – the closing of schools – Kennedy's economic views were at stark odds with the health advice, and he didn't mince his words. 'You start closing schools and you immediately take five million people out of the economy.'

When it was Lowe's turn to talk, he explained that unlike during the GFC, the central bank's monetary policy levers were extremely limited with interest rates already at a record low, and the RBA having no desire to go to the negative interest rates that some countries had moved to. Outside of quantitative easing – colloquially known as 'the printing of money' – the RBA had little room to manoeuvre.

His message to the premiers was as unvarnished as Kennedy's: 'Let the stabilisers work; do not tighten your fiscal policy [don't raise taxes]; do what you can on infrastructure, schools program, roads; and provide stimulus to support businesses.'

In effect, he urged them to pump-prime their own economies. The federal government had done the right thing, now the states needed to follow.

Lowe's sense was that the premiers and chief ministers understood the health issues but had not yet fully grasped the virus's economic impacts.

It would not be long before they found themselves rushing to catch up.

COAG meetings were always long and intense but that Friday, a parallel narrative was unfolding elsewhere.

Berejiklian, seated next to Morrison, kept getting texts from her staff updating her about new case numbers, which were being relayed by the NSW chief health officer, Kerry Chant, and she shared them with Morrison. The virus was in lift-off mode.

*

Power struggle over health advice

Around 2pm the leaders had broken for lunch. Louw found the PM and passed him a note revealing what had happened in the AHPPC.

This would affect that weekend's sport, pubs, cafes, the lot.

'Where the hell did this come from? You'd better get Murphy back in here,' the PM said to Louw.

When Murphy came back down, Morrison left the room to talk to him privately.

'What the hell?' he snapped at the CMO. 'This is a 180-degree turnaround!'

Morrison then took a minute to process what he was hearing.

'We have always said we would take the health advice,' he then said to Murphy. 'But you'll need to explain this to them,' he added, pointing into the room where the state and territory leaders were.

Fuming, Morrison went back into the main room and ordered all staff and advisers to leave. He didn't want anything about to be said in the room to get leaked. Even the representative of the local government association was asked to go. 'COAG is over, mate. It's just me and the premiers now,' Morrison told him.

He then gave Murphy the floor.

The AHPPC was now recommending that all outdoor gatherings of more than 500 people be banned with immediate effect and it wanted to place restrictions on indoor gatherings, too.

'[The announcement] came out of nowhere,' Morrison recalls. '[The AHPPC] hadn't even told [us] they were contemplating it or [that it] was even on the agenda. We were getting ready to go and do a press conference, and then this thing comes and just drops in the middle.'

Murphy told the premiers that the proposal was a response to the coronavirus numbers they'd been seeing throughout the day, and that several state chief health officers were even more aggressive, pushing for a complete shutdown, no events at all, indoors or outdoors.

Like everybody else, they were witnessing what was happening overseas, where in some countries the virus was spreading apparently unchecked with hospitals being overwhelmed. They were determined to prevent a repeat of those scenes in Australia.

Victoria's CHO Brett Sutton and Queensland's Jeannette Young were among the most vocal in calling for immediate and draconian measures.

Murphy picked up on the exasperation in the room and he undertook to go back upstairs to tell the AHPPC that if they were going to advise the leaders to start closing the country down, they needed to explain the what, the where and the how to them first.

Before Murphy left for his shuttle diplomacy, he heard Morrison and his state counterparts come to an agreement: they would continue to follow the AHPPC's recommendations. They believed they needed to stay true to the medical advice and maintain a unified position. That was a benchmark Morrison had made a virtue of from the beginning and the other leaders had signed up to it. But, Morrison stressed to Murphy, that pledge by the politicians didn't absolve them of their duty to question the medical advice. It was obvious, he said, that the leaders couldn't go out that afternoon and simply announce these immediate restrictions. There would be reasonable questions – plenty of them – about the practical aspects. As of now, he told Murphy, the leaders needed to wrap their heads around the details. To foresee and discuss the ramifications.

Murphy returned to the AHPPC to flesh it out.

When he came back to the politicians, the advice he brought gave a little more time for the public to adjust. So as not to force the cancellation of every major event planned for the weekend, the AHPPC suggested pushing the 500-person limit for outdoor gatherings to start from the following Monday, 16 March.

Despite reservations that the AHPPC was making things up on the run, all the leaders agreed to the 500-person limit, but they wanted more time to talk through the 100-person limit on indoor gatherings. Dramatically restricting crowds at sporting events and concerts was one thing but affecting gatherings of significance to families, like weddings and funerals, was another. Clamping down on the big moments in their constituents' lives wasn't being taken lightly. Ultimately, they would take that decision – on 18 March – but not before a lot more wrangling.

The AHPPC stressed that the limits they were proposing were only the starting point of social restrictions. In Murphy's opinion, while it wasn't a hard lockdown, it would be enough to give the state public health systems time to scale up their response measures including contact tracing capabilities.

*

A national cabinet is born

WA's McGowan believed the AHPPC's advice was too ad hoc and that it was essential for the states and the Commonwealth to reach a coherent position before the meeting broke. 'We are going to have to meet more regularly,' he told his colleagues. 'We've got to work this out now; we can't just go out there and make these decisions having not worked through all the consequences.'

McGowan's words struck a chord with Morrison. The COAG structure, operating since 1992, was driven by bureaucrats, a bottom-up approach. Its processes were slow and cumbersome, and with multiple jurisdictions, getting to a consensus was like herding cats. Morrison had already come to the conclusion that COAG was not armed to deal with a pandemic.

This was a watershed moment for the prime minister. Nodding, he said, 'We will need to be meeting on everything from now on. We *will* need to be meeting very regularly.'

And, on the spot, he made his call and proposed a national cabinet.

This was met with unanimous support from the premiers and chief ministers.

As of that moment, the management of the crisis changed.

At that point the national cabinet was a concept without a legal structure, but whatever the formal shape would turn out to be, the premiers and chief ministers had just decided on a mechanism though which they could make quick decisions. Rightly or wrongly, they placed the AHPPC – itself an amalgam of unelected health bureaucrats – at the peak of their decision-making.

'Let's meet on Sunday and get a formal recommendation back from the AHPCC that answers all these questions we have for them,' said Morrison.

Collectively, the leaders' heads were spinning.

In Morrison's words, they had just gone 'from zero to 100'.

He looks back at that meeting in astonishment. A meeting that began mostly concerned with economic impacts, especially from the existing border closures with China, South Korea, Iran and

Italy. 'We were anticipating that there would be more [closures]. This was already hurting the economy and we were very glum on the March quarter.'

Morrison's $17.6 billion stimulus package was already on the table. 'That seemed enormous at the time,' he says. 'There had been a lot of debate about how big it needed to be. Its final composition just came down to the aggregate measures and what it added up to.'

The AHPPC's advice to shut down large parts of the domestic economy had taken them all by surprise.

The meeting was well over time, but before they left they workshopped what they would say at the press conference. Several premiers prompted Morrison to consider how he'd answer questions about whether he was still planning to go to the football the next day. It was the NRL season opener: the PM's beloved Cronulla Sharks were taking on the Labor leader Anthony Albanese's favourites, the South Sydney Rabbitohs at ANZ Stadium. In a surreal moment, Morrison found himself on the receiving end of advice from both Liberal and Labor premiers, all in good faith. It was a measure of the unique sense of unity and purpose that had emerged from that meeting.

'They're going to ask if you're going to the football,' Andrews said to him, adding that he should go. Others concurred.

As for the messaging around the constraint on outdoor gatherings, the newly formed national cabinet was treading a delicate balancing act: to inform the public without inciting panic or anger.

Louw had been waiting outside the main function room with the PM's other advisers for the meeting to wrap up when the doors opened and Morrison hustled out.

'We are doing a presser,' Morrison bluntly told his team, sending his media staff into a flurry. There would be no prep time. They were straight into it.

As expected, the unanticipated cap on numbers at sporting, concerts and other events drew a big media response at the press conference. Murphy, as the CMO, took to the mic to explain it.[1]

'Most of our cases still are imported, but we know that some of those imported cases have led to some community spread.' He spoke at length about the risk Covid-19 posed to the Australian community: how it was currently low, and how the nation's state and territory health officials and ministers were determined to keep it that way.

'... all the international evidence suggests that if you have some community transmission, the way in which it can be spread more rapidly is in very large events. You might only have one or two people at a very large event who might be carrying the virus, and the chances of that being spread at those large events accelerates the rate of progression of this virus.' That was why, he continued, there would be limits from the Monday on large outdoor events.

'We're not suggesting that people should interrupt their normal daily work. It's just avoiding those particular circumstances where transmission can be accelerated.'

The other topic was equally a sensation, the historic agreement to form a national cabinet.

Morrison talked the press through it – that it would be a regular meeting of the premiers, the chief ministers and him, and no one else. 'We will be meeting on a weekly basis to ensure that we get coordinated response across the country to the many issues that relate to the management of the coronavirus,' he said.

'Each and every state and territory that is represented here is completely sovereign and autonomous in the decisions that they make. But what we've agreed to do together is to work together and be unified and to be as consistent and coordinated as possible in our national response. That means from time to time sharing resources. It means if there is a need to assist each other with various needs, then this group will work closely together to achieve that end.'

As Andrews had warned, Morrison was peppered with questions, including whether he was still going to the football on Saturday and to church on Sunday. He answered truthfully: yes, to both. The media made much of his responses, especially this one,

'The fact that I would still be going on Saturday speaks not just to my passion for my beloved Sharks; it might be the last game I get to go to for a long time.'

If he had his time over again, Morrison comments, he would have rethought his answers. 'The media didn't get it … they were thinking in a binary mode,' he says. 'I was following the medical advice … the AHPPC wasn't saying you can't go to the football this weekend. What the media were finding hard to grasp, failing to get their heads around … was how can it be medical advice today for Monday and not Saturday.'

Even so, Morrison was starting to second-guess his decision to attend the NRL game, which up until then he'd been looking forward to immensely. For the time being, however, he needed to keep moving at a fast clip.

*

'Shouldn't you ask cabinet to agree?'

Louw could see where the rest of the day was headed, even if others hadn't. An economist by training, he'd worked for the Productivity Commission from his mid-20s before joining Treasurer Joe Hockey's office as an adviser, then moving into Morrison's office when he was Treasurer and being seconded to go on the road with him during the 2016 election campaign.

Such was Morrison's regard for the cool-headed whizz, he created the role of executive officer to bring the then 28-year-old across to his office permanently when he became prime minister in August 2018.

No one on Morrison's team spent as much time with Morrison as Louw. He quickly developed a keen sense for when things were about to go wrong. Straight after the press conference, he pulled Morrison aside to remind him that his own ministers would need to be brought into the loop.

'You should probably call a cabinet meeting to agree what you've just announced,' he told his boss.

Though it was Friday, and well into the afternoon, any hopes of an early weekend for the PM's team were dashed.

As Louw watched C1, the PM's Commonwealth car, pull away from the stadium, with Morrison and Kunkel, his unflappable chief of staff, inside, he realised none of them would be going home just yet. He had already called ahead for another car to ferry the rest of the PM's crew, including Carswell, Caroly and media adviser Ben Wicks, back to Kirribilli House.

*

With Parramatta's high-rises receding into the distance, Kunkel took a call from Craig Maclachlan, chief of staff to Home Affairs minister Peter Dutton.

Eyes wide, Kunkel turned to his boss: 'Dutton has Covid.'

Neither man could believe it but their chaotic day had just got worse.

Kunkel made a flurry of calls. One of the first was to the cabinet secretary, Andrew Shearer, to brief him on the outcome of the meeting. After covering off the broader themes, Kunkel dropped what to Shearer – who was in Canberra and hadn't seen the press conference – was a bombshell: 'They've also decided to set up a national cabinet.'

'What's that?' asked Shearer.

'That's your problem now, mate,' Kunkel quipped.

*

With community transmission starting to move, Morrison had to rapidly redirect his focus. The first thing he did when he got back to Kirribilli House was to set up a phone hook-up with his cabinet.

Louw, Carswell and other members of the PM's media team milled around trying to design the government's communications strategy to explain what had happened that day as Morrison held court with his ministers on speaker phone from the comfort of a cream fabric armchair in the lounge room.

Morrison knew his cabinet colleagues would be wary about the role of the new national cabinet, and fearful that the existing cabinet would be subordinated to it. Morrison assured them that even though it would meet weekly, it would not remove or affect the sovereign decision-making for either the Commonwealth or the states.

He characterised it as a clearing house for advice from the AHPPC and the NCM, and a means to show the country there was a national unified leadership dealing with the crisis. On top of that, he pointed out, this national cabinet would help him rein in any erratic state leaders and provide him with a useful forum to keep up the pressure on the states to provide their own fiscal support. Lastly, he flagged his intention to go to the football the following day, justifying it as based on the heath advice and a bid to maintain public confidence.

Hunt could be overheard on the call raising the 'Dutton thing'.

'What Dutton thing?' Louw whispered to Kunkel, who quickly brought him up to speed.

The Home Affairs minister had tested positive for Covid after a trip the previous week to Washington, where he had been conferring with officials from the Five Eyes intelligence alliance at the White House.

That morning, Dutton woke with a high temperature and sore throat. He immediately and correctly suspected coronavirus. News of his eventual diagnosis led to a mild panic in the White House. As well as his Five Eyes counterparts, he had also met with Ivanka Trump and US attorney-general William Barr. All this within the same 24 hours that President Trump had declared a national emergency.

As it turned out, no one Dutton had been in contact with in Washington DC was sick, leading White House officials to deduce he had contracted the virus elsewhere. US deputy press secretary Judd Deere released a press statement, '[Dutton] was asymptomatic during the interaction … Exposures from the case were assessed and the White House Medical Unit confirmed, in accordance with CDC guidance, that Ivanka is exhibiting no symptoms and does not need to self-quarantine. She worked from home today out of an abundance of caution until guidance was given.'

Staff needed to follow up on all of Dutton's contacts since his return, including his ministerial colleagues at the cabinet meeting he attended the day after, as well as passengers and crew on his commercial flight back to Brisbane that evening.

Hunt informed his colleagues on the cabinet call that after Paul Kelly, Murphy's deputy chief medical officer – a world-renowned epidemiologist – had conducted a tele-health consultation with Dutton, the minister admitted himself to hospital, as required under the Queensland government's guidelines.

For the communications team that Friday 13th, the list of sensitive topics they had to navigate had ballooned. Carswell suggested holding off until the next day before making Dutton's situation public.

Carswell was a former journalist and chief of staff with the Sydney newspaper *The Daily Telegraph*, before taking the leap into politics and joining Morrison when he was Treasurer in 2018. He shared a common bond with the PM through their shared Christian faith and Morrison trusted his judgement.

Carswell knew how the Dutton story might play out if not managed well. His instinct was to not add to the media drama of the day by announcing Dutton's diagnosis. That might have been fine except for a coincidence: actor Tom Hanks and his wife, Rita Wilson, had been admitted to hospital the day before, having contracted the virus while filming on the Gold Coast. The international press was pursuing the celebrities' story, which meant substantially higher chances that Dutton's hospitalisation would hit the media radar.

After consulting via phone with Dr Kelly, Louw conducted his own contact tracing for the Tuesday 10 March cabinet meeting. 'The first step was trying to work out where everyone was,' recalls

Morrison. 'So, we called everyone and said, "You're all out."' They all had to isolate. Predictably, the domino effect was big. Deputy prime minister and Nationals leader Michael McCormack was due to attend his party's centenary dinner that night. Morrison phoned him and told him he couldn't go. Mathias Cormann, who had committed to attend a political fundraising event in Perth, had to cancel as well after receiving a similar call.

By 7.30pm that day, Kelly gave the cabinet the all-clear: Dutton, he'd determined, would not have been infectious at the time of the meeting earlier that week.

Carswell approved a media statement that Dutton, who that morning dropped a scheduled media appearance because of what was described as a 'stomach bug', was now known to have contracted Covid.

'In advice provided to the Prime Minister this evening, the deputy chief medical officer has reiterated that only people who had close contact with the Minister in the preceding 24 hours before he became symptomatic need to self-isolate. That does not include the Prime Minister or any other members of the cabinet.'[2]

This illustrated a new reality Australians were only now coming to grips with: the danger the virus posed before it was detected, and the need to self-isolate following exposure.

If Morrison was in two minds about going to the football game the next day, Dutton's diagnosis settled it. At 7.30pm the PMO posted a tweet: 'After further consideration and [because of] the potential for the prime minister's attendance to be misrepresented, the prime minister has chosen not to attend the match this weekend.'

*

Cabinet secretary Andrew Shearer was under pressure. The new national cabinet was holding its inaugural meeting on the Sunday afternoon, so he spent his Friday night, all of his Saturday and early Sunday working out how best to construct it.

Shearer's first thoughts were to establish it under resolutions passed by each of the state and territory cabinets. But he was troubled by the possibility of leaks and wanted to find a way to impose confidentiality on the premiers, given they'd be seeing sensitive advice from not only the AHPPC but, for example, the National Security Committee. Shearer was struggling with this, and then he had a brainwave. If it was formally established as a subcommittee of the federal cabinet the state and territory leaders would be bound by cabinet confidentiality. He set the processes in train.

Soon after Morrison's announcement of the national cabinet, Albanese was demanding a seat at the table. 'A national cabinet would involve representation from the opposition,' he said. 'Any time there's been that form of national cabinet or war cabinet, that's the way it has operated.'[3]

But if Albanese was to be admitted, the state and territory opposition leaders would likewise make a claim, and like Morrison, none of the premiers or chief ministers – even those from Labor – had any appetite for that.

On Sunday morning, Morrison's hopes of maintaining public calm were shattered when he saw a story on the front page of the *Sunday Herald Sun* newspaper. Brett Sutton, Victoria's CHO – who later claimed he was misrepresented – was warning the public to start stocking their pantries with two weeks' worth of supplies.[4] The sudden and 'extraordinary levels of demand for groceries' forced Woolworths to temporarily suspend deliveries from its Victorian supermarkets.[5]

Toilet paper wasn't the only commodity to spike in demand. That night, television news bulletins showed long queues outside liquor stores.

Before long, the queues would also be forming outside the government's welfare agencies.

CHAPTER 6

Outbreaks on land and at sea

AUSTRALIA'S FIRST OFFICIALLY recorded death from Covid-19 was on 1 March, and the transmission had been at sea.

While troops packed into overcrowded vessels returning from war had helped spread the Spanish flu, a century later it would be tourists aboard cruise ships who helped spread the first wave.

Retired Perth travel agent James Kwan had contracted the virus aboard the 18-deck *Diamond Princess* during a cruise around Asia over the Lunar New Year. Unaware he was infected, he returned home. By the time Kwan succumbed, the vessel – overrun with cases – had been making global headlines for weeks. It was the biggest outbreak outside mainland China.

Cruise liners have a reputation – deserved or not – as seaborne disease incubators. This became a stark reality for the *Diamond Princess* and its 2600 passengers and 1000 crew.

The passengers joined *Diamond Princess* cruise M003 in Yokohama, Japan. The 16-day itinerary took in Hong Kong, Chan May and Cai Lan in Vietnam, Keelung in Taiwan, then Naha in Japan.

It turned out that the index (first known) Covid case was an 80-year-old male passenger from Hong Kong. Oblivious that he carried the virus, he travelled to Yokohama, boarded the *Diamond Princess* on 20 January then disembarked in Hong Kong on 25 January.

Hong Kong health officials notified their Japanese counterparts as soon as his Covid diagnosis was confirmed, but the subsequent handling of the escalating crisis was erratic. The outbreak ultimately killed nine people and infected more than 700 passengers and crew and even some of the health personnel who assisted with the poorly implemented quarantine.

With hindsight, cruise M003 and its subsequent quarantine process was a global super-spreader event. Not only did the *Diamond Princess* deliver Covid into all the ports on the itinerary, but on release from quarantine, sick and healthy passengers mingled freely on emergency repatriation flights. Given that passengers and crew were from around 50 different countries, authorities were posed with an almost impossible task of tracing the chains of transmission.

It was a global wake-up call for the cruise-ship sector and for public health authorities. For the Australian government, the immediate fear and the most pressing concern were that a domestic outbreak of significant scale would overwhelm the state and territory hospital systems. How easily and quickly this could happen became obvious, first as Italy's health system ground to a halt, then when the same thing happened in Spain, France and the UK and in parts of the US.

'We were seeing all these systems collapse: in primary care, in aged care and in their hospital systems. The view was that if it could happen to them it could happen to us,' Hunt recalls. 'They were also seeing doctors and nurses dying.'

Morrison and Hunt quietly discussed the risk that Australian GPs might shut their doors for fear either that their surgeries could become transmission points for the disease or that they might catch the virus themselves. The possibility of this triggered a rush to establish Medicare-funded tele-health consultations – to keep patients out of GP clinics.

By Hunt's reckoning, a reform like that would ordinarily have taken a decade to implement: yet it was done in 10 days in the second half of March. Within a year, the new system would clock up 60 million consultations.

Seeing what systemic failure looked like in other countries made Hunt determined to ensure that such a collapse wouldn't occur in

Australia. Uppermost in his mind was the best-case scenario – the one with every possible plan in place – which was that Australia could well see 30,000 dead.

'All that early planning was scaling up with masks, test kits, ventilators,' recollects Hunt. 'Through all of that we were running a stealth procurement team – ahead of anyone else in the world.'

Patients badly affected by Covid-19 needed assistance to breathe, so top of Hunt's list was ventilators. 'What we would do in cabinet was model the outbreak – the curve versus the capacity. We kept working on it until the worst-case curve would be below the worst-case ventilator capacity.'

Nationwide, there were 2200 ventilators available at most, and many of those were old or on their last legs. Based on the modelling projections, if Covid started running rampant in the community, the intensive care units (ICUs) in the state- and territory-run hospitals would be overrun within a month. The planning determined that the magic number for ventilators was at least 7500. Re-engineering some existing equipment would help to achieve this but, plainly, new ventilators had to be sourced, and quickly.

In all, close to 10,000 new ventilators would be manufactured in Australia. Surplus stock was given to Indonesia and India when they got into a grave state. But the Health minister was also mindful of the deployment and resources to operate the ventilators. Hunt recalls, 'We had to build the nursing reserves, so we embarked on the upskilling of non-ICU nurses to ICU capacity and started bringing back retired nurses.'

The public messaging about the virus had become even more of a consideration. Morrison wanted to strike a balance between alerting people to the scale and severity of what could happen and providing a pathway out of it. He wanted to offer hope.

A junior staffer in Hunt's office, Nathan Hershey, came up with the line that formed the basis for the government's communications campaign: 'We are not immune but we are prepared'.

Morrison and Hunt were also starting to build the national language around 'flattening the curve' of the infection rate – a graph which showed the intersection between rising numbers and when hospitals would get overwhelmed. It was a term that Australians would soon become very familiar with.

Underlying all this was a deep concern at the Commonwealth level that the state hospital systems might not cope in a crisis. New South Wales was deemed the best prepared. For the past 20 years it had been rotating staff through the public health units as a quasi-internship for dealing with major disease outbreak. The other states and territories, however, were considered to be less equipped. Victoria was regarded as particularly exposed.

But it wasn't just the public health units that were of concern. The viability of the private hospital system would be on the line if there was a lockdown and elective surgery was put on hold.

*

Signs of frustration began emerging at the start of March between Morrison and Hunt on one side and the state chief health officers on the other, with Murphy stuck in the middle. It started with containment measures.

In line with the border closure with China, Australia had moved swiftly to impose restrictions on those arriving from Iran. But case numbers were mounting in Italy and Korea too. At that point, the Australian Health Protection Principal Committee baulked.

On 6 March, the AHPPC made a public statement against closing the borders to countries in the high-risk category: 'AHPPC believes that, in general, border measures can no longer prevent importation of Covid-19 and does not support the further widespread application of travel restrictions to the large number of countries that have community transmission.'[1]

Referring to 'detailed modelling', the AHPPC seemed satisfied that the couple of border measures introduced had 'helped to delay entry of [Covid-19 into Australia] and buy time for health sector and societal preparedness'. Further, according to the statement, data showed that self-isolation by travellers arriving in Australia was an effective containment measure. In other words, AHPPC was backing domestic isolation and community cooperation to limit the spread of coronavirus.

Morrison and Hunt were stunned by this pushback from the chief health officers. While they never said it at the time, they suspected Victoria's reticence to close the borders to Italy was based on its concern that it would impact the upcoming Formula 1 Grand Prix in Melbourne.

As CMO, Murphy chaired the AHPPC meetings, and the prime minister asked him to go back to the state CHOs. While Morrison wanted to maintain faith with the medical advice, he couldn't reconcile the risks he was seeing with the AHPPC's reluctance to extend border closures to countries other than China, known to be in the grip of mass outbreaks.

Border closures were but one issue Morrison and Hunt pushed back on. The AHPPC had also earlier recommended against the use of face masks and would later resist political pressure for mandatory vaccination of the aged care workforce.

'You have to put your hands to your head and say "What?"' Hunt recalls. 'There were three areas we had to lean in on heavily with the AHPPC. We went back for second and third opinions. Brendan [Murphy] had to drag them over the line on Italy and Korea and the final closures. Brendan would have to wrangle them to a consensus.

'And we had to keep going back to them on masks. We thought it was obvious that masks would make a difference. There wasn't resistance from us; there was resistance from parts of the AHPPC.'

*

The *Ruby Princess*

The run-up to Australia's first Covid-19 wave was slow, just as it was during the Spanish flu. As of Sunday 8 March 2020, there were 83 active cases across the country, and the daily case numbers were running in single digits. Suspected cases from Wuhan were still active, plus recent cases from Iran and Italy.

With almost 20 per cent of the 3711 passengers and crew aboard *Diamond Princess* eventually contracting Covid-19, cruise-ship operators the world over, alert to the potential for mass infections of coronavirus on their vessels, had instituted strict safety protocols.

Despite this, no alert was triggered on 8 March when the *Ruby Princess*, a sister ship to the *Diamond Princess,* docked at the Overseas Passenger Terminal at Circular Quay after a two-week round-trip cruise to New Zealand.

Passengers waiting to board the ship's next cruise, scheduled to depart at 6.45pm, began gathering at Circular Quay around 8am. Princess Cruises, owner of the cruise line, informed customers there would likely be delays as a deep-clean was underway after the previous passengers had disembarked, and NSW Health officials were conducting an on-board assessment.

Aside from that apparent glitch, embarkation proceeded smoothly. The Port Authority of NSW's daily report shows passengers boarded the *Ruby Princess* between 5.25pm and 9.07pm on 8 March 2020. The cruise liner departed at 10.59pm, with 2671 passengers and 1146 crew members on board, according to the report of the Special Commission of Inquiry into the *Ruby Princess*.[2]

On day six of its voyage, when the ship docked in Wellington, New Zealand, ship doctor Ilse von Watzdorf informed NSW Health about 'a few cases of the sniffles and Influenza A'. The following day, 15 March, Dr von Watzdorf told NSW health officials the ship was now 'in the early phases of an Influenza A outbreak onboard'. In Wellington, the ship had tested five passengers for Covid-19 – its medical centre had brought with it only 27 viral swabs – but all had returned negative results. Another 13 viral swabs were taken over 16–18 March, of which four tested positive for coronavirus.[3]

By then, the Commonwealth had issued a directive banning international cruise ship movements in Australian waters. The *Ruby Princess* cut short its voyage and returned to Sydney. It was one of four ships given a special exemption to dock under strict conditions.

On 18 March, Morison announced new restrictions, including cancelling Anzac Day celebrations and limiting the numbers who could congregate in non-essential indoor and outdoor gatherings.[4]

On 19 March 2020 at 2.29am, the ship berthed again at Sydney's Overseas Passenger Terminal. Before 3am, NSW Ambulance paramedics arrived to transport two passengers, Lesley Bacon and Anthony Londero, to Royal Prince Alfred Hospital, where both tested positive for Covid-19. Lesley Bacon subsequently died.

What happened next that day demonstrated a failure by officials to absorb the lessons from the *Diamond Princess*. A combination of incompetence and breakdown in communications involving multiple Commonwealth and state agencies allowed the *Ruby Princess* passengers to depart the vessel just after 7am.

Covid-19 doesn't show itself immediately: by the time NSW health officials realised that 663 passengers, including 367 from New South Wales itself, had contracted Covid-19, as had 191 crew plus several Overseas Passenger Terminal (OPT) staff, it was too late to contain the spread.

Most passengers saw it as a standard disembarkation, where no 'special procedures were put in place'.[5] Australian Border Force officers and Department of Agriculture officials collected incoming passenger cards and distributed 'Information for International Travellers' fact sheets as people left the vessel.

It wasn't obvious that the 11 passengers from whom Covid-19 swabs had been taken were kept isolated on board until all other passengers had disembarked.

By allowing passengers to return home immediately, NSW Health had effectively facilitated a mass spreading event. The *Ruby Princess* quickly became known as the 'plague ship'.

An outbreak at Tasmania's North West Regional Hospital, resulting in 138 confirmed cases and ten deaths, was linked to two passengers from the *Ruby Princess*. As the nation's trickle of community cases became a crescendo, an estimated 10 per cent of the infections could be traced back to the *Ruby Princess*.[6] Data is hard to come by for the almost one third of passengers on the

Ruby Princess who were international guests, although of the 28 deaths recorded as being associated with passengers from the *Ruby Princess*, eight occurred in the US.

As all this came to light, community rage welled up, and the finger-pointing began.

*

Everyone stuffed up

Responding to growing public pressure, the NSW government on 15 April established the Special Commission of Inquiry into the *Ruby Princess*, led by eminent barrister Bret Walker SC. The high-profile Walker – he had recently represented Cardinal George Pell when Pell's child sex abuse convictions were overturned in the High Court – was Australia's first Independent National Security Legislation Monitor. He had become the go-to legal expert for federal and state governments.

Under the terms of reference, Walker's primary objective was to determine the roles, communication and decision-making of the lead Commonwealth and state agencies – the Australian Border Force, federal Department of Agriculture, NSW Health, NSW Police and the Port Authority of New South Wales – in allowing 2700 passengers to disembark and return to their home bases.

Walker was also instructed to analyse the 'knowledge, decisions and actions' of the *Ruby Princess*'s crew, medical staff and owner, Princess Cruises (owned by Carnival Corporation), 'with respect to cases or potential cases of respiratory infections on the ship'.[7] And he was given just under four months to do all this.

In his final report, released on 14 August 2020, Walker catalogued numerous serious mistakes made by NSW Health. For instance, they 'should have ensured that cruise ships were aware of the change to the definition of a "suspect case" for Covid-19 made on 10 March. This would have resulted in the identification of such cases on the *Ruby Princess*. 101 persons fell within the suspect case definition by 18 March, and 120 by the time the ship docked. NSW Health should also have ensured that such persons were isolated in cabins.'[8]

Walker also said passengers had been 'incorrectly advised by the ABF during the cruise that their 14-day period of self-isolation would commence from the date of departure from the last overseas port visited by the *Ruby Princess*, being Napier on 15 March. This inaccuracy was later clarified during disembarkation at the OPT on 19 March, when passengers were provided with a fact sheet published by the Commonwealth Department of Health which relevantly instructed them to self-isolate for 14 days from their arrival in Sydney.'[9]

Walker found that allowing passengers to travel interstate and internationally after disembarkation on 19 March had been a breach of the terms of the Public Health Order that came into effect on 17 March 'which required all cruise ship passengers entering the State from any other country to isolate themselves in suitable accommodation for 14 days. Under the terms of the Public Health Order, the State Government should have arranged suitable accommodation for all passengers who were not residents of the State.'[10]

Declaring that 'It is inappropriate and unhelpful to make recommendations to experts that in truth amount to no more than "do your job",'[11] Walker made few recommendations.[12] In his assessment, NSW Health had acknowledged the mistakes made and he was sure they would do things differently if they had their time again.

To illustrate the inconsistencies in the ship's health protocols, Walker's final report also contained case studies of passengers who contracted Covid-19 on board. Paul Reid, who experienced influenza symptoms from 14 March, visited the *Ruby Princess* medical centre and was given a nose swab. Though his throat was examined, it was not swabbed.

'Shortly afterwards he was told by a male doctor he had influenza, that "it wasn't Corona, and more likely to be a common cold". The ARD (Acute Respiratory Disease) logs compiled by the

medical staff of the *Ruby Princess* and sent to NSW Health record
that Mr Reid tested negative for Influenza A and B. He and his
wife later tested positive for Covid-19,' the Special Commission of
Inquiry report said.[13]

Others, including Lynda De Lamotte, Lynette Jones and Wendy
Williams, had similar experiences, plus they wondered why they'd
had to pay to attend the ship's medical centre – and were concerned
that it had issued poor health advice that contradicted standard
Covid-19 screening measures.[14]

NSW premier Gladys Berejiklian formally apologised[15] and
Morrison acknowledged the public hurt and anger but took a
pragmatic line. 'There are a lot of complications that have come
from that rather terrible event. But ... there are going to be failures
in the middle of a crisis. There certainly has been here. No one is
walking away from that. We've got to keep focused on the next set
of problems,' he said.[16]

The *Ruby Princess* and *Diamond Princess* weren't alone in
finding themselves at the epicentre of Covid-related disease, death
and mass spreading events. After dozens of other international
passenger liners – including the Australian Antarctic expedition
vessel *Greg Mortimer* – encountered countries refusing to allow
vessels carrying infected passengers to dock, the global cruise ship
market collapsed. Some cruise ships, including newly renovated
vessels, were sent to graveyard sites across the globe for scrapping.

For Australians, the *Ruby Princess* debacle became a symbol
of unambiguous systemic failure. It was also the first sign of the
emerging tensions in the federation that were to follow.

CHAPTER 7

Things get serious

BY 18 MARCH, Covid-19 was spreading internationally and in the Australian community. Global numbers hit 30,000 new cases and just over 1000 deaths per day. Australia's daily case numbers were running in triple digits. Morrison decided he would need to relocate to The Lodge and run the crisis from the nation's capital, to be close to the infrastructure of government and to project an image of a leader in control.

The pace of the virus was accelerating and with vastly more serious measures likely to be required, Morrison was worried that even national cabinet might not always be able to act quickly enough.

He and Hunt had been considering a drastic measure, invoking the emergency powers – the so-called trumping provisions – under the little-known section 475 of the Biosecurity Act which would empower the Governor-General to declare a 'human biosecurity emergency'.

They were envisaging a worse-case scenario that swift action might be required, whether it was to direct people's movements, lock off suburbs or close down a premises, even shut the skies and clear the ports. Anything that would effectively require the suspension of people's ordinary rights and freedoms to combat a national threat – in this case a virus.

A declaration under section 475 gave Hunt as Health minister exclusive and extraordinary powers. He, and only he, could personally make directives that overrode any other law and were not disallowable by parliament. He had authority to direct any citizen in the country to do something, or not do something, to prevent spread of the disease. One of the only things he couldn't do would be to give directions to a state or territory government official.

Morrison knew that if he asked the Governor-General to invoke section 475, he effectively would be handing Hunt control of the country.

The pair understood the enormous implications of these wide-reaching powers – that had never been used – and they'd been privately discussing this possibility since February.

Given the sweeping nature of the biosecurity powers, Hunt had observed how odd it was that there was no controversy when, in 2015, parliament supplanted the Quarantine Act of 1908 and its numerous amendments over the course of the century and enacted the Biosecurity Act.

That new legislation represented the most far-reaching codification of reserve powers. To Hunt, it was up there with the divine right of kings.

Morrison and Hunt were acutely mindful that to maintain national unity and stability, anything that might seriously impinge on the states' or territories' powers – and use of these emergency powers could definitely do that – needed to be done with their cooperation. They'd been consulting with Attorney-General Christian Porter. If they were going to use them, Morrison wanted protocols set up as well as a formal process to impose constraints.

Porter publicly flagged the possible use of these powers weeks earlier on 2 March, in an interview on ABC TV, warning people that they could see troops on the street and be forced by law to stay in their homes: 'Under the Biosecurity Act, you could have the prevention of movement from persons in and out of particular places,' Porter said. 'You might have a major sporting event where people would be in very, very close proximity to each other and … it might be determined that the risk of transmission at a venue like that was too high.'[1]

The protocols Porter set about designing required the minister to provide written medical advice and advance notice of his intentions to the NSC.

However, Morrison wasn't satisfied, feeling that there needed to be more checks and balances before any single minister could wield such powers. One option was to delegate the powers to cabinet, but Porter's advice was these powers could not be delegated and could only reside with the Health minister.

*

Morrison's secret plan

Morrison then hatched a radical and until now secret plan with Porter's approval. He would swear himself in as Health minister alongside Hunt. Such a move was without precedent, let alone being done in secret, but the trio saw it as an elegant solution to the problem they were trying to solve – safeguarding against any one minister having absolute power.

Porter advised that it could be done through an administrative instrument and didn't need appointment by the governor-general, with no constitutional barrier to having two ministers appointed to administer the same portfolio.

'I trust you, mate,' Morrison told Hunt, 'but I'm swearing myself in as Health minister, too.'

It would also be useful if one of them caught Covid and became incapacitated. Hunt not only accepted the measure but welcomed it.

Considering the economic measures the government was taking, and the significant fiscal implications and debt that was being incurred, Morrison also swore himself in as Finance minister alongside Cormann. He wanted to ensure there were two people who had their hands on the purse strings.

In the first week of March, Hunt, Murphy and several departmental officials visited Governor-General David Hurley at Yarralumla to brief him early about the 'human biosecurity emergency' that Morrison and Hunt might later ask him to declare.

That day came on 18 March, two days after Victoria declared a state of emergency under its public health act and NSW issued a series of public health orders. Other states and territories scrambled to follow suit. The declaration by law could only be enforced for three months, after which the governor-general's approval was needed to keep rolling it over. It would be repeatedly extended throughout the pandemic.[2]

With infection rates – globally and in Australia – beginning to soar, Morrison and Hunt knew the first thing they had to do was deal with the cruise ship crisis. Almost immediately on asking the Governor-General to issue the declaration that morning, Hunt used the powers to forbid any foreign flagged ship entering an Australian port.

A week later he used the powers a second time, to completely lock down the country with a declaration that banned any Australian from leaving Australia by air or ship. The penalties for violating these directives carried jail sentences of up to five years.

Just as critical was the health of remote Indigenous communities, considered particularly vulnerable. Tragically, during the Spanish flu pandemic, some communities had been hit especially hard. Murphy and Hunt saw significant risk to Indigenous communities and, from February onwards, this was a chief concern.

In consultation with elders and community leaders, Hunt used his new emergency powers to effectively lock down the communities to prevent the virus getting in. To implement this policy, the Health department deployed mobile testing kits, which were then in scarce demand. It was a step that initially saved many lives.

The powers under Hunt's dominion, however, would spark vocal protest among some sections of the community a year later when he used them to prevent potentially infected Australians trying to re-enter the country from India when the Delta wave first hit.

*

As Australia was racing towards lockdowns, UK prime minister Boris Johnson was preparing to jettison Britain's short-lived herd immunity approach, where his government had been relying on the vast majority of the population becoming immune to the disease after first being infected. It was becoming obvious that this policy would overwhelm the UK's hospital system. The speed with which Johnson was pivoting was impressive. It cemented a view within the Australian political establishment that while Johnson had a 'river boat gambler' way about him, he still got things done.

Herd immunity was not something Morrison ever considered as a serious option for Australia.

On 14 March, a week before Johnson would eventually plunge his country into lockdown, and 13 days before he contracted the virus himself, he and Morrison spoke by phone, comparing notes. It was the first of many conversations between the pair over the course of the pandemic. They'd struck up a rapport at their last in-person meeting, in November 2019 at the G7 summit in Biarritz, a grand beachside resort on France's Atlantic coast. The relationship would be useful throughout the Covid crisis but also beyond. It was instrumental to the formation of the AUKUS agreement that the two of them announced with the new US president, Joe Biden, in September 2021.

By now, shutdowns to prevent the spread of the virus were becoming commonplace around the globe, and the rates of Covid-related illness in some of the world's economies were seriously restricting workforce participation. Morrison and Johnson saw eye to eye on the need for an international approach to manage the economic damage and shock to global supply chains. They agreed to use the international G20 forum as the vehicle to drive it.

Morrison had already been pushing Josh Frydenberg to energise the G20's finance ministers and central bankers to start meeting regularly. They, in Morrison's opinion, were far better placed to address the virus's impact on financial markets than the leaders, not least because central bankers were hard-wired to be focused on impact, not so much on politics.

After recruiting support for his approach from India's prime minister Narendra Modi, Morrison also got Johnson on board.

*

'That is not who we are as people'

On Sunday afternoon, the day after his call with Johnson, Morrison chaired the inaugural meeting of the national cabinet. Conducted by secure video link, it was a precursor to the new way the entire world would be doing business.

Numerous social restrictions were being imposed. Chief among them was the four-square-metre rule for indoor venues, and limiting patrons to less than 100.

The leaders knew that if they were going to start closing down large sections of the economy, including forcing people to stay in their homes, they had to explain why and bring the community along with them.

In New South Wales some pubs and clubs would initially defy the new rules, with the state government finding them difficult to police. And this was just the start of restrictions.

At that meeting Murphy was brought in again to brief the premiers and chief ministers. 'Flattening the curve' would become the new mantra – the curve being a graph highlighting the different rates of infection depending on the intervention, and the point at which the infection peak could crash Australia's health system: ie the interval at which Covid-19 patients would outnumber available hospital beds. The possible futures looked so bleak that the leaders shared a common concern: the health system would not cope with an uncontrolled outbreak.

The leaders were still coming to terms with the AHPPC's dramatic recommendations of Friday so there was vigorous discussion about the kinds of restrictions that could be imposed. What would be effective? Would Australians comply?

Morrison was adamant, 'We have to rely on people to do the right thing,' he told the meeting.

Looking back, he is still incredulous at some of what was canvassed. 'We were talking about pubs, and having discussions around pubs of certain sizes, the idea of people only being allowed in for two hours, how would you rotate them in and out – with wristbands or stamps.

'We were trying to get to very practical measures. But the idea of getting young people to stand a metre and a half apart in a pub seemed ridiculous. I was expecting stronger decisions to be made on that Sunday but that was okay, they weren't ready yet.

'My view was that we've done that, so now let's see how it goes. If we keep closing something every day, we will be scaring the hell out of people. We need to keep a pace that people can absorb.'

If any of the premiers were tentative at Sunday's national cabinet meeting, all bets were off within a matter of days. With case numbers worsening, they reconvened on the Tuesday and again on the Thursday and grappled with a slew of tough decisions.

Some of the discussions bordered on the inane – for example, an incredibly detailed debate about hairdressing – but in the context of trying to keep the public's peace of mind, they too were important.

'There are still some things that people have got to do and, yeah, there might be a risk attached to it but if everyone was walking around like woolly mammoths it will affect people's psyche,' Morrison argued.

Murphy too understood the practical implications. He agreed that some businesses, including personal grooming, had to be kept open. Maintaining a sense of humanity was important. It became evident, though, that not all the state CHOs were as nuanced as Murphy. Victoria's Brett Sutton was regarded as having the most hawkish views of all the AHPPC members; he was angling for a full lockdown of the economy and society.

Other levers were also being pulled. On Wednesday 18 March, the RBA made an extraordinary out-of-cycle move to cut interest rates again, to a new low of 0.25 per cent. Its view was that while it might have a negative impact for people relying on income from deposits, lowering rates would boost cashflow for businesses and households more generally while supporting asset prices and protecting trade-exposed industries through a lower exchange rate.

The following day, Morrison moved to close Australia to the rest of the world and, with some limited exceptions, announced a ban on all foreign nationals entering the country.

But as quickly as Morrison was moving to protect the nation at the borders – his domain – he couldn't keep pace with the premiers' rush to lock down the country internally – their domain.

Within seven days of the national cabinet's first meeting, life for Australians had changed beyond recognition, and something had happened to the public mood, something dark.

Kunkel recalls a phone call from a nervous Steven Cain, the CEO of the Coles supermarket chain. Cain was worried about public disorder at supermarkets as people pushed the panic button and began hoarding essential items. 'I think we're going to need police down here,' Cain told him.

Media images of people flocking to iconic Bondi Beach on the balmy Sydney Saturday morning – contrary to the new social distancing rules – were unsettling, shocking even.

On the day those pictures were being broadcast, Hunt recalls he was holding a press conference by the Balcombe Creek Estuary, near his home at Mount Martha.

'The locals down there know me ... and a few started to gather to watch the press conference.' Suddenly, it struck the Health minister that there were 30 people present and they had all socially distanced themselves – in stark contrast to the Sydneysiders who'd been photographed at the beach. 'I thought, "Wow!" The level of community fear and awareness was nothing I've ever seen.'

Eventually, purchasing limits had to be imposed on toilet paper, limits on pharmaceuticals enforced and curfews on shopping only for essential items put in place.

At a press conference on 18 March, Morrison issued an extraordinary plea to Australians to behave themselves. 'I can't be more blunt about it. Stop it. That is not who we are as people,' he said.[3]

Four days later, he warned Australians to comply with the public health orders or be prepared to face consequences, and that tougher restrictions were on the way.[4] 'What happened at Bondi Beach yesterday was not okay and served as a message to federal and state leaders that too many Australians are not taking these issues seriously enough,' Morrison said.

'So the measures that we'll be considering tonight means that state premiers and chief ministers may have to take far more draconian measures to enforce social distancing, particularly in areas of outbreaks, than might otherwise need be the case.

'... if there have been pubs and clubs that are heaving with people on the weekend, that is simply an invitation for the states and territories to shut them down. And if [people at those venues] are unable to get a handle on that, then they are bringing on what would be their worst outcome. And there's a responsibility, both of those who run those venues and the patrons, I underscore, and those who are going to these venues ... I mean, coronavirus is not a secret. It is very serious. It is deadly serious.'

*

Cracks in the cabinet

On Saturday night, 21 March, NSW premier Gladys Berejiklian phoned the prime minister. She was troubled. Australia's infection trajectory was rising steeply – approaching upwards of 500 new cases in a single day, and most were in her state. Berejiklian felt she was coming under great pressure to force NSW into a widespread lockdown.

She asked if the national cabinet could meet again, ideally the next day. 'Of course,' replied Morrison, and he set up a meeting for early evening on the Sunday.

The first rip in the fabric of the new Commonwealth–state alliance was already discernible. Everyone in the national cabinet knew Morrison favoured an orderly move to social restrictions and was reluctant to move quickly to a 'survivalist' lockdown. As Berejiklian had told him, the pressure was on her to go into lockdown. It was similar with Victoria. The states with the two biggest cities were experiencing the highest Covid numbers.

Morrison was hearing an echo of the parochialism that saw the state premiers withdraw from the November 1918 agreement during the Spanish flu and go their own way. The big question for him was how to get a national baseline approach amid the conflicting concepts of centralism and federalism.

As the instigator of the national cabinet, the question would preoccupy Morrison considerably. There was only so much he could do. The Commonwealth, despite possessing overarching powers both constitutionally and under the Biosecurity Act, had to be content with the states running public health, as was their usual province. The best Morrison could hope for was to establish a set of national principles to which all the states could agree while respecting the division of powers.

In football parlance, Morrison found himself juggling the dual roles of being the captain of the team and the umpire of the game. Being both at once, however, was about to be proven a challenge.

With hindsight, it's obvious that most of the state and territory leaders had decided to protect their turf. The smaller states moved first. Tasmania's premier Peter Gutwein announced that as of 20 March, all 'non-essential travellers' to Tasmania would be required to quarantine for 14 days.[5] The Northern Territory, South Australia, Western Australia and Queensland quickly followed.

But it was Andrews and Berejiklian who caused widespread panic and confusion when they allowed news of their plans – a virtual lockdown of their states – to be leaked to the media ahead of the national cabinet meeting.

Morrison found out at a press conference earlier that day when a journalist asked him about a list of services New South Wales was planning to shut down.[6]

It was a so-called 'white list' of the businesses that could remain open but it was silent on which needed to close. It was so vague it created immediate confusion and chaos.

Morrison was furious. He believed it was prepared so hastily that it unnecessarily cost people their jobs.

The Victorian approach was even more proscriptive: any enterprise not deemed to be an essential service was to shut down.[7]

After being shown the list by Carswell, who had received an email from the NSW premier's office notifying him of a press release it was about to issue, Morrison immediately got on the phone to Berejiklian. He was calm but direct about how ill-thought-through New South Wales's plan was. He then texted Andrews and stressed that all members of the national cabinet needed to stick together to make it work.

Neither premier had provided an exhaustive definition of what an essential service was. In New South Wales's case, that would change over the course of the day. But many businesses were kept guessing as to whether they would be allowed to open their doors the next day.

Morrison would walk into the national cabinet that afternoon with one question to the state premiers: are you committed?

It was a pivotal moment for the federation and how it would bind to manage the crisis.

'I believe in this [national cabinet]. It is the only way to manage the most important issue we have ever faced,' he told them. 'Today's events have made it difficult.'

Everyone declared their fidelity to the national cabinet, but not before the other premiers and chief ministers took Andrews and Berejiklian to task.

Queensland's Annastacia Palaszczuk was particularly aggrieved by the pair's failure to consult her and fellow national cabinet colleagues. It was insulting, she told them.

WA's Mark McGowan was furious and let Andrews and Berejiklian know it.

Partisan politics was absent as Labor premiers rounded on Labor premiers and Liberals on Liberals.

Morrison managed to calm the waters after their frustrations were vented.

Berejiklian apologised if she had offended anyone then explained that she believed New South Wales had a unique issue because of its size and the problems cruise ships had introduced. She also attributed some of the cause to her frustration that 'people were ignoring the government' on its social distancing rules.

With the meeting back on track, it was time, said Morrison, for them all to 'unscramble the egg'. If the national cabinet was going to work, he told them, this kind of chaos could not erupt again.

And they moved on.

*

Political observers were keeping a keen eye on the national cabinet. Some likened it to the war cabinet of 1939, if not in structure, then in function and significance. Others were critical, questioning its legitimacy.

For many of Morrison's ministers, its effect of elevating state premiers to a national platform was not only undesirable but a dangerous devolution of political authority for the federal government.

Over time it would become the subject of derision from conservative and left-wing commentators alike. Yet it endured, and in spite of its politicisation by all its participants at various points, it kept the state, territory and Commonwealth leaders in the same room throughout the crisis – avoiding the failure of a century earlier.

And largely because no one had proposed a better alternative.

The federal Labor opposition kept changing its tune. Initially, Albanese wanted in, and when that was denied, he became dismissive then highly critical of it.

Albanese argued that the body could have no authority without opposition representation, which, he claimed, was the tradition of past war cabinets.

This wasn't strictly accurate. The 1939 war cabinet comprised only members of the United Australia Party (UAP) government, then under the leadership of Robert Menzies. A year later, a War Advisory Council was established and while it did have opposition membership, it had no executive powers.

Other political watchers suspected Morrison was trying to suspend democracy. A Senate select committee looking into Covid-19 – three Labor senators, two Coalition senators, a Greens senator and one Independent – were similarly critical. 'Despite claiming the protection of cabinet processes, the National Cabinet has not functioned in accordance with longstanding Westminster conventions on cabinet government in relation to collective responsibility and solidarity,' it said in an interim finding.[8]

It accused Morrison of fracturing the process in his criticism of the premiers and using the national cabinet as a vehicle to 'avoid transparency'.[9]

Jennifer Menzies, a research fellow at Griffith University, wrote in *The Conversation* that, 'Executive federalism forums such as the national cabinet can be criticised for being undemocratic and unaccountable, with the role of the parliament marginalised. However, these forums are undertaking different roles. The national cabinet deals with negotiation and compromise between states, which recognise difference and diversity. The parliament is about majority will.'[10]

*

Schools out for Covid

From late January to March, state and territory governments had been assessing the potential impacts of Covid-19 on schools.

The first public orders issued in the education space came on 29 January, when Queensland chief health officer Jeannette Young –

who in 2021 became the state's governor – ordered children and staff who had recently been to China or Hong Kong to stay home from school.

On 10 March, the Queensland and WA governments introduced similar restrictions, banning international excursions for students.

Despite health advice that children had low susceptibility to Covid-19 and that closing schools and childcare centres would negatively impact economic productivity, the South Australian government on 13 March announced it would shut schools for a minimum of 24 hours in the event of a positive case, and that health advice would guide when they could reopen.

The consequences of keeping kids home from school were inestimable. In the majority of cases, their parents would have no choice but to stay home to look after them, setting off a cascade of repercussions: disruption to learning, loss of work participation and income, economic downturn, and physical and mental health pressures, for starters.

These prospects worried Morrison who, with backing from Murphy and Kennedy, could see no reason *not* to follow the health advice, which had never changed: attending school was both safe and sensible. The economic advice was keeping schools open was an enormously powerful cog in the engine of everyday life.

If there was one issue that could cause the collapse of the national cabinet, it was schools.

Andrews came next, on Sunday 22 March, making an announcement before that day's national cabinet that Victoria's schools would close four days before the start of the scheduled holidays.[11]

Berejiklian told the meeting that day she was coming under pressure from the teachers' union and the powerful NSW Catholic education lobby to shut down schools.

Hearing that, Morrison acted. He rang the Catholic archbishop of Sydney, Anthony Fisher. 'I need you to keep the schools open,' he said.

The archbishop gave his word.

If the private schools could be persuaded to stay open, there would be greater pressure on the premiers to not shut down public schools.

And it appeared to work. At the national cabinet meeting, all the state and territory leaders came around to Morrison's way of thinking. The statement issued afterwards said, 'All leaders agreed that children should go to school tomorrow ... we cannot see children lose an entire year of their education as a result of school closures caused by Covid-19. Leaders committed to the AHPPC advice that says that it is safe to keep schools open ... All leaders have committed to re-open schools at the end of the school break.'[12]

The apparent solidarity on schools remaining open was breathtakingly short-lived, however. That same day, the states and territories were preparing themselves for mass school closures ahead of the Easter holidays.

Within a week, the ACT, Victoria, Queensland, Northern Territory, Tasmania and South Australia closed their schools and brought forward holidays to give teachers time to prepare for online learning in Term 2.

Looking back, the weekend of 21 and 22 March 2020 was a turning point in the life of Australians.

It would also be the last weekend that people could to go a pub, club, restaurant or movie for a long time. Both the NRL and AFL seasons were suspended.

*

'We are up to this challenge'

That Sunday night, after the national cabinet, Kunkel was handed the draft of a speech Morrison was due to deliver to parliament the next day, announcing the House would adjourn 'until a date and hour to be fixed by the Speaker'.

Kunkel thought the speech needed more work. He was looking for an antidote to the uncertainty and fear that reflected the events of the past fortnight. While no one could know what would play out over the course of another year, he felt the moment called for a message of resilience and hope. Kunkel asked Louw to see what he could do with the speech. Already exhausted, Louw grabbed a bottle of whisky and a glass and got to work.

The next morning Morrison scribbled a new introduction minutes before he walked into the chamber. Before an empty public gallery, he called on the nation to 'steel' itself for crisis[13]:

We gather today at a time of great challenge for our nation and, indeed, the world. We are a strong nation and a strong people, but in the months ahead this will put us all to the test, as at no time like this since the Second World War. But together, Australia, we are up to this challenge.

The Coronavirus that is sweeping the world will continue to change the way we live, but we must not allow it to change who we are as Australians. I know – we all know – that Australians are very concerned at this difficult time. It is the understandable fear of the unknown, and there is much that is not known about the Coronavirus, but we must not let that fear overtake us. We must focus instead on what we do know, what we can control.

We know who we are as a people and the legacy and inspiration that has been given to us from those who have come before us and shown us the way through challenges and tests just like this. So we summon the spirit of the Anzacs, of our Great Depression generation, of those who built the Snowy, of those who won the great peace of the Second World War and defended Australia. That is our legacy that we draw on at this time.

CHAPTER 8

Hibernation

ON 28 MARCH 2020, Josh Frydenberg was taking a brisk morning walk around the external perimeter of Parliament House when on impulse he phoned John Howard. Clouds were beginning to gather on an otherwise sunny and mild autumn day in Canberra.

The dimensions of the economic enterprise he was about to embark on were weighing heavily on his mind.

He had gone from a mindset of fiscal restraint to Keynesian stimulus within a matter of weeks. The call was less a request for advice than an appeal for reassurance.

'As a Liberal, this isn't the type of intervention that I ever thought I'd be announcing,' Frydenberg said to the former prime minister.

'Josh, in times of crisis there is no ideology,' Howard replied.

Three days earlier, a voicemail he'd received from former colleague and Liberal senator Bill Heffernan was no less supportive but his language was far more earthy: 'Josh, you know you'll be immune from any virus because you have to eat so many shit sandwiches.'

Lessons in humility were coming thick and fast for the then 49-year-old: his ambition of being the first Treasurer in a decade to deliver a surplus had long gone extinct.

That day, at a COPC meeting, Morrison had briefed key portfolio ministers on the next, and third phase of the economic response.

In his update, Treasury's Steven Kennedy had painted a bleak picture of what the country was facing. The current circumstances would precipitate the largest fall in production since the Second World War.

A week earlier, the morning before the 22 March national cabinet meeting, Frydenberg and Morrison had unveiled the government's second stimulus package.[1] With a total stimulus of $172 billion it not only eclipsed the previous $17.6 billion stimulus announced ten days earlier on 12 March 2020,[2] but also signalled the significant shift in the government's thinking in the rapidly changing environment. While the first round of intervention reflected a belief that a short, sharp injection of money into the economy would get the country through, it was fast becoming evident that the economy would need to be protected from a deeper shock.

Because the first stimulus package – $17.6 billion – was such a large out-of-budget-cycle announcement, Frydenberg felt compelled to ring key economists to background them on the rationale.

That cautious optimism lasted barely a week and a half: Frydenberg, Morrison and Cormann announced the second stimulus package when it became clear that the states' moves towards full lockdowns would have devastating economic effects. The states' decisions to shut down schools were only making it worse.

The advice was that welfare recipients would most likely spend any extra income so doubling JobSeeker payments, the Coronavirus Supplement, in theory was going to ensure that cash was still pumping through the economy.

As a greater sense was emerging that the economy was starting to shut down as a result of the state-imposed restrictions and the recommendations that people cease all unnecessary travel within Australia, it became obvious that more would need to be done.

Philip Lowe had been advocating for a dramatically increased stimulus – to build the proverbial bridge to the other side. At that stage, though, it was still expected to be relatively short-lived. What the government needed to do was boost economic activity and make sure businesses survived.

The government had asked the major banks to defer interest and principal on small business loans, and the banks were playing ball, provided the government gave them an underwriting for their eventual losses. Frydenberg was willing to share the risk 50/50 and no more.

He was also crafting a policy to allow people to have emergency access of up to $10,000 from their superannuation accounts. More than $34 billion would be taken out of the superannuation system that way.

The RBA had already moved, on 19 March, to an extraordinary out-of-cycle interest rate cut to 0.25 per cent – the lowest on record. For the first time, the central bank would also start buying government bonds on the secondary market, to achieve quantitative easing, while offering $90 billion in loan facilities at 0.25 per cent to the banks, if they used those funds as loans to small and medium-sized businesses.

Lowe indicated that he could not predict how bad things could get, other than to say the central bank expected a major economic hit with significant job losses.

'Before the coronavirus hit, we were expecting to make progress towards full employment and the inflation target, although that progress was expected to be only very gradual,' he said when announcing these unprecedented moves. 'Recent events have obviously changed the situation.

'As our country manages this difficult situation, it is important that we do not lose sight of the fact that we will come through this. At some point, the virus will be contained and our economy and our financial markets will recover. We are in extraordinary times, and we are prepared to do whatever is necessary to make sure ... the supply of credit is there for Australian businesses and households. We feel like at the moment we've done enough. If it turns out not to be the case, there are other measures we can consider.'[3]

The ABC described the stimulus as a lifeline as the 'nation braces for an end to life as it knows it'.[4]

Among the measures were a government guarantee over unsecured small business loans up to $250,000, a reduction in the deeming rates by a further 0.25 per cent and a second $750 payment to around 5 million people. Not-for-profits and small businesses with a turnover under $50 million would receive a tax-free cash payment of up to $100,000, with a minimum payment of $20,000 for eligible companies. The expectation was that almost 700,000 businesses employing around eight million people, as well as 30,000 not-for-profits and charities, would be eligible.

The number and scale of measures, including pausing responsible lending obligations and mutual obligation rules for the unemployed, had already been significant. There had also been a $715 million assistance package for the aviation industry and a freeze on insolvencies and tenancy evictions.

On 20 March, Cormann had lifted the debt ceiling in anticipation of the significant borrowing that would be needed to pay for the stimulus.[5]

Then Morrison announced that the May budget would be delayed until October.[6]

But the ink wasn't even dry on all of this as Frydenberg, Cormann and Treasury got to work on the third and most significant package.

If the first was a stimulus and the second a bridge, then the third would become what Frydenberg reluctantly and privately referred to as the Doomsday plan.

While he, Morrison and Cormann never believed that the second stimulus package would be the end of it, none of them had a true grasp of the scale of what they would need to do next.

The UK had recently adopted wage subsidies and the federal Opposition was mounting the public case for Australia to follow suit.

On the day before the announcement of the second stimulus package, Treasury had given Frydenberg a critique of the UK model – which subsidised workers' wages at 80 per cent of their usual pay. Treasury's assessment was that it was unwieldly, impossible to cost and difficult to administer.

On 24 March, after parliament had passed the bills for the stimulus measures, Frydenberg got his first hint of what might be needed next.

In a phone hook-up, Kennedy and deputy Treasury secretary Jenny Wilkinson warned Frydenberg that they were expecting gross domestic product (GDP) to fall by between 10 and 12 per cent in the June quarter. If Frydenberg thought that was extraordinary, and it was, they went on to tell him that if the pandemic required further and ongoing social restrictions, GDP could fall by as much as 24 per cent in a single quarter. That was equivalent to $120 billion in economic activity being lost in the space of three months.

If Frydenberg and Morrison needed a clue of what they were facing, they only had to look at the queues of people lined up outside Centrelink offices, supermarket shelves emptied of toilet paper and the 'Closed' signs dotted around Bondi Beach, now an emblem for social disobedience.

*

'$130 billion ... My God!'

Over 25 and 26 March, Frydenberg set up shop in the Treasury building located on Langton Crescent in Parkes, within what is known geographically as Canberra's parliamentary or national triangle encompassing most major landmarks of the capital, to work up the options for a wage subsidy. By Friday 27 March, Kennedy and Wilkinson offered him three choices for a flat fortnightly payment: $1000, $1200 or $1500, with the last representing 70 per cent of the median wage or 100 per cent of a hospitality sector worker's median wage. For some casual workers, payments of such magnitude could exceed their normal take-home pay.

Only minutes before, Frydenberg had been consoling one of his own staff, who had burst into tears on learning that her husband had just lost his job. 'This is a break-glass moment,' he said. 'I'll take the $1500. We need to give people hope.'

Frydenberg decided to test what the government was planning by seeking feedback from an eclectic group of key business leaders. One by one, he personally phoned retailers Solomon Lew (Premier Investments), Richard Murray (JB Hi-Fi) and Rob Scott (Bunnings and Officeworks), Justin Hemmes (hospitality) and cosmetics queen Jo Horgan. He wanted to know what it would take to avoid shedding jobs in the key retail and hospitality sectors.

All of them told him they were preparing to let staff go. Frydenberg knew that once that happened, and people's employment connections were broken, the unemployment queues would stretch longer and, on the other side of the crisis, not all the staff would get reemployed.

Frydenberg asked them what they thought of his plan. Their response gave him confidence that the payments he was considering – but had yet to take to colleagues – would be enough for those companies to keep their employees on their books.

The frenetic pace of his activity that week is hard to convey. At one point, Frydenberg was glued to multiple phones. He describes one afternoon: he was talking on his mobile phone to the head of the Australian Prudential Regulatory Authority, Wayne Byres, about the regulatory changes that they needed to make to get liquidity flowing through the banking system; at the same time the Commonwealth Bank's CEO, Matt Comyn, was on his office line, telling him that the bank was moving on loan deferrals. So commonplace were extreme exhaustion levels becoming among his staff he would see them taking naps at their desks before they pushed on.

That Friday 27 March was a day of high drama. Sensationally, UK prime minister Boris Johnson confirmed he had contracted the virus.

Stepping out following a national cabinet meeting via video link, Morrison announced that further social restrictions were being imposed, including a two-person rule for outdoor gatherings, a six-month moratorium on evictions for commercial and residential tenancies in distress and the first instalment of a mental health and domestic violence funding program. As for the economy, he told journalists he was putting the final touches to a plan to effectively put the economy into 'hibernation'.

As Frydenberg prepared himself to give the PM more detail on the wage subsidy package, he found himself nervous about telling him the cost. Taking a deep breath, he picked up the phone in his Parliament House office and rang Morrison, who by then was back at The Lodge. They were both about to join a video meeting of the ERC, which included Kennedy and Wilkinson from Treasury, Australian Taxation Office (ATO) commissioner Chris Jordan, and Jeremy Hirschhorn, the deputy tax commissioner, who had been working with Treasury to develop the model.

'It's going to cost $130 billion,' Frydenberg told Morrison.

'My God,' replied the PM.

Morrison was not only cognisant of the government's imperilled budget position but of the significant debt levels they were exposing the country to.

At the ERC's video meeting everyone was in favour of Frydenberg's proposal. The Treasury officials maintained Australia was well placed to absorb the costs, with interest rates their lowest in a generation. Reassuringly, despite the pandemic, the demand for the government's ongoing bond issues remained very strong. The last was oversubscribed by four times.

What was troubling Morrison was the mobility data, which anonymously tracked people's movements via different modes of transport. While reflective of the broader social acceptance of lockdowns, the data was catastrophic for the economy as it showed the nation's cities grinding to a halt.

Channelling the wage subsidy payments through the tax system was going to be the quickest and most effective way to deliver them to people in need. When Morrison asked ATO commissioner Chris Jordan if he could actually do that, Jordan was positive.

Morrison and Frydenberg spoke again multiple times over the weekend and during the course of two more ERC meetings before landing on a policy.

Initially Treasury's proposal was for the subsidy to last for three months, but Morrison was adamant it should be six months. He wanted to give recipients some greater peace of mind and also avoid a debate in three months' time, as he couldn't be sure where the pandemic would have taken them.

Morrison also felt strongly that it should be a flat payment.

The new policy served two purposes: it kept workers tied to their employers as businesses went into hibernation, and it would prevent millions of people transferring from the workforce into a welfare system that would buckle under the strain.

He remarked that in a decade's time, historians might look back and criticise him for making the package too generous, but in his opinion that was far better than the other way around.

Frydenberg had also sought advice through Treasury on the treatment of casual workers before landing on a definition of a permanent casual: someone who could demonstrate 12 months of continuous employment.

Frydenberg's chief-of-staff, Martin Codina, came up with the name – JobKeeper – over lasagna in the PMO, as the final touches were being applied to the package before it was taken to cabinet.

'It's not so much JobSeeker but JobKeeper,' Codina said. By then it seemed obvious the country was heading towards recession. But this was unlike any ordinary downturn as the economic shocks were both on the supply side and demand side. The supply shock came when entire sectors – such as tourism, hospitality, retail and transport – were effectively shut down. The demand shock followed. The key to recovery would be in restoring confidence.

'Things were moving so fast,' Morrison recalls of that period.

'We weren't opposed to a wage subsidy. We had been thinking about it. We also knew JobSeeker wasn't going to be sufficient.

'We thought we are going to see a lot of people coming out of work because of [the coronavirus] and we are going to have to expand the safety net, loosen some of the rules because we are going to see a lot of people come on to this payment.

'We knew that if people had to go on this payment, it wasn't going to be a month or two or three, they were going to be on it for a while. So, we had to make it a sustainable income support payment.

'At the same time, we were already thinking about how we do something in the private payroll that would work. What was clear was that the wage subsidy would be needed because the social security system was not going to be able to cope with the volume.

'We weren't opposed to a wage subsidy; we were just opposed to the UK model of wage subsidy. We looked at the UK measure and Kennedy's advice was very clear that this wasn't going to work in Australia. Because it was impossible to cost: it was sitting down the entire labour force at 80 per cent of their wage.

'This always grated on me. I felt it wasn't a very egalitarian view. We weren't even sure they were going to do it or how they would do it. In an economic event like this, there is no rank. If the taxpayer is going to help an Australian, they help every Australian equally. You don't get more because you earn more.'

New Zealand and Canada announced similar schemes but without costing them. Morrison's view was that they were hastily assembled, with little thought as to how or whether they would even work.

'Josh's view and my view was that you aren't going to get away with that in Australia. When you announce something, you've got to explain how it's going to work. Otherwise, you cause chaos. And equally the media wouldn't have put up with it ... Our response was set up around principles: we must use existing mechanisms ... The UK wage subsidy violated half of these principles, so it went in the bin very fast.'

Morrison was pragmatic about the politics. What he and Frydenberg were proposing was a nationalisation of the private payroll to deliver a welfare benefit. There was little argument from his own Liberal Party colleagues, who in other circumstances would have been expected to baulk.

He and Frydenberg believed the private sector payroll system was going to stand up to the pressure better than the government welfare payment system would. Even though the money didn't flow for several weeks, people understood it was coming and could plan around it.

Frydenberg also needed to persuade the banks to provide bridging loans to businesses to keep them afloat until the JobKeeper scheme kicked into gear.

Morrison recalled 'the big challenge in the early part was to protect the country from despair. The other purpose was to buy time, to buy businesses time, about their decisions ... no one knew what the economy would look like in two weeks, let alone two months.

'I knew if we didn't get on top of this, we would be in freefall,' Morrison said.

None of this had yet gone to cabinet and the deliberations were held very tightly to just a handful of ministers and advisers.

*

While Morrison, Frydenberg and Cormann spent the final week of March developing an Australian model of wage subsidy that would not only work but be fiscally responsible – as much as that was possible during a crisis – Hunt found himself dealing with a separate crisis: the potential crumbling of the entire private health system.

While this may seem like an exaggeration, during the second half of March 2020, the risk that Australia's primary health care system could also wind down was real considering the experience of other countries. Italy and later Brazil experienced the almost complete collapse of their health systems due to the high number of cases requiring hospitalisation.

Getting the tele-health network up and running was a complex and intense project, and to Hunt it looked like it would be accomplished with astonishing speed and with remarkably few problems given the technological and regulatory issues that had to be grappled with. He and his colleagues were working on it when Covid-19 case numbers began to rise alarmingly and the states looked like they'd be shutting down non-urgent elective surgery.

Hunt felt that the state CHOs were forcing elective surgery shutdowns through the AHPPC without understanding the consequences, and the Commonwealth would be forced to backfill.

Private hospitals had a workforce of almost 100,000, including 57,000 nurses. Cancelling elective surgery placed those jobs and the businesses themselves at risk. While larger private hospital organisations might have survived, the smaller providers, including the Catholic hospitals, would struggle to recover.

On top of this, there were legitimate concerns about the supply of PPE, and about infection control and freeing up beds and ventilators for the public-system Covid patients.

For a five-day period, Hunt worked on a plan to save the private health system. At the same time, he was trying to push the ERC to sign off on the immediate national rollout of the tele-health plan.

Hunt was still on ERC at the time, which had made it easier for him to argue the case with colleagues. But without the support of Cormann, highly skilled at talking people around, he may never have won the necessary approvals.

Cormann was instrumental in getting Morrison and Frydenberg on side with the funding of tele-health.

Hunt's private hospital plan – which involved a viability guarantee that would effectively involve a soft nationalisation of the entire system, albeit on a temporary basis – was unpalatable to both the Treasury and Finance departments, which cited matters of principal and also budgetary concerns.

Initially, it looked as though Hunt's plan could cost $1 billion, but ultimately the scheme was accepted with no cap.

In the end, it cost less than the $1 billion because elective surgery was one of the first services to resume in the Covid recovery phase.

Hunt was convinced that if his scheme had not been implemented, tens of thousands of nursing staff might have been stood down, crippling a national health workforce needed for the Covid response. That capacity was also needed to handle the post-Covid backlog waiting lists and overflow from the public system.

*

'The biggest decision in our political lives'

In the run-up to the JobKeeper announcement, Kunkel was becoming anxious about a looming gap in the practical management of the crisis. While the National Coordination Mechanism was running well, under direction from Home Affairs deputy secretary Paul Grigson, he spotted a troubling disconnect between the bureaucracy and industry.

Frydenberg had established a special business liaison unit to provide a link between business and Treasury on economic issues, but Kunkel was seeing a lack of coordination with industry at a practical level, for example, in crucial areas like making masks, getting hand sanitisers, manufacturing and supply chains into supermarkets. Kunkel believed this could be solved if industry was given a bigger role in the overall management of the pandemic.

He came up with the idea of a National Covid Commission that could feed advice into the system alongside the NSC, ERC and the AHPPC. It would be run directly out of PM&C. After the idea was workshopped at several ERC meetings, Frydenberg suggested WA mining boss Nev Power, the former CEO of Fortescue Metals, to run it.

Morrison got on well with Power. He'd met him through his WA-based assistant minister, Ben Morton, and Cormann. Not only was Power a problem solver but he was a straight talker. In Morrison's view, people from WA usually came without the 'bullshit'. If you've run a mine you've got to be pretty practical.

Kunkel and Morrison sat down to work out who else to put on the commission. Kunkel produced a list including David Thodey, former Telstra boss and chairman of the CSIRO. He had headed the 2019 review of the public service. Catherine Tanna was on the list. She was managing director of EnergyAustralia and an RBA board member. Others were businessman and former managing director of courier company Toll Holdings, Paul Little; the former Productivity Commission chairman, Peter Harris; and Jane Halton, a former career public servant who had served as secretary of both the Health Department and Department of Finance.

Morrison also wanted to call in Greg Combet, the former ACTU boss and Labor minister in the Rudd government. He was already working with Industrial Relations minister Christian Porter and the unions on industrial relations reforms.

Morrison personally called Combet and appealed to his sense of patriotic duty.

'Your country needs you,' Morrison told him. 'I need people to solve problems fast.'

What Morrison liked about the Covid Commission was that it brought in people directly at the coalface of industry, cutting industry groups like the Business Council of Australia and the Australian Chamber of Commerce and Industry out of the loop.

It also put together a group of experts, in finance, health and business and industry, who went looking for problems to solve rather than waiting for them to appear.

Morrison knew that from time to time, they would step on some ministerial and bureaucratic toes. And he was happy for them to do so.

*

On Sunday 29 March, Morrison addressed his cabinet and briefed them on the package he knew would force many Liberal and National Party colleagues to test their ideological principles and values against this one-in-a-hundred-years crisis.

The infection rate had spiked again, with 528 cases recorded that day – the second highest of the pandemic to date, with the overall number of cases now close to 4000.

Morrison told them that the JobKeeper package would save hundreds of thousands of businesses and keep millions of people in work.

'This is the biggest decision we will make in our [political] lives. Countries that get this wrong will take a generation to recover. We have to get as many Australians through this as we can.'

Morrison said that even though it had been barely three weeks, the first stimulus package was now 'old world' thinking.

For many around the cabinet table, the enormity of what Morrison was putting to them had a definite sense of the surreal.

Not for the first time, Morrison allowed himself to become emotional when pondering what the cabinet, having been forced to a point that had been previously unthinkable, was about to do.

He took the Treasurer aside and, in a quiet and solemn moment, said, 'Josh, I thought we would be building the nation, not saving it.'

The following day, writing in *The Australian* newspaper, Paul Kelly declared that with this latest package[7] the government had 'averted a depression'.[8]

'This is the most momentous and unprecedented fiscal decision in our history,' he wrote.

'There has never been anything like this. Past ideological prescriptions are annihilated.

'No Liberal government has remotely contemplated such spending before. The deficits and debts will linger for years and maybe decades.'

CHAPTER 9

Flattening the curve

LITERALLY OVERNIGHT, AUSTRALIA'S cities metamorphosed from thriving centres of human pursuit and endeavour into empty concrete and glass monuments to what life was like before the virus. 'This is getting very, very real,' Morrison declared to an apprehensive nation on 2 April 2020,[1] barely days into a nationwide lockdown.

A mass social experiment was underway. As well planned as it might have been, it would also have unintended and unforeseeable consequences. For the economy, for society, for industry, livelihoods and the mental wellbeing of millions.

People were locked away in their homes while parents were working out how to school their children. Malls were drained of shoppers, the skies empty of aircraft, and streets stripped bare but for freight, garbage trucks, essential workers and the postal services, which still ran on time.

In the regions and the bush, life threatened to retreat even further into bucolic isolation.

Amid the confinement and enforced separation, there were few remaining links to the largely unremarked daily rituals of the past. The sick had even stopped going to the doctor for fear of getting Covid.

'Today, emergency powers are in place across all the states and territories and at a commonwealth level with a very clear message when it comes to the measures we need to have in place, to continue to save lives and to save livelihoods,' Morrison said. 'Stay at home unless you're out there exercising, getting medical care, you are going to work or education, these are important, or getting things that you need at the shops.'[2]

It was another echo of 1919 and the Spanish flu when, before radio and television, it was up to the daily newspapers to bugle government decrees of social restrictions through to the public. Historians were already making comparisons. Universities around the globe were collaborating to crowdsource a digital archive of Covid, *Journal of a Plague Year*, inspired by Daniel Defoe's account of the 18th-century bubonic plague that ravaged London.[3]

No one was exempt from the changes sweeping the world, not even the PMO. Plans were drawn up restricting the numbers allowed to be in the office at any time. Ministers' personal cars, idle due to the absence of MPs, were allocated to transport Morrison's staff from their Canberra flats to the office instead of taxis and Uber, to maintain as much of a Covid-safe bubble as possible. Cabinet secretary Andrew Shearer installed hand sanitiser at the entry to the cabinet room.

By and large, Australians were adapting, as they had before. And for the most part, it seemed to be working.

Even though much of the country was seized with fear or uncertainty, or forced into solitude, the daily infection rates began to fall dramatically. It was back to double digits almost immediately and, within days, single digits.

Australia had entered its 'suppression phase', effectively code for nothing is normal and no one has a clue how long that will last.

'I really want Australians to understand that we need to be in this for that haul. It will be months,' Morrison said. 'We are fighting a war on two fronts. We are fighting this virus and we are fighting the economic threats that it carries for us.'[4]

Privately, the phrase that kept coming to Morrison was that 'humans are not animals', in a pejorative sense at least, and were capable of adapting rapidly to change. Even if the experience was unpleasant, when they got to the other side of lockdowns their behaviour would likely be different.

It had been only 21 days since the WHO had officially declared the global outbreak of Covid-19. It was reporting more than 1 million people infected across 171 countries, and almost 6000 deaths every day. Murphy had told Morrison he believed the true number of deaths was likely ten times that.

On 3 April, Morrison spoke with Indonesian president Joko Widodo, whose concerns for his country gave Morrison pause for thought. Australia had 4704 active Covid-19 cases and 25 people had died. Indonesia had little early reporting but there was a sense Covid there could be catastrophic.

The call drained Morrison emotionally. The magnitude of what was happening sat heavily upon his shoulders amid his fears for a neighbouring country that could be devastated by the virus. 'I just can't go home yet,' he told Morton, who had relocated from Perth several weeks earlier and would barely leave Morrison's side for the next few months. 'I think I need a beer.'

Morrison would become even more troubled when three days later he heard that Boris Johnson had been moved to an intensive care unit.

In this first wave, Australia was faring much better than other countries but Morrison's attitude was 'plan for the worst and hope for the best'.

*

Bringing them home

In the last weeks of March, one of Morrison's greatest worries, which would only intensify, was the conundrum over returning Australians, including those who were resisting the government's advice that they should come home.

Thousands stranded overseas were confronted with flights being cancelled and inadequate quarantine places in Australia, with many unable to pay exorbitant airline ticket prices.

Morrison and the premiers were also apprehensive about the upcoming school holidays and families still seeking to go overseas for them. The last week of March and the first week of April were shaping up to be critical.

WA premier Mark McGowan was extremely concerned that families would fly to Bali and bring chests full of Covid back with them.

Even the closure of international borders appeared to bring no guarantee of safety. To the surprise of Morrison – as well as Murphy and Hunt – US case numbers were on the rise and that was after the US had shut its own international borders.

With Australia now effectively shut to the world, Morrison believed that there was only a narrow window to get Australian residents back. But there was a burning competing issue.

As the health experts kept pointing out, the bulk of Covid-19 cases Australia was recording came from people coming home. At that stage, 20,000 to 30,000 people were entering the country every day.

Possible solutions were roundtabled by the national cabinet. Options floated included placing stickers on house windows to indicate they were temporarily out of bounds or mandating the wearing of wristbands or armbands to enforce self-isolation.

As the national cabinet examined the issues from all sides, its stance shifted from imploring people to come home to 'we don't want you home'. The concern was that the longer people stayed overseas, or delayed their return, the greater the risk they would contract the virus and bring it home.

Morrison put forward the idea that returning travellers should do mandatory quarantine in their home states. The premiers and chief ministers embraced the proposal and, to Morrison's surprise, agreed to not only run quarantine for returning travellers but wear the cost. It was unanimous that the best way to run quarantine would be under state and territory health orders. From this discussion, hotel quarantine was born. To help run it effectively, the PM offered them all the ADF personnel they needed.

Once the scheme was announced, however, the number of arrivals dropped markedly. The idea of 14 days quarantine had a significant deterrent effect.

*

A twin crisis

Australia had moved early – and ahead of most other countries – in establishing the Covid-19 response as a twin crisis of health and economics. While both were distinct problems of their own, they were indissolubly linked.

It was an important association that was not universally shared around the national cabinet table. Some premiers argued that any measures taken on the health side were justified no matter what the economic cost.

Morrison took issue with this position and had made the point emphatically from the outset. At one meeting of the national cabinet that month, he had studies on the correlation between suicides and economic contractions run into the room so he could read them out to the premiers to convince them.

'I said, "You know people commit suicide in depressions",' he recalls. '"So let's not assume an economic effect doesn't have a human effect, potentially for a generation ... they are equally important and you can solve both at the same time." Some of them believed that you only had to solve the health problem.'

The deeper they dug into the myriad issues the pandemic triggered, the more consumed Morrison became with data, numbers, projections, the verifiable. He would increasingly demand of the bureaucracy better and more real-time material to be printed on the data 'placemats' he was given every day – A3 pages comprising the relevant data and information on a particular problem. For a while, he was receiving up to eight placemats a day, providing an almost real-time coverage across the spectrum of the health effects of the virus and the economic decisions being made.

Primed by phone conversations with former Australian of the Year and University of Melbourne psychiatrist Patrick McGorry, Morrison turned his attention to the mental health impacts, which, he was warned, would be significant. Ian Hickie from the University of Sydney's Brain and Mind Centre was also among the mental health experts warning that suicide could kill more people than Covid. The PM set Australia on a path to get ahead of the curve on that problem too.

The federal government laid claim to being among the first governments in the world to recognise this emerging problem.[5]

'I thought that the more data I can get, the better I can target the responses and effort,' Morrison recalls. 'I wanted to build a system in real time ... to get out of the lockdown you needed to allow for a higher-functioning economy and a health system that can respond instantaneously to outbreaks. We wanted to get an economy that can live with the virus, so when it goes bang and you get an outbreak, you can smack it down really fast.

'For that you needed a testing regime, data systems, and resources ready to scramble.'

In a nutshell, the emphasis on health bureaucrats making decisions with profound economic implications had to swing back the other way. The economists had to have more of a say. But the premiers didn't necessarily share Morrison's preoccupation with keeping the two in balance.

There arose a feeling in Canberra that the states had subjugated leadership to their chief health officers while sidelining their own treasuries and economic advisers.

Morrison worried that New South Wales and Victoria were going too hard on enforcing their lockdowns and risked losing public support. Potentially it could lead to civil unrest.

Fortunately, between JobKeeper kicking in and the tripartite group of the NCM, the business liaison unit and the overarching Covid Commission hitting their strides, things started to settle down. Efforts as granular as ordering local councils to lift their night-time curfews to allow trucks through suburban streets to deliver goods helped.

That wasn't to say that the unity of the national cabinet wouldn't be sorely tested, like when Kennedy warned the premiers that closing schools delivered a near-fatal shot to the economy. The issue gnawed at Morrison. When he met with the Australian Education Union, which he found cooperative, he was surprised how little sway they had with the powerful teachers' unions. The posture of the states was being driven by the unions rather than science.

His response – which he would later admit may have been ill-timed – was to try to bypass the premiers and deliver a public appeal to parents and teachers to keep students in school. While he may have convinced parents, yet again, the two largest states were implacable.

McGowan and Marshall had been sympathetic to Morrison's view that schools were integral to reopening the economy, but Andrews and Berejiklian were less so.

On the health front, Morrison had been working on an idea he got from a conversation with Japan's prime minister, Shinzo Abe: placing strike teams into hotspots to extinguish clusters as they emerged. The premiers didn't warm to the PM's proposal to have the military lock down suburbs. Khaki on the streets was not the way forward. Back to the drawing board they all went.

*

A question kept arising at national cabinet: were they pursuing a suppression strategy or going for eradication, as Victoria's chief health officer, Brett Sutton, seemed to be pushing for. This was at odds with Murphy's assessment that in the absence of a vaccine, such a strategy was implausible. Eradication, or elimination, such as had been achieved 30 years earlier with smallpox, for example, meant a complete absence of the virus. By definition this meant stopping all Australians from returning home. No one else was suggesting that just yet.

Murphy and Hunt suspected Victoria's hawkish posture was borne from a fear that its contact tracing abilities would not stand up in the face of a significant outbreak.

Contact tracing was a long-established system for hunting down sources and potential spreaders of communicable and highly contagious diseases in a community. Identifying anyone who may have had contact with an infected person. Victoria was still using paper-based contact tracing systems requiring manual input into a database. Under a high-caseload scenario, such a system could be quickly overwhelmed.

With all that in mind, and conscious of the economic and social dislocation that even a few weeks of lockdown would deliver, on 3 April, Morrison signalled that the government was now looking at the next phase of the crisis, the way out, the road to recovery.[6] By now, he'd taken his obsession with data to another level, introducing to the national cabinet a dashboard that would also feed in daily data from the states to track the progress of the virus and the response.

'... had the virus kept growing at the same rate it was 12 days ago, we would now have more than 10,500 cases in this country,' he said. 'There'd be over 5000 more cases. And in fact, some commentators who were doing the maths were suggesting that we would have had 8000 cases just as recently as last weekend. That is a tribute to the work that has been done by Australians in getting around and supporting the very sensible measures that are being put in place all around the country by the state and territory governments.

'But we must continue to do this. It doesn't matter what the temperature is. If it's a warm day, don't go in masses down to the beach. That's a simple instruction that all Australians expect other Australians to abide by. It isn't just the government asking you to do this. It's your fellow Australians asking you to do this ...'[7]

*

More from Moore

Already the federal government had announced more than $200 billion in economic supports, a figure that would eventually grow to more than $320 billion when all measures were taken into account.

Morrison was constantly reminded of Kennedy's warning from the outset not to repeat the mistakes of the GFC, of which he had intimate knowledge since he was in Treasury at the time. 'Whatever you do, don't invent anything new,' Kennedy told Morrison. 'Don't let the perfect be the enemy of the good.'

He was speaking chiefly about the funding of stimulus initiatives, not confined to the failed Home Insulation Program (aka the Pink Batts scheme), which funnelled billions of dollars of taxpayers' funds into ill-devised and politically skewed projects with often disastrous fiscal and social consequences.

There were still challenges in getting the broader bureaucracy to comprehend that Covid was going to have a far greater material impact on the real economy than the GFC. People simply wouldn't be going to work.

So, pumping cash directly into the economy wouldn't suffice on its own. After all, there were no guarantees people would spend it.

Treasury briefed Frydenberg on 13 April that if the government hadn't created JobKeeper the national unemployment rate would have hit 15 per cent. Despite the unparalleled fiscal and monetary intervention, Frydenberg was coming under pressure from industry as well. Several large organisations were demanding specific and sizeable assistance outside the JobKeeper payments and the other remedies already available to them.

The most publicised example was Virgin Australia. On 2 April, VA chief executive officer Paul Scurrah confirmed he was seeking $1.4 billion in government assistance to stay in the air. Initially, Frydenberg was sympathetic.

But Morrison was convinced there were 'Melbourne politics' involved and, from the outset, believed that the issues facing Virgin were not sector-wide. Cormann was equally as hostile to company specific bailouts. Virgin had been in commercial trouble prior to the pandemic. Morrison took the approach that he was not going to 'get played' by the big end of town.

Qantas was reacting aggressively to rumours that the government was considering assistance for Virgin. Qantas CEO Alan Joyce claimed that if Virgin got public aid Qantas should get the same.

The future of the nation's second airline became a vigorous topic of discussion over several ERC meetings. Morrison didn't want to bail out Qantas any more than he wanted to bail out Virgin. He didn't buy the argument put to him that governments around the world were bailing out airlines. They were bailing out national carriers. Virgin, a foreign-owned carrier, didn't fit the bill.

Even though the message to market was that there would be no corporate bailouts, Morrison did go in to bat on Virgin's behalf. He called Singapore's prime minister, Lee Hsien Loong, to test the waters on whether Singapore Airlines had any ambitions to take over VA. It already owned a 20 per cent stake. He told Lee that if Singapore Airlines was interested, Australia could discuss further air rights. Lee's response was that, after already pumping $20 billion into Singapore Airlines to keep it alive through its sovereign wealth fund Temasek, they weren't in 'acquisition mode'. By then, Morrison's view, eventually accepted by Frydenberg and others, was that VA's best option was to go into voluntary administration, which it did on 21 April.[8]

The government wanted two airlines to survive post Covid – to ensure competition – but if there was only going to be one, it had to be Qantas. Morrison and Cormann remained firm with VA. If it genuinely was a fair dinkum airline with a future, as VA was arguing, the government believed commercial money would be out there to ensure it survived. Frydenberg brought in former Macquarie Bank CEO Nicholas Moore to assess Virgin's viability and the options for government assistance.

Now realising there would be other industries of national significance facing the same fate, he widened Moore's brief, to quietly head up a unit in Treasury to assess businesses deemed critical to the economy.

*

Another vexing issue facing Morrison and the premiers was commercial tenancies. Morrison was hearing – from friends, MPs as well as the premiers – about landlords maltreating tenants who had lost business due to the lockdown. Mark McGowan was also vocal about this, and spouted some of the horror stories he'd been hearing. The hibernation strategy was all about keeping businesses alive, albeit at a low level of activity, with creditors giving them space.

Morrison and the premiers kicked the issue back to their Treasurers but when only weak proposals came back from them Morrison started having private and very heated conversations with some of the larger commercial landlords.

He left them in no doubt as to what he thought of their behaviour. Then, having given up on the Treasurers, he sat down and wrote the policy himself, on an issue over which the Commonwealth had no jurisdiction.

The principles included a system of waivers and deferrals on rent, which would see landlords share a proportion of reductions in turnovers of their tenants. It was limited to companies with a turnover under $50 million, with the view that big players could look after themselves.

There would be a moratorium on evictions. It didn't mean landlords couldn't demand rent; they just couldn't throw their tenants out for not paying it.

*

By mid-April, Morrison was already getting frustrated about how long the recovery was taking and he wanted to turn the conversation to what was needed to start opening up again.

The consequences of lockdowns on people's mental health were playing out as warned, and there were increased incidences of domestic violence. At several NSC meetings, Home Affairs minister Peter Dutton reported that the Australian Federal Police were seeing a spike in online child sexual abuse and grooming. These were all gut-wrenching matters no pandemic plan could have foreseen.

There was an ever-growing list of things to consider. Ensuring childcare centres stayed operational for essential workers, home delivery service for the National Disability Insurance Scheme (NDIS), changes to temporary visa holders to allow workers to stay and even tax considerations for people working from home. There were also the temporary structural changes to the industrial relations system that were needed to allow employers to reduce workers' hours to keep them in their jobs. The daily task of triaging the economy and the impacts of the hibernation policy across every aspect of modern life was nothing that could have been predicted.

On 14 April, the International Monetary Fund released its world economic outlook declaring that the world economy in 2020 would suffer its worst year since the Great Depression.[9]

The number of recorded global cases had passed 2 million. More than 130,000 had died. But again, Australian officials considered that was a significant underestimation.

Encouragingly, Australia seemed to be managing the crisis better than most other countries. It certainly was faring better than the world's other advanced economies. Three months into the crisis, there was some cause for optimism when it seemed that the draconian measures taken early were indeed 'flattening the curve' of the infection rate.

By then the world was demanding answers as to how it had got to this point so quickly. The focus began shifting back to the World Health Organization. And to China.

CHAPTER 10
The Middle Kingdom

AS BAD AS the pandemic was, the concern that kept Morrison awake at night was China. He knew that Covid would eventually recede, but the 'Middle Kingdom's' ambitions would be the enduring strategic issue that Australia would still be dealing with 50 years from now.

Morrison said as much to Andrew Shearer one afternoon at Kirribilli House when he confided in his cabinet secretary that he believed the world was entering a dangerous geo-strategic shift that the West had failed to grasp fully.

Shearer was regarded as a China hawk. A national security adviser to John Howard and Tony Abbott, he was appointed deputy director of the Office of National Intelligence (ONI) by Malcolm Turnbull.

After Morrison won the 2019 election, he made Shearer cabinet secretary, and would eventually promote him to the top of the intelligence community pile in November 2020, as director general of ONI.

When it came to national security, Shearer's experience and political judgement helped to stiffen the resolve of any handwringers in the ministry. He was regarded as more fearless in his views than Morrison's national security adviser, Michelle Chan, a respected former Australian diplomat.

As early as February 2020, concerns were raised in cabinet about the potential that China might aggressively engage in economic coercion and increase military activity in the region under cover of the pandemic.

On 24 February, the secretary of PM&C, Phil Gaetjens, briefed cabinet on a planning document that dealt with Chinese economic coercion, which Shearer had advised on and which had been in development long before the pandemic. Gaetjens characterised Covid as a 'stress test' in the two countries' relationship and predicted Australia should expect friction from China.

The assessment was that China could respond to Covid domestically and continue with its coercive tactics internationally. In other words, China would not be weakened by Covid; rather, it would be empowered, if only temporarily. Australia should expect more cyber-attacks and increased militarisation in the region.

It was Morrison who raised in cabinet the subject of the public mood towards China. He felt sure it was one of both concern and acceptance that Australia was exposed. He reiterated a long-held view that it remained important for Australia to diversify its trade relationships and deepen strategic partnerships.

It was critical, he said, for the government to find ways to support the Australian Chinese community while, at the same time, working more closely with the US through the Indo-Pacific as well as the EU to counter any supply-chain threats. It was prudent planning, he argued, to find pragmatic ways to deal with China without creating vulnerabilities.

He was fully aware that some agricultural industries would be exposed, and their businesses risked becoming collateral damage. At the same time, the government couldn't allow the taxpayer to act as the risk insurer for every company that had China as its major customer or supplier.

'We will cop some pain but we can't let it undermine our national security,' Morrison told his colleagues.

It wasn't until 6 April, at a full meeting of the NSC, that the national security implications of Covid were laid out for the first time. The view from the intelligence community was that the pandemic would accelerate strategic tensions in the region. China could be expected to make the most of the situation.

Fragile states in South-East Asia would be hardest hit by Covid. There were deep concerns for Indonesia, where the estimates were that 'millions' of its citizens could die. Covid was set to be the most traumatic event since the Second World War for many of the nations in the region. The strategic assessment was that Beijing would see it as an opportunity and could take advantage. It would try to seize the initiative.

Morrison believed that Australia would need to counter this and fill any vacuum China would seek to exploit. But there was no misapprehension that it wouldn't come at a cost.

'Don't doubt China's capacity and will to exploit Covid-19,' Morrison told the meeting.

*

Rise of the Dragon

To choose the point when the relationship with China started to change would be like trying to nominate the first autumn leaf to fall. The greater question was who had changed: Australia or China?

There had been low points before. Relations soured in the wake of the Tiananmen Square massacre of 1989, and again in 1996 over Taiwan.

By the time Xi Jinping addressed the Australian Parliament in November 2014,[1] becoming only the second Chinese president to do so, the bilateral relationship had endured a 40-year diplomatic courtship, punctuated by periods of deep mistrust, clashes over China's human rights abuses and strategic pressures prompted by the deepening of the Australia–US alliance, all set against several resource booms which underpinned the prospering trade partnership.

The pre-Xi view of China was set against a different world but one that was susceptible to the recalibration occurring in the Indo-Pacific region. China had been expanding its influence throughout the region through its sheer economic size.

But then it was a foreign policy rooted in soft-power diplomacy more than overt military projection, as Singapore's first premier, the late Lee Kuan Yew (a man regarded as one of Asia's seminal leaders of the 20th century) had said of China more than a decade ago, regarding the choice the world was faced with in the new century:

> Peace and security in the Asia-Pacific will turn on whether China emerges as a xenophobic, chauvinistic force, bitter and hostile to the West because it tried to slow down or abort its development or is educated and involved in the world, more cosmopolitan, more internationalized and outward looking.
>
> As China's development nears the point when it will have enough weight to elbow its way into the region, it will make a fateful decision – whether to be a hegemon using its economic and military weight to create a sphere of influence or to continue as a good citizen ...
>
> If States or enterprises do not accept China's position and pay appropriate deference, they are faced with the threat of being shut out of a rapidly growing market with 1.3 billion people. [2]

Lee's view then was that China understood it could never hope to match the US with its significant technological advantage. There would be no point in a military confrontation.

Ironically, the stability of the region provided by the US since the end of the Second World War was also the very foundation for the rapid economic advancement of the Asian Tiger economies as well as China.

This provided the greater disincentive for confrontation.

'China knows that it needs access to US markets, US technology, opportunities for Chinese students to study in the US and bring back to China new ideas about new frontiers,' said Lee. 'It therefore sees no profit in confronting the US in the next 20 to 30 years in a way that could jeopardize those benefits.'[3]

Lee's summation might have been right at the time but for an underestimation of Xi.

At the 19th People's Congress in 2017, Xi's ambitions for a nationalistic revival could not have sent a clearer signal as to which direction the foreign policy pendulum was oscillating. China would be at the 'centre stage' by the middle of the century, he declared.[4]

Lowy Institute senior fellow Richard McGregor, in his 2019 paper 'Xi Jinping: The Backlash', said Xi's 'clarity of purpose provided a sharper lens through which the rest of the world could view China's actions'.[5]

'Not only had Beijing become more powerful and less willing to hide its disdain for its critics' views, Xi has articulated a willingness to leverage Beijing's elevated power to press the ruling Communist Party's ambitions with a force and coherence that his predecessors' lacked,' McGregor wrote.[6]

McGregor, an expert on China's political system and a former China correspondent for the *Financial Times* and *The Australian*, commented:

Xi has not just reenergised the ideological state that Mao ruled over in a more primitive form. Under Xi, as with Mao, the personal is political as well.

Xi's ideological bent underpins the hardening foreign critique of China, of a hostile power more interested in surpassing the West than working with it. It also helps explain the reaction at home. The backlash against Xi inside China is less visible, for obvious reasons. Xi has made it perilous to oppose him openly. Even lofty members of the Politburo are careful to routinely pledge fealty, lest they fall foul of the leader.

To be sure, Xi is in no danger of being toppled from his perch. As long as China's economy remains reasonably healthy, he can count on sufficient support to retain his hold on the system.[7]

Under Xi, the CCP pumped record spending into defence hardware and soft-power economic programs spearheaded by the Belt and

Road Initiative. The modernisation of the nation's military, a process started under Deng Xiaoping in 1978, would reach new levels under Xi.

China built its first aircraft carrier, the *Liaoning*, and invested heavily in ballistic missile capability in a direct challenge to US strategic air power in the region, facilitating the withdrawal of the continuous presence of US bombers on the strategic island of Guam.

Their cyberwarfare capacity, an industrial-scale operation dwarfing similar state-sponsored set-ups in Russia, Iran and North Korea, maintains a 24/7 transnational assault targeting the critical infrastructure of countries and companies, and stealing information from governments across the spectrum.

Trump's 2016 election victory, which ushered in a new US unilateralism amid the backdrop of terrorism and the rise of Islamic fundamentalism and fractures in the European Union, bracketed by Brexit, provided cover for China to grow its influence among developing nations.

Xi's hardline policies on the South China Sea, Taiwan, Hong Kong and Uighurs in the Xinjiang province would ultimately shift the global view of China. But it was a gradual awakening rather than immediate for most western countries. Australia came to the realisation before most.

Brookings Institution fellow Rush Doshi, in his book *The Long Game*, outlined China's strategy of displacing American order in the world.[8] He talks of China's 'blunting strategy', a policy built on diminishing US influence internationally rather than taking them head on.

Since the Second World War, the US has used international institutions to advance its strategic interests. Doshi makes the case that China set about a long game by infiltrating the international fora, including the WHO, by stacking them with their own numbers, with member countries that China had effectively bought off whether through BRI investments or direct investment in critical infrastructure. The effect was the blunting of US influence.

The world was now not only seeing the impact of the blunting strategy but witnessing the transitioning to a new phase of China's strategic ambitions – the sharpening of its military and technological capability.

*

'The Australian people stand up'

The genesis of Australia's recent troubles with China can be in part traced back to China's recalculation during the GFC that the financial collapse was not only the beginning of the decline of America but a crisis that would undermine the integrity of the free market more broadly and damage the pre-eminence of liberal democracies. This swung China's outlook to a more emboldened one. The election of Xi in 2012 put this new foreign policy posture on steroids.

But it wasn't until Australia's sovereignty was challenged that a new and darker element was injected into the Australia/China relationship, which changed the game.

For Morrison, the first signs emerged in early 2015 when then Treasurer Joe Hockey began to raise concerns not only about the level of foreign investment coming from China but its nature. The investments were shifting from the purchase of prime agricultural land to bidding for sophisticated telecommunications, port infrastructure and energy distribution assets as the state and territory governments began privatising their state-owned assets.

One of Morrison's first forays into this space was after he was awarded the Treasury portfolio in September 2015, after Turnbull successfully challenged Tony Abbott for the Liberal Party leadership and became prime minister. Morrison appointed David Irvine, a former director general of both the Australian Security Intelligence Organisation (ASIO) and the Australian Secret Intelligence Service (ASIS), as well as a former ambassador to China, to the Foreign Investment Review Board (FIRB) in the wake of the Northern

Territory government's controversial Port of Darwin lease-sale to the Chinese-owned Landbridge group.[9]

This was the first signal that everything had changed and that the Australian government was thinking in a completely different way.

From then on, FIRB applied a new national security lens to all foreign bids for state-owned critical infrastructure.

One issue that hastened the breakdown was the collapse of talks about a formal extradition arrangement between Australia and China, following years of negotiations.

With a treaty first signed in September 2007, the Turnbull government was ready to push the button in 2017. At the highest levels, Beijing believed the extradition treaty would be ratified despite national security hawks warning Australian officials about the ramifications and precedent of such a deal.

The issue was that under Xi, Chinese authorities had launched a global purge of rivals not seen since Mao, under Operation Fox Hunt.[10] Launched in 2014 it was promoted as being focused on weeding out corruption but China hawks saw it being used to run covert domestic and global operations, targeting Chinese dissidents living abroad. In addition, the intelligence services viewed Xi's operatives to be engaging in clandestine overseas tactics to identify and eliminate anti-CCP operatives.

Following a Coalition backbench revolt and Labor's decision to team up with Liberal Party defector Cory Bernardi in the Senate to oppose the extradition deal, the Turnbull government pulled it within days of a visit to Australia by Chinese premier Li Keqiang.[11]

After decades of bilateral leaders' visits between Beijing and Canberra, Li's trip would be the last.

Xi and senior officials effectively slapped a ban on all high-level contact between Australian and Chinese leaders and ministers, which remains in place to this day.

The collapse of the Australia–China extradition treaty initiated the first of Beijing's retaliatory measures, with the imposition of trade sanctions on Australian meat exporters.

When the Turnbull government released its Foreign Policy White Paper in November 2017,[12] adopting a hard position on Beijing's aggressive behaviour in the South China Sea, the deterioration in relations continued at a rapid pace.

Tensions reached new levels ahead of the 16 December 2017 Bennelong by-election, when Malcolm Turnbull announced his government would legislate the biggest overhaul of Australian espionage and intelligence laws in recent history.

Standing alongside former tennis champion John Alexander, who'd been forced to recontest Bennelong after being caught up in the parliament's citizenship crisis, Turnbull famously compared Australia and China, incurring fierce and enduring hostility from Beijing: 'I tell you this,' Turnbull said, 'modern China was founded in 1949 with this, with these words: "Zhōngguórén men zhànqǐlai", "The Chinese people have stood up." It was an assertion of sovereignty; it was an assertion of pride. And we stand up, and so we say: "Àodàlìyǎren men zhànqǐlai", "The Australian people stand up."

'Chinese people stand up for their sovereignty, and they expect Australian people and particularly Australian leaders to stand up for theirs. That is why we respect each other and that is why they respect me and my government.'[13]

Political commentators were inclined to view Turnbull's move on foreign interference through the prism of domestic politics: his was a minority government, after all. But this belied the actual nature of the threat, which was exposed earlier, in April 2016, when Turnbull approved a public declaration that Australia now had an offensive cyber capability.[14]

The significance was not appreciated at the time. But few, if any, western governments had made public admissions about military capability in this grey zone before. It was a not-so-subtle message to foreign actors including China that Australia would respond to cyber intrusion.

The height of the foreign interference debate came amid a series of scandals engulfing rising Labor star Senator Sam Dastyari over his dealings with political donor and Chinese businessman Huang Xiangmo. At a press conference for Chinese media outlets, attended by the billionaire, he contradicted Australian – and Labor – policy on the South China Sea.[15] It ultimately ended his career.

The backlash from Beijing was swift. Senior figures slammed Turnbull's 'stand up' remarks and the handling of the Dastyari affair. China swung into full 'wolf warrior diplomacy' mode.

Within weeks, officials in Beijing made threats about a consumer-led boycott of Australian exports, tourism and universities. In May 2018, Chinese customs held up shipments from Treasury Wine Estates, producer of premium wine labels such as Penfolds and Wolf Blass.[16]

Next the government banned Chinese tech giant Huawei from supplying Australia's infrastructure for the 5G telecommunications network.[17] Turnbull had been an early mover on the perceived threat posed by the Shenzhen-based 5G vendor. To China's fury, this sparked a domino effect: Australia's partners in the Five Eyes security alliance – Canada, the US, Britain and New Zealand – and other western democracies started pushing back against Chinese infiltration of their critical infrastructure and telecommunications networks.

On 23 August 2018 – the day before Turnbull's demise as prime minister – a statement was released by then Communications minister Mitch Fifield and Morrison, who was acting Home Affairs minister following Peter Dutton's resignation from the ministry to contest the leadership.

'The government considers that the involvement of vendors who are likely to be subject to extrajudicial directions from a foreign government that conflict with Australian law, may risk failure by the carrier to adequately protect a 5G network from unauthorised access or interference,' their statement said.[18]

The release did not name Huawei but its message was clear: going forward, Australia would not allow the Chinese telecommunications giant to have involvement in the nation's 5G rollout.

Turnbull's departure did not ease the souring of Australia–China relations.

In 2019, Beijing blocked Australian coal exports[19] and was linked to a cyber hack on the Australian parliament.[20]

The petty tactics and rhetoric levelled against Australia – interpreted as China making an example of Australia to dissuade other nations – were beginning to attract the attention of European nations, the US and Indo-Pacific countries.

By the end of 2019, shortly before the first cases of Covid-19 were reported in China, plans to reboot the Quadrilateral Security Dialogue (the Quad) were already well advanced. The alliance of the US, Japan, India and Australia – despised by Beijing – would no longer sit idly by and watch Xi go unchallenged in the Indo-Pacific.

Morrison took the view that everything had changed with Xi. It was China that had shifted but Australia was perhaps the first country to appreciate it, understand it and take action against it.

His critics would ask why Australia had to be the first to act, why it couldn't fall behind someone else.

To that, Morrison would simply ask who that someone else would be. And who was more at risk than Australia? Who was being targeted more than Australia?

CHAPTER 11

The long game

O N 20 APRIL, Morrison took a decision to up the ante with Beijing. He told a meeting of the NSC that the time had come for Australia to be more strident in its language about China's conduct.

It was a decisive moment. The NSC met virtually and was provided with an oral update on the latest Chinese-sponsored cyber-activity.

Morrison, acting as commander in chief, gave a sweeping interpretation of the brief, telling his most senior minsters that Australia's democracy was being 'infiltrated' and that it had to be resisted.

'We need multiple points of pushback on this increasing aggression,' he told them.

China's military activities in the South China Sea was one of those fulcrums. Morrison told the meeting that the government needed to start calling out the behaviour in a more forceful manner.

Frydenberg then told the meeting that while China was a great source of economic prosperity for Australia, it was beginning to behave like an adversary.

The two were taking a long-term view based on a strong sense of national interest they weren't going to deviate from. They felt that if they were clear and consistent, their position would earn respect. If they let China shift the goalposts over every dispute, the game could be lost.

Morrison had already risked provoking a showdown with Beijing over the outbreak in the days preceding that meeting, when in an interview with *The Australian* newspaper, he began building a case for a formal investigation into the origins of the virus. 'There must be transparency in understanding how it began in Wuhan and how it was transmitted. We also need to fully understand and protect against the global health threat posed by places like wet markets,' he said.[1]

All around the globe, the WHO's judgement was being called into question, especially after its lacklustre response to even calling this a pandemic, and in particular when it sanctioned the reopening of wet markets in Wuhan.

Morrison found the decision absurd and said as much publicly.

Accusations that the WHO's leadership was heavily influenced by China and was politically compromised were surfacing. This was occurring at the same time US president Donald Trump announced that the US would freeze its funding for the WHO.

On 19 April, Foreign Affairs minister Marise Payne had been despatched to ratchet up the pressure. Interviewed on the ABC's *Insiders* program Payne called for a review into the origins of the virus, suggesting it needed to be independent of the WHO since it would be 'poacher and gamekeeper'.[2]

The clarion call received bipartisan support from Labor but provoked a choleric response from Beijing, which accused Canberra of 'panda bashing'. Via an editorial in Chinese propaganda outlet the *Global Times*, it issued threats that the bilateral relationship, which was underpinned by the comprehensive strategic partnership agreed to by Xi and Abbott in 2014, could be irreparably damaged, and called Australia 'gum stuck to the bottom of China's shoe.'[3]

The prior month, Frydenberg had already taken one significant step prompted in part by Dutton, at the time the minister for Home Affairs, who pointed out that Chinese companies had been buying up bulk PPE in Australia and sending it back to China – just one example of commercial activity at the expense of Australians.

Frydenberg had phoned David Irvine, chair of FIRB, to give him a heads-up over his worries that foreign investors could raid distressed Australian assets during the pandemic. The government needed to do more, Frydenberg warned. Legislating a national security test on all foreign investment was on the cards, he told Irvine. And on 29 March he announced he was temporarily increasing FIRB supervision.[4] Until then, FIRB only had a veto over large acquisitions, deals over $1.2 billion. Frydenberg dropped the screening threshold so it became a zero-dollar trigger. No foreign acquisition whatsoever could now occur without prior FIRB approval.

At the prior NSC meeting of 6 April, Morrison had raised the idea of leveraging the G7, the intergovernmental forum of the UK, US, Canada, France, Germany, Italy and Japan. Australia had become a quasi-member under a loose 'G7-plus' banner.

Australia's position, he told colleagues, needed to be firm but not aggressive, even-handed and defensible, to strike a strategic balance.

He was pushing for a stronger collaboration of like-minded democracies that shared the same world view. The only way to counter the coercion and Chinese adventurism, he argued, was for greater intelligence and strategic cooperation among aligned democracies.

In Morrison's view Australia had done a lot of retreating to placate China in the past and it was time to hold its ground.

At the 20 April meeting, the NSC proceeded to map out a plan to address the calls for an inquiry into the virus and problems with the WHO.

Morrison would write to like-minded countries to solicit support for increased transparency over the health agency. He flagged using a technical committee of the World Health Assembly (WHA), the WHO's 194-member governing body, whose policies were set by the health ministers of member states. Getting the numbers was going to take considerable diplomatic effort.

With the task set, Morrison concluded the meeting, 'Let's get working on that. I'll call the UK prime minister.'

Boris Johnson, however, was still on leave after a life-threatening bout of Covid-19. It wasn't until 3 May before Morrison got to Johnson, out of hospital but still convalescing, asking if the UK would lend weight to Australia's push for an inquiry into the origins of Covid-19.

'Yes, of course. I want to know where it came from as much as you,' Johnson replied emphatically. 'The thing almost killed me.'

By then, Morrison had already approached dozens of world leaders to enlist their support for the cause, one that would test European and African resolve in the face of immense pressure from China. Some countries were reluctant, publicly at least, claiming that mid-crisis – with the virus ticking over 2.5 million cases and 176,000 deaths worldwide – the time was not right for such an inquiry.

That said, they were all happy if Australia front-ran it.

Kunkel later likened the situation to a biological crime scene. 'You couldn't just say, "Look, here's a crime scene, and we'll come back to it 18 months later when the evidence has evaporated."'

DFAT officials on the ground in Geneva identified a mechanism Australia could use to pursue the issue: a resolution the Europeans had drafted ahead of May's WHA meeting. It called for action on Covid-19 and cooperation, but it fell short of demanding an investigation. Morrison and Payne saw an opportunity to piggyback an investigation onto it via an amendment.

On 21 April, Morrison spoke to German chancellor Angela Merkel and French president Emmanuel Macron. While both leaders were in favour of an inquiry they believed their bigger priority was getting on top of the significant outbreaks in their countries. For most of Europe at that stage, it was a horror show. France had more than 120,000 cases and was still recording up to 5000 a day. The UK and Germany were experiencing similar numbers with upwards of 1100 deaths every day.

Undeterred, Morrison continued lobbying. The following day, 22 April, he called Trump.

The two leaders had had similar talks in the past, and would continue to do so. But Trump's initial position, dismissing China's culpability for the virus, had shifted dramatically since the outset of the pandemic. He opened the call by unloading on China with a colourful articulation of his anger at Covid's economic impact.

'They could have stopped this,' Trump told Morrison. 'But they didn't. It's worse than a depression. Countries are cracking.'

Morrison told the US president that he was glad they had both cut off travel to and from mainland China when they did, which had some effect in stopping the spread of the virus.

Various theories had been circulating from the beginning – a lab leak or even a deeper intrigue that the virus was engineered – but Morrison had seen no official intelligence from the US or from Australia's intelligence agencies to give those rumours any credence. That said, Morrison and Trump were on the same page; they wanted answers.

On the call, Morrison raised his idea for an independent weapons inspector-type role for the WHO. Global organisations like the WHO had been held to the lowest common denominator and needed greater transparency, he told the US leader. Before they ended the call, he repeated the need for allies to hold together in the face of punitive economic tactics, like those being meted out to Australia.

Trump finished on a personal note. 'Your family must be very proud of you,' he said. 'The job's a little tougher than you thought, I bet.'

Morrison was taken aback. He got on well enough with Trump but was wary of his unpredictable nature and his tendency to change topic quickly.

*

Beijing's revenge

On 26 April, China's ambassador to Australia, Cheng Jingye, issued a warning from Beijing that the Morrison government's pursuit of an independent investigation into the origins of Covid-19 could trigger a boycott of major export industries, students and tourists.[5]

Two days later, in a break with diplomatic protocol, the Chinese embassy leaked details to the media of a phone call between Cheng and Frances Adamson, secretary of the Department of

Foreign Affairs and Trade, in which she assured the ambassador that Australia's actions were not politically motivated.[6]

The leak signalled the depth of Beijing's anger and, from Australia's standpoint, a complete breakdown of trust. Beijing's pressure campaign against Australia, which was building long before the pandemic, was moving into uncharted territory.

On Wednesday 29 April, Morrison's message to reporters was that Australia was merely exercising prudence.

'This is a virus which has taken 200,000 lives across the world. It has shut down the global economy. It would seem entirely sensible and reasonable that the world would want to have an independent assessment of how this occurred so we can learn the lessons and prevent it from happening again. I think that is a fairly obvious and common-sense suggestion.'[7]

Coincidentally, the same week that Australia was leading the call for an inquiry US officials were pushing the theory of a lab leak from the Wuhan Institute of Virology. There were commentators who linked Morrison's decision to adopt a lead role in the global calls for an inquiry into the origins of the virus with the aggressive approach taken by Trump, calling it a 'Chinese virus' because 'it comes from China'.[8]

As diplomats were keenly aware, nothing would convince China that Australia and the US weren't conspiring or that this wasn't about strategic competition.

While it was an easy assumption to make, Morrison maintained that he never asked Trump for direct support for the Australian initiative. If anything, Trump's move to withdraw from the WHO provided Morrison with a convenient point of difference with the Trump administration. Morrison was adamant that Australia did not support such a move.

Despite Morrison's intent, Beijing's ferocious response – both rhetorical and material – continued over the course of the following months.

'I was quite deliberate in saying this could have happened anywhere,' Morrison recalls of that period. 'And that it could happen again. Marise [Payne] and I discussed it. The problem was that too many people would try to see it through the prism of strategic competition between the superpowers.

'And China tried to pitch it as us in that context. Our view was that it shouldn't be a competition between the US and China. We wanted to take it out of that context and say, well, there can be no disagreement about the need to find out where this started.'

On 28 April, Morrison got a sympathetic hearing from the president of the EU commission, Ursula von der Leyen, a German physician, and also from Canadian prime minister Justin Trudeau two days later.

Morrison was either making or receiving these calls on an almost daily basis. One call in particular stuck with him. Netherlands prime minister Mark Rutte opened up to Morrison about his mother's illness and how, because of the European lockdowns, they had been kept apart. A few weeks later, she died.

Unlike other world crises, the human dimension to this one left few people untouched, including the leaders themselves, who were facing the task of imposing previously unimaginable hardships on their citizens to save their lives.

Through his calls, Morrison was getting a good sense of how other leaders were feeling. The consensus was that they were happy for Australia to lead, and they would support it. Critical to an outcome was an assurance that any resolution did not point the finger directly at China.

Morrison's task was to draw the support and avoid the counterpoint that this was just about the US. Fortunately, Trump's ongoing stridency enabled Morrison to give a defence of WHO through a local lens and create an impression, at least on this issue, that Australia and the US stood apart.

Ironically, it was the US's aggressive position that effectively gave the Europeans permission to ultimately back the Australian proposal.

*

China – 'the biggest challenge in a generation'

By 4 May 2020, China had become a constant theme at both the National Security Committee's Covid group – a slimmed-down security meeting that dealt only with Covid-19 related issues – as well as the NSC's full meetings. On that day, Morrison assembled the NSC for a secure video call to discuss the escalating threats from China.

'There is no more serious issue facing the NSC,' he told them. 'Our relationship with China and the deterioration of the wider strategic situation is the biggest challenge in a generation.' He used the 1930s as an analogy. Having chosen to defend its national interests and sovereignty, Australia had to accept that this was a long-term campaign. 'We can't be naive,' Morrison told them. 'The game has changed in the past five years.'

The nation, he said, would need to put up a shield, build up its defence capability, strengthen cyber-defences and counter foreign interference abilities. Yet Australia's alliance with the US would be its ultimate protection. Without it, resisting China's coercion would be difficult.

Morrison's attitude, shared by every NSC member, was that Australia had to hold its ground, and work with traditional allies and partners so the rest of the world was aware of what was at stake.

This included the state and territory governments, which also needed to wake up to what was going on.

*

First Movers Club

The First Movers Club was an exclusive group of countries that had so far succeeded in suppressing the virus. Spearheaded by Austrian chancellor Sebastian Kurz, then 34 years old, it initially included Australia, Austria, Israel, Greece, Denmark, Norway, the Czech Republic and Singapore.

Its inaugural meeting, on 24 April, was Morrison's last scheduled event in a long, exhausting day of back-to-back meetings, including the national cabinet. He was sitting in the secure international room in Parliament House, late in the evening, with the other leaders on a large screen on the wall in front of him.

So far as the others were concerned, considering it was morning for most of them, Morrison was sipping a tea from a mug that he'd asked his official photographer, Adam Taylor, to fetch him. What they didn't know was that Morrison had asked Taylor to fill it with beer.

Israel's prime minister Benjamin Netanyahu may have been the elder statesman of the group but Australia was the largest country at the virtual table: the other members' populations were broadly between five and 10 million.

This was an informal gathering and talk quickly moved from how each participant had got ahead of the curve – Morrison explaining how shutting international borders had largely kept the virus out of Australia – to how to keep it that way while safeguarding their economies. But it was obvious to all that there were still many unknowns, and discussion bounced from whether children were carriers, to what testing technology each country was using, what they were doing about aged care and hopes for a vaccine.

By the second meeting, on 7 May, joined by New Zealand, the group was wrestling with a wider range of topics. Singapore's Lee spoke of the need to maintain supply chains, while others raised the challenge of local outbreaks, locking down suburbs and even plans for reopening their economies.

Morrison brought up the WHA resolution and Australia's push for an inquiry into the origins of the virus. There was genuine need for a thoroughgoing investigation, he argued, so the world could understand how the pandemic happened and how to avoid it happening again. He reiterated that this wasn't directed at any one country. It could have happened anywhere, but the world needed to learn the lessons.

He told them he had written to G20 leaders seeking support for the European resolution with Australia's amendment calling for an inquiry.

When the storm from Beijing hit Australia, the ferocity would ultimately work in Morrison's favour. While it didn't feel that way for the Australian industries and exporters who China targeted, it forced open the eyes of European nations that, until then, had been less aware of the geopolitical chess game being played.

China's first tangible actions against Australia began on 10 May, with a threat to impose hefty tariffs on Australian barley exported to China.[9] Two days later, Beijing suspended four Australian meat exporters, citing historic and technical issues around labelling and health certificates.[10] A week after that, China's Ministry of Commerce made the barley threat real, levying an 80.5 per cent tariff.[11]

Chinese authorities were also instructing state-owned power plants to shun Australian coal, and instead prioritise domestic coal or coal from other markets. By the end of the year, no Australian coal was entering China, despite the country's insatiable demand to keep its steel mills pumping and support Xi's post-Covid economic recovery strategy. But by late the following year, with a power crisis in China due to coal shortages, sales began to resume.[12]

A flip side was that China, while harbouring long-term plans to mine iron ore in Africa, had no choice but to continue purchasing record quantities of Australian iron ore, with Brazilian iron ore giant Vale crippled by the country's unfolding Covid-19 disaster.

Setting aside its backflip on coal, China managed to inflict economic pain on Australia. The fallout eventually fractured the bipartisan support that Labor had initially offered over the WHO inquiry. Then shadow minister for agriculture and resources, Joel Fitzgibbon, accused Morrison of offending the Chinese. His view wasn't shared by all in the opposition and it jarred with broader public opinion. But some of Albanese's front bench saw an opportunity to start building a domestic political narrative blaming Morrison for the trade tensions.

Many European and Asian countries were watching to see how China would react when Australia pushed back. Some of them, like the Netherlands, had their own supply-chain issues with China and were concerned. Morrison was also wary of how China and indeed the US might try to misrepresent the Australian position for their own agendas.

While Morrison and Payne were successful in strengthening the WHA resolution to include an inquiry, they had to concede to watering down the language. On 19 May 2020, the WHA passed resolution WHA73.1 – as sponsored by Australia and with unanimous backing – to instruct the WHO to lead a multi-agency probe identifying 'the zoonotic source of the virus and the route of introduction to the human population, including the possible role of intermediate hosts'.[13]

That Russia, Indonesia and the African bloc all supported the resolution came as a shock to China. Ironically, despite Trump's disavowal of the WHO and therefore its absence as a sponsor of the resolution, the US voted in favour.

In the end, China was the country at risk of being isolated. Ultimately, it was left with no choice but to endorse the resolution too.

The passage of the resolution was a diplomatic triumph, one that took a full-court press by Morrison, Payne and the diplomatic corps.

Soon after, on 8 June, China issued a travel alert for Australia, claiming a 'significant' increase in racism because Australians were blaming its citizens for the coronavirus.[14]

Addressing the NSC again on 25 and 26 May, Morrison reiterated that the most important issue the government was facing, aside from Covid-19, was managing the relationship with China

Following the WHA vote, China's attitude had only sharpened. Plainly, the CCP was bent on taking a particular path.

Morrison told colleagues that it was time for a 'reality check'. It was going to be a long game.

CHAPTER 12

It's the economy, stupid

JOSH FRYDENBERG'S DIRECTOR of communications, Kane Silom, was sitting alone in his parliamentary office watching on a monitor as his boss delivered the government's first major economic statement on coronavirus to the House. It was 12 May 2020, the day the budget would have been delivered, had Morrison not postponed it to October.

Delaying the budget was one of the key decisions early on in the pandemic. When he made that announcement on Friday 20 March, Morrison said, 'The idea that you can actually put together any sort of forecast around the economy at this time is simply not sensible.'[1]

But even choosing a firm date for the budget – traditionally held on the second Tuesday of May – was a source of internal debate. Morrison's first choice was the final week of September. But Frydenberg told him this would have conflicted with the most important religious holiday in the Jewish calendar, Yom Kippur, which fell on 28 September, a day before the Tuesday Morrison had in mind.

'I respect the need for religious observance as much as anyone. But I need you to deliver a budget and your country needs you to deliver a budget,' Morrison had told Frydenberg at the time.

Frydenberg told him flatly, 'No.'

Morrison then agreed to push it a week later, to 6 October.

The Treasurer was barely minutes into his speech when he began coughing uncontrollably.

'Bloody hell, what's wrong with this bloke?' Silom thought out loud. His phone began to light up like a Christmas tree with colleagues calling and texting to ask if Frydenberg was okay.

When the Treasurer walked back into his ministerial office, he found Silom and his chief of staff, Martin Codina, together, trying not to laugh, but also concerned whether Frydenberg was indeed well. Frydenberg had simply choked on a glass of water, he told them, but he paced back and forth through the office wondering what he should do.

He rang Hunt. On the health minister's suggestion, he called deputy chief medical officer Paul Kelly. Kelly, with an abundance of caution, suggested the Treasurer immediately leave Parliament House and go to his Canberra apartment and wait for a registered nurse Kelly would send to test him for Covid-19.

The Treasurer's short-lived malady – he didn't have Covid-19 then, but would succumb to the virus in January 2022 – provided light relief for some, in stark contrast to the gravity of his speech's central theme that while the country seemed to have dodged a bullet as to the pandemic's health impacts, the bullet was definitely hitting the economy.

For politicians, delivering negative economic news is always a challenge, not only politically but because excessive pessimism can become self-fufilling by denting consumer and business confidence. The International Monetary Fund had declared two weeks earlier that 2020 would be remembered as the year the global economy suffered its worst shock since the Great Depression.[2]

While Frydenberg had to be up front and honest, he and his team wove some positivity into the narrative around the impact the government's support measures were having on people's lives and overall community sentiment.

Given Treasury's forecasts, compared with the numbers that actually unfolded later, some sanguinity was justified. Treasury's forecast was that Australia's GDP would fall more than 10 per cent for the June quarter, the largest fall in output on record for a single quarter.[3] (It would actually be lower, at 7 per cent.[4]) Household consumption would also fall 16 per cent. Unemployment was expected to reach 10 per cent, although the effective rate – taking into account those who were on JobKeeper – was closer to 15 per cent.

(Unemployment actually peaked at 7.5 per cent, still the highest in over twenty years, but lower than the forecasts.) Business investment was expected to fall by 18 per cent, mainly in the non-mining sector, and housing investment was tipped to fall similarly.

And then there was the debt. The country would have to pay back the borrowings that were funding the government's eye-watering $320 billion in life support for the economy and the population.

Frydenberg told the chamber, 'Australia finds itself at war against a faceless and flagless enemy. The coronavirus has created a one-in-a-hundred-year event. A health and economic shock the likes of which the world has never seen.

'While there will be a significant increase in Government debt which will take many years to repay, our measures have been designed in a way that protect the structural integrity of the budget. Australians know there is no money tree. What we borrow today, we must repay in the future.'

Frydenberg described the government's economic actions as a 'race against time'. Presciently, he also outlined the cost of what would happen if the states and territories had to go into a second round of lockdowns.[5]

The following day, Hunt told parliament he was extending his three-month declaration of the human biosecurity emergency period for another three months.

With Australia's mortality rate one of the lowest in the OECD, the tone of Hunt's speech was that Australia appeared to be through the worst of it, but that the states and territories needed to be vigilant in maintaining low case numbers and containing outbreaks.[6]

Morrison had already publicly floated the idea of Australians getting 'an early mark' and was steering the national conversation towards a deadline for easing restrictions. Confidence needed to be restored, and he was doing what he could to facilitate that.[7]

In mid-April, he had tasked Murphy to get the AHPPC to set out the preconditions for the states to emerge from lockdown. It identified the need for additional ventilator capacity, ICU nurses, and rigorous testing and tracing capability. At that stage, only New South Wales met the AHPPC standards but Murphy was confident the others had ample time to prepare. Every state, apart from Victoria, assured the AHPPC that it had a scaled-up workforce and had good contact tracing systems in place, and Victoria's lag would, a month later, have tragic consequences.

On top of the work being done to fortify public health units, Attorney-General Christian Porter was working with Greg Combet, then chair of Industry Super Australia but formerly a respected ACTU secretary and minister in the Rudd and Gillard governments. The task was to develop protocols to ensure Covid-safe workplaces that would be practical and acceptable to the unions and employers.

The COVIDSafe app was launched on 26 April, and Morrison intended to use the speed of its uptake as a benchmark in the thinking about the reopening of the economy. But like a number of tools deployed to combat the invisible scourge, the app's utility was questionable and would be short-lived.

To all around the national cabinet table, another big piece of the reopening puzzle was behavioural. Would people go back to work? Would they comply with social distancing rules? How would they feel about mask wearing? Would they leave their homes to go to shopping centres?

The leaders knew that these important measures of a functioning society could only happen if their governments could help to create a sense of safety in the community.

*

The three-step plan

The momentum for reopening had been building for weeks. The public were yearning to get back to as normal a life as possible.

In the first week of May, Morrison pushed the premiers to agree to a three-step plan for easing restrictions and reopening within a week.[8]

The three steps were for a phased increase of the sizes of allowable gatherings – at work and socially – based on social distancing and depending on case numbers. The first phase allowed 10 people at work and 5 visitors in the home, then it might go to 20, and then to 100.

Australians were going to need hope, he explained, especially when the next round of unemployment figures landed the following week. The country needed to see a path out of the dark and it was up to the leaders to show them the way. The premiers and chief ministers all agreed.

Morrison recalls, 'It was going to be the first set of numbers that really say, "We are heading toward recession, or near one."

'The unemployment figures were an important deadline for us because we knew how bad they were going to be. But we didn't need data to tell us that things were completely stuffed and we had to get out of it. That's why the three-step plan was so important.'

This marked the crossover from the health crisis to an economic one. It was on that basis the AHPPC gave the green light to reopen the country, domestically at least, and gradually.

So instead of standing up every day and talking about Covid case numbers, Morrison shifted to articulating a way forward, to the opening up of the economy.

It wasn't just the general public who were crying out for some return to normalcy, it was business too.

Business leaders had been bombarding the business liaison unit Frydenberg had established within Treasury, with daily phone calls wanting details on a path out of hibernation.

JobKeeper and JobSeeker, which were about to kick in, were highly appreciated but business saw the country needed a broader roadmap.

Rolling meetings were held with the Covid Commission, the National Coordination Mechanism and the business liaison unit.

And Frydenberg's phone never stopped. He became the government's intelligence gatherer of industry and business sentiment. One business figure in constant contact with Frydenberg was CBA's Matt Comyn, and when Comyn took a position it would often lead the market.

For Morrison, whose demand for hard data became an obsession, Frydenberg's networking became invaluable.

Morrison wanted the deadline for all three stages to be completed by the start of July. Some of the states were angling for the end of July. Victoria's Daniel Andrews was putting 'in July'.

Morrison was feeling confident about timing because Murphy's state and territory counterparts on the AHPPC were assuring him that their public health response systems were all up to speed. That assurance was the critical underpinning for the roadmap. If any state couldn't deal with a local outbreak and contain the case numbers, it could be a disaster.

With Morrison's moves towards agreeing a roadmap, the focus was shifting to the states and away from the federal government and the politics started to turn. By the end of April, according to a Newspoll conducted for *The Australian*, even before the national cabinet signed off on the roadmap, his approval ratings climbed to the highest level for a prime minister since 2008.[9]

*

Even so, Morrison and Hunt could not stand back with their arms folded. The mental health of people in isolation was one area they zeroed in on.

Pat McGorry, a leading mental health clinician, called Morrison personally, asking him to consider the issue as a top priority. Morrison took it seriously and raised it with Hunt.

Soon after, on 7 May, Sydney University professor Ian Hickie released modelling that forecast a rise of up to 50 per cent in the rate of suicides due to the economic and social impacts of the coronavirus. Given the low mortality rate from Covid so far, the modelling was suggesting that ten times more people might die from suicide than from the virus itself.[10]

Murphy and Mental Health commissioner Christine Morgan had for some time been pushing for a mental health role to sit alongside the CMO.

And mental health had been a priority of Hunt from the time Turnbull appointed him Health minister in 2017. His mother Kathinka had suffered from a serious mental health condition of which he rarely spoke.

In under a week, Hunt appointed the country's first deputy chief medical officer for mental health, Ruth Vine – the health department's chief psychiatrist – to steer a new plan for mental illness associated with the pandemic.

*

Thursday 14 May 2020 was one of Morrison's toughest days, and it ushered in what was going to be a particularly difficult week. The employment numbers, at 6.2 per cent, revealed that almost 600,000 people had lost their jobs.

'Terribly shocking, although not unanticipated,' Morrison said as he stood next to Frydenberg to address the Canberra press gallery. 'We knew there would be hard news as the pandemic wreaks an impact on Australia as it is on countries all around the world. And so it has been the case. And in the months ahead, we can brace ourselves and must brace ourselves for further hard news for Australians to take.[11]

The pain was felt most acutely by women, 325,000 of the 594,000 job losses. And the young. The youth unemployment rate rose from 11.5 per cent to 13.8 per cent. Unsurprisingly, the participation rate – the percentage of people in the working-age population who are in the labour force – had fallen to 63.5 per cent.[12]

Frydenberg added, 'There is still a long way to go and the economic numbers will get worse before they get better.'

Yet the May numbers could have been worse. The market had been expecting an unemployment rate of 8.2 per cent. Regardless, the lower 6.2 per cent just printed was no silver lining on the economic front.

*

Exhaustion was setting in for Morrison. Desperate to spend time with his family, he flew back to Sydney. There, on Thursday night 21 May, he took a call from Frydenberg, who sheepishly told him there was a problem with the $130 billion JobKeeper program, one that would become a free kick for the Labor opposition.

The ATO and Treasury had learned that – due to an ambiguity in the application form they had designed – some firms were misstating the numbers of their staff eligible to receive payments under the program. The original forecasts had set the figure of eligible workers at 6 million. This was now being revised down to 3.5 million, and as a result the scheme would cost $60 billion less.

The *Sydney Morning Herald* senior economics correspondent Shane Wright described it the next day as the 'biggest policy miscalculation in Australian history', and Labor leader Albanese quipped that the error was so big 'you could see it from space'.[13]

Morrison, livid, let Frydenberg know his displeasure on that call.

'You need to fix this,' he told his Treasurer. Not only was the mistake a major embarrassment to a government that prided itself on economic management, but that coming weekend Morrison was heading to the NSW south coast to start campaigning ahead of a federal by-election on 4 July in the bellwether Labor-held seat of Eden-Monaro.

Morrison's only defence publicly was to suggest that it was a good problem to have since it meant the economy was doing better than expected.

*

Hawke's ghost in Kirribilli House

That same week Morrison secretly hosted a guest at Kirribilli House, a person whose presence would once have been unimaginable and, if the media got wind of it, might have caused problems for both of them.

Sally McManus, secretary of the Australian Council of Trade Unions (ACTU), was self-isolating in the Blue Mountains west of Sydney when Morrison reached out to the peak union leader to invite her to Kirribilli House.

It would be an historic meeting.

Unlike the industrial accords of the 1980s, this time it was a Liberal leader rather than a Labor one offering a seat at the table when it came to mapping out an industrial relations reform agenda.

The pair had met before but this would be the first time they would meet one-on-one. They agreed to keep the meeting private and low-key.

On arrival, and like any guest to Kirribilli House, McManus was greeted by Morrison's dog, Buddy, a black schnoodle that makes a point of accosting visitors with demands for attention.

McManus ran considerable political risk just being seen with Morrison, as he did by being seen with her, especially with the hardliners in the Liberal Party who were already irritated by Morrison's occasional positive references to Bob Hawke, forgetting that his acclaim for the Silver Bodgie wasn't so much over his policies, rather his ability to win four elections.

As Morrison said at Hawke's funeral, he was far from the perfect man but what had endeared him to people was that he didn't indulge pretence, he didn't seek to be something he wasn't.

Morrison would never admit it but it was clear that he admired Hawke for the same reason he did the former US president Theodore Roosevelt and Joe Lyons, Australia's oft-forgotten Depression-era prime minister, as leaders who genuinely sought to find ways through the problems besetting their nation by bringing people together.

In this olive branch he was offering to McManus and the union movement in a time of crisis, Morrison saw both common sense and political opportunity. Sidelining the Labor opposition was undoubtedly appealing.

From her brandishing performances in the media, the McManus who Morrison expected to meet would be feisty and adversarial. Yet, after they settled into the armchairs in the lounge room looking out over the southern-facing lawns towards the city, he found her polite and personable. Throughout their discussion, and over tea, McManus was constructive, pragmatic and straight. Willing to engage but not yet commit.

Morrison was equally accommodating, and not unsympathetic to the plight of casual workers, but unequivocal about his intent. The unions could become a partner, but he was going to do what he was going to do.

Morrison saw the economic crisis brought on by the pandemic as an opportunity for significant industrial relations reform.

Unions and employers had holstered their weapons and agreed at the height of the pandemic to changes to some workplace conditions to save jobs.

But Morrison believed he could take that further.

They discussed the Federal Court decision on entitlements for casual workers, the *Workpac v Rossato* case.[14] The court had just decided that if a casual employee worked regular shifts their employer owed them entitlements like holiday and sick leave despite already paying a loading intended to compensate for the worker missing out on those benefits. Employers were apoplectic.

Porter had built a constructive relationship with McManus. And while Morrison had harboured lofty ambitions for an industrial pact, both Porter and McManus were grounded in political reality.

After a two-hour meeting Morrison and McManus agreed to approach the negotiations in good faith and see where it went from there.

Morrison had always maintained that business and industry had to make the public case for labour market reform rather than have government do the heavy lifting and wear the political pain.

Bringing the unions to the table was a major step forward in his ambition to secure meaningful reform, with Morrison acting as broker.

There would be significant political dividends for the government in achieving reform through a consensus model. And in the early stages it had looked possible. In the end it was a waste of time. A set of working groups subsequently established between employer groups and the unions, brokered by Porter, made initial progress but, constrained by unconquerable ideological divisions, failed to agree on a unified reform package.

CHAPTER 13

The road to recovery

THE PANDEMIC KEPT making Australian history, and it wasn't good. On 3 June 2020, Frydenberg told the country that for the first time in 29 successive years of economic growth, Australia was tipping into recession, words no modern Liberal Treasurer expected to utter on his watch. It was an 'economist's version of Armageddon', he said.[1]

The official figures revealed that the shutdowns had contracted the economy by 0.3 per cent in the March quarter and, with Treasury forecasting the June quarter would post significantly worse results, the technical definition of a recession – two consecutive quarters of negative growth – was a given.

Frydenberg could have danced around the issue – since this was only one quarter of negative growth – but he decided to own it, after workshopping with Silom what he might say if asked by reporters.

When probed that day at a press conference by veteran Canberra journalist, Channel 7's Mark Riley, if Australia was in recession for the first time in three decades, the Treasurer bluntly answered, 'Yes'.[2]

He went on to say, 'Less than 100 days ago, our nation was on the edge of an economic cliff. The number of coronavirus cases was increasing by more than 20 per cent per day. Treasury was contemplating a fall in GDP of more than 20 per cent in the June quarter.

'This was the economists' version of Armageddon. In response to this one-in-100-year global event, we put in place a series of health measures that have hit the economy hard. These were tough decisions, but these were decisions we had to take.'

The job numbers had also deteriorated. The 600,000 lost jobs announced in May had grown to around 950,000.

Despite that, the economy was already starting to show signs of recovery. It was strange to many, but consumer spending was lifting and confidence returning.

Reserve Bank governor Philip Lowe commented that the economy was faring better than even the central bank had predicted. Treasury secretary Steven Kennedy was also cautiously optimistic.

Australia, compared with most of the rest of the world, was doing well. China's economy had contracted 9.8 per cent, France was down 5.3 per cent, Germany 2.2 per cent, Britain 2 per cent and the United States, 1.3 per cent.[3]

*

Sleepless nights

In the face of presiding over a recession, this qualified success was of no comfort to Morrison, who hadn't been sleeping.

He'd often wake at 3am, wrestling with the scale of what was facing the country and his responsibilities in dealing with it. He'd rouse in a fitful state and look at the ceiling for hours on end, saying to himself, 'I have to sleep or I won't get through this week.' More than once, so he could function the following day, he would take a mild sedative.

Morrison had always been a bit like that. When he was Treasurer and preparing the budget he'd suffer similar bouts of insomnia.

It had been no different for him the night before he convened what he believed was one of his most important strategic cabinet meetings, not just during the pandemic but for the entire term of his government. He took half a sleeping pill to make sure he was fresh for the next day.

The 3 June meeting lasted a gruelling four hours. In his hand he held a single A3 sheet of paper that outlined what he,

Frydenberg and Cormann had decided was the roadmap – not only for restarting the economy but to finally unshackle it from the industrial constraints that had for decades characterised prevailing ideological and political divisions. They'd already introduced JobSeeker and JobKeeper, and now Morrison was proposing a JobMaker plan.

Up until then, the focus was entirely on the here and now, bringing in emergency economic supports and management of the health crisis.

But Morrison, Frydenberg and Cormann believed they needed to shift gear by thinking about the longer term.

While the PM was holding twice-weekly meetings with Kennedy, Lowe and the economic advisers, he also began regular meetings with Porter on industrial relations reforms, and with Energy minister Angus Taylor, Industry minister Karen Andrews and Employment minister Michaelia Cash.

The previous week he also held a long meeting with Andrew Liveris, the former Dow Chemical CEO who had advised the Obama administration on advanced manufacturing. Morrison had appointed him to head up the National Covid Commission's manufacturing taskforce.

Morrison had already begun talking of Australia's need to dramatically boost its sovereign manufacturing capability in light of the supply chain issues the pandemic had exposed.

Critical to that would be an energy policy that delivered a cheaper cost base for industry, and gas becoming the government's preferred option for the transitional base-load supply.

Morrison's emphasis on sovereign capability and reinvesting in local manufacturing had sparked a running joke among some of his colleagues that he was turning into a socialist.

*

The 3 June cabinet meeting was, as far as Morrison was concerned, a crucial and binding moment for the government. As he introduced the JobMaker plan, he was overtaken by the gravity of the events that had led them to that point.

'I was talking about this plan and I was talking about what we now had to do. I started reflecting where this sat largely in terms of the country's economic history,' Morrison recalls of the meeting.

'It was all coming down to us, in this room, to make some critical decisions in the next six months that would determine how we as a country would go for the next five to 30 years.

'I reflected how much we had done to get the budget back into balance and I said Matthias and I had been doing it for six years and we had seen all the fiscal numbers coming back. We had created half a million jobs. Mathias and I, we probably knew more intimately than anyone else in the room how hard some of those calls were. But here we were, we had got back to surplus. And it had been wiped out in a fortnight.'

Not that Morrison saw this as an exercise in Sisyphean futility. He believed he had to give people hope, though he admitted to his colleagues that day he was shattered by what had happened.

'This is just devastating where we are now, with the number of people out of work,' he told them. 'People are relying on us like no other government in 80 years. We have to come together and get this right and not be distracted by anything else.'

Other ministers sitting around the cabinet table have attested to Morrison's uncharacteristic display of emotion. How he appeared genuinely heartbroken by what had happened to the country, by what had happened to jobs, and the hardships imposed on the nation. It was one of those rare moments when a leader goes beyond the numbers and the brief and allows the full human catastrophe to swamp them.

It wasn't disabling, but Morrison was completely affected by it.

'Going onto a discussion like this, I allowed myself to do it because I'm usually disciplined with this sort of stuff, but I was happy for the cabinet to do the same thing. To reflect on it. Take yourself out of the moment, the politics, out of the media cycle, the government and ambitions,' he recalls.

'I said, "None of that matters now. The next election, nothing matters. What matters is that we have to get this right. And it's only us, there is no one else and this better be the right plan."'

*

The general tenor through May and into June was that the country was positioning well for the recovery, but everything was delicately balanced, and there was quarrelling between the states over who was signed up to the national plan.

The First Movers Club was facing similar tensions. On 27 May, Morrison dialled in for his third virtual meeting with the group.

In hindsight he'd see it as a benchmark for the end of the pandemic's first wave and a lesson about complacency.

Morrison told the meeting that he felt they all, including Australia, needed to remain vigilant and ensure their citizens did likewise.

Denmark's prime minister, Mette Frederiksen, reported that her country was almost back to normal, except for restrictions on large gatherings. The issue she was grappling with was reopening Denmark's borders.

Greece was in a similar situation, with very little if any community transmission; fatigue over social distancing and mask wearing was an issue.

In Israel, everything was open except for movie threatres and sporting events. Netanyahu told the meeting that they all had a common challenge: that success bred expectations. 'People think it's over. I keep telling them it's not,' Netanyahu said. He added that he would use the group's discussion to give a message to Israelis that he and other leaders had shared concerns about people relaxing their discipline.

Domestically in Australia, the data showed consumer confidence was coming back strongly. The mood was that businesses might be able to hang on as long as Australia stayed on the current path and kept the virus under control; there was a general sense of optimism.

*

The Australian way

Morrison, a reader of history, began to acquaint himself with analyses of past crises and, through that, started using the term the 'Australian way'. Uppermost in his mind was how prime minister Joseph Lyons successfully guided Australia out of the Great Depression ahead of and in relatively better shape than most other countries.

Apparent to Morrison was that Australia's relative success wasn't due to luck or happenstance, rather to a series of hard decisions and disciplined economic principles, and not all of them universally shared.

This came through loud and clear from a series of eight lectures from almost 90 years ago. Given by a celebrated economist, Douglas Copland, to an eager audience at Cambridge University in late 1933, they were entitled 'Australia in the World Crisis, 1929-1933'.[4]

Copland, New Zealand born but Australian by choice, and most remembered for his stewardship of the Premiers' Plan of 1931, is said to have helped steer the country through the crisis.

His assessment was that Australia found its own way through the Depression, and consequently was able to emerge sooner and more intact than most other countries. He likened the Australian approach to what the country had done in other disasters, including war.

'Not unlike the Allies in the war, Australia was ill prepared to meet a resolute foe,' he wrote.[5] 'There was much controversy and delay before a successful offensive could be launched and it was planned only after traditional methods of attack had been to a large extent discarded and new weapons devised.

'Australians earned a reputation during the war for bold and unorthodox strategy. Their economic struggle of 1930 and 1931 gave them opportunity to show once more those qualities that made their shock tactics so successful in the war.'

Quite unlike the open, strong economy that faced the pandemic of 2020, Australia entered the Great Depression with both a debt and a credit problem.[6]

The federal system was the same, namely state governments and a Commonwealth often at odds with each other, a structure that isn't particularly well adapted to a rapidly changing economic environment.

Had it not been for Lyons, a prime minister often lost to history and political nostalgia, the achievement lauded by Copland may never have been realised.

After serving five years as Labor premier for Tasmania, Lyons was elected in 1929 to Federal Parliament as part of a landslide victory led by James Scullin, who returned Labor to government after 13 years on the opposition benches following a split over conscription in World War I.

In 1930, Scullin appointed Lyons acting Treasurer while he went overseas. Lyons' plan to deal with the Depression was based on returning the budget to balance, cutting government spending and lowering wages, among other things including price control. A plan wholeheartedly rejected by the Labor caucus. Lyons eventually resigned from the cabinet in frustration, prompting a second spilt in the Labor Party. He helped form a new party, the United Australia Party, which defeated the Scullin government at the 1931 election.

Lyons, the first prime minister to die in office, would eventually be succeeded by Menzies. And the UAP would later became the Liberal Party.

Morrison saw himself governing in a similar fashion, a leader unchained from orthodoxy, ideologically uninhibited and politically licensed to employ dramatic fiscal intervention as leader of a conservative party.

Lyons' legacy bequeathed Morrison a set of guiding political principles to steer Australia out of economic despair once again, including his central theme of leveraging private enterprise rather than government.

Two books became pivotal to shaping Morrison's thinking. A biography of Lyons by Australian writer Anne Henderson,[7] and American Amity Shlaes' conservative critique of Franklin D. Roosevelt's New Deal in her book *The Forgotten Man*, which helped Morrison contrast Lyons' approach to emerging from the Great Depression with the New Deal.[8]

Shlaes' central thesis was that rather than dragging America out of depression, the New Deal prolonged it. The New Deal, she wrote, would be remembered as a 'grand failure' of government intervention.

She concluded that it was the advent of the Second World War that lifted the US out of depression – rather than any of the grand schemes of the New Deal – when American industry kicked into gear following the Japanese bombing of Pearl Harbor on 7 December 1941.

Morrison drew heavily from Shlaes' controversial challenge to the popular notion that the New Deal saved America. He saw it as a 'what not to do' guide for framing Australia's economic response to the pandemic.

For Morrison, it was not government intervention versus no government intervention. It was about the type of intervention.

As Copland wrote, Australia chose a policy in the 1930s that contained a large degree of social justice with 'sound economic effect. She pursued a middle course that had hitherto not been fully explored.

'It was the inherent fairness of this course that appealed to people.'[9]

Copland was suggesting that Australia had found its own unique path, an Australian way.

Morrison was determined to frame 2020 as a catastrophe borne from a pandemic rather than an economic crisis made of itself. It was nothing like the GFC. It was not a collapse of marked-based economic systems or a failure of capitalism.

For Morrison, the key lesson from the Depression was that while there had to be a plan to get out of it, what was vitally important was what it was going to look like on the other side. A plan could not be dictated by crisis thinking. Which in turn highlighted for him the danger of making economic policies a prisoner to ideology.

'In Australia during the Depression, Lyons took us out of recession far earlier than the US, and he did things around budget discipline and not overextending,' said Morrison.

'Commodity prices were not as they are today, and our ability to repay loans was critical to Australia's economic future at the time. So over-borrowing and defaulting, which was the Lang adventure, could have totally destroyed Australia at a time when it was enormously vulnerable to UK lenders.

'Lyons' approach as acting Treasurer in the Scullin government and then as PM in his own right was to actually be the voice of economic responsibility. He was desperately concerned about unemployment and what people were going through. He had a strong empathy for that but at the same time he wasn't splashing money all over the place.

'He wasn't engaged on some sort of ideological adventure, as was occurring with the New Dealers in the US.

'And we came out of it a lot earlier than they did.'

Which would become Morrison's mission for Australia in coming out of the Covid-19 pandemic.

CHAPTER 14

We are all federalists now

IN HIS MAIDEN speech to the Federal Parliament on 14 February 2008, Morrison likened the federation to a three-legged dog, hobbled by the incompetence of state and territory governments.

'We must cast our eyes forward and embrace a new round of economic reforms. Of particular significance is the need to reform our federation.

'However, we must proceed carefully. The realignment of our federation, particularly in priority areas such as water, taxation and infrastructure, must be about delivering a better system of governance for our population and our economy. It should not be done to cover for the inability of state governments to do their jobs, especially in health and education.

'Commonwealth, state and local government should operate like a three-legged stool, each supporting the other. At present it is more like a three-legged dog.'[1]

At the time, he pointed particularly to the incompetence of the then Labor government of his home state of New South Wales.

The pandemic presented Morrison with a challenge he could not have envisaged when he gave his critical assessment of the federation 16 years earlier. But in 2020, and determined to leverage the lessons of history, he reflected that if William Watt couldn't bind them together during the Spanish flu crisis, nor Joseph Lyons when he was acting Treasurer heading into the Great Depression, then he needed to find a new way.

The national cabinet he formed on 13 March 2020 was part of that.

The approach fascinated Canadian prime minister Justin Trudeau, who faced similar issues with a federation of provinces. Of all the western leaders Morrison would speak to during the pandemic, Trudeau's experience was most similar, and in late March the pair empathised over each other's lack of control over school closures, for example.

Morrison's formation of a wartime-like national cabinet was heavily criticised by the federal Labor opposition, but no one embraced it more enthusiastically than the state and territory leaders themselves. They were soon pushing to make it a permanent leaders-only forum, unencumbered by the armies of folder-bearing bureaucrats and advisers who had been a permanent and sclerotic feature of the federation's then-suspended forum of COAG, the Council of Australian Governments.

By May the economic and health agendas were coming together and with equal prominence, and the leaders were talking about broader reform issues, such as the national skills agenda, the NDIS and childcare.

They saw the national cabinet as a better pathway to actually pursuing some of these agendas and, by 15 May, all the premiers and chief ministers were advocating for the complete abolition of COAG.

'Look, I don't disagree,' Morrison told them, 'but we actually have to work out what it is that it is going to be replaced with.' He undertook to do further work and bring back a plan.

He went back to his office and told Kunkel the leaders had agreed to make the national cabinet permanent. COAG, which Paul Keating set up in 1992 to replace the Premiers' Conference, was dead.

Morrison pulled out a folder of A3 sheets and began penning his own chart on how it would work – he preferred to pen his thoughts and ideas rather than using a digital tablet – and two weeks later, on Wednesday 27 May, he took the idea to his own cabinet, where he got it endorsed. At the next national cabinet meeting, two days later, it was settled.

One of the agreements struck between Morrison and the other leaders was that only one voice would speak on behalf of the national cabinet, and that was to be the prime minister's. And the new protocol began that afternoon, when Morrison faced the media.

After confirming the three-step plan was well underway and announcing a $134 billion five-year hospital agreement with the states, on top of the $8 billion of Commonwealth funding already provided during the pandemic, he revealed the decision.[2]

'The other thing we agreed today is a major change in terms of how COAG will work in the future ... COAG is no more. It will be replaced by a completely new system and that new system is focused on the success that has been yielded by the operation of the national cabinet. What we'll be doing is keeping the national cabinet operating and particularly during the COVID period, we'll continue to meet on a fortnightly basis. In a normal year it will meet on a monthly basis.'

Morrison made the point that the national cabinet had already met more times in its first two months than COAG had met in a decade. Morrison saw the opportunity in crisis to drive reform of the federation.

While it wasn't its primary objective, the national cabinet served a secondary political purpose for the PM. Having sidelined the federal opposition from the 'war' cabinet, Morrison achieved political bipartisanship on the management of the pandemic through the federation rather than the Federal Parliament. From that perspective, it had its partisan advantages.

But as he would discover over time, the national cabinet would not necessarily deliver the political dividends he had expected.

Despite the exhilaration of the premiers that they could drive the agenda, over time, flaws in the national cabinet began to reveal themselves. There were still limitations to delivering on the expectations it created, stresses along the faultlines of who dealt with what. And later, even its legitimacy as a subcommittee of the federal cabinet would get tested through the courts.[3]

A misconception about the national cabinet was that, through it, the Commonwealth was handing power back to the states. Political power, yes. Actual power, no. The states already had immense power, especially in the administration of public health. Other than their unanimous decision to administer quarantine within their states under agreed public health orders, nothing much had really changed power-wise in 100 years.

Morrison was acutely aware of the limitations of the country's constitutional power-sharing arrangements. For example, he was worried about the potential for massive civil disobedience against health orders, and he privately complained to Hunt that if he wanted to send in troops from the Australian Defence Force (ADF) to marshal compliance, the states could order their police forces to arrest the soldiers for breaking state laws.

'Chaos at the curb' was how a senior official described the power impasse operating during the pandemic. Theoretically, the Commonwealth could allow international visitors or returning Australians into the country but, under a state public health order, a premier could stop them leaving the airport.

Chaos was the last thing the PM wanted. The best Morrison could hope for was to get all the state and territory leaders in a room together and press them to agree to nationally consistent measures.

In the early days of national cabinet, he got his wish and the collaboration was remarkable. Party politics seemed to be left at the door. The national cabinet was meeting every second day, by telepresence, with a determined effort to put in place a set of common Australia-wide restrictions.

It had been largely working, until it didn't.

In a virtual repeat of the events of 1919, there had already been fractures with states starting to go their own way on some issues – sometimes out of political expediency, sometimes in sheer terror that their local public health system wouldn't cope with an outbreak.

Australia was getting engulfed in border wars.

*

Border wars

Morrison may have control over the international borders but he found out the hard way that he had no sway over what the states and territories did with their own.

One by one the premiers and chief ministers shut their internal borders to keep the virus out of their states and territories.

Tasmania had been the first to close, on 17 March,[4] with the Northern Territory,[5] South Australia,[6] Western Australia[7] and then Queensland[8] following suit: all used powers under declarations of a state of emergency.

New South Wales eventually closed its southern border to Victoria on 7 July.[9] In an eerie echo of similar action in 1919 responding to the Spanish flu, hundreds of ADF personnel and police officers were deployed to border towns to enforce a containment line restricting the flow of trucks, planes and trains between Australia's two most populous states

While annoyed with all of them, Morrison took particular exception to Queensland slamming its borders shut. There had been no consultation and, unlike other states, the closure had been abrupt. More importantly, it drew a hard line down the middle of a heavily populated border – the Gold Coast and Tweed Heads, creating instant havoc for people going about their daily lives.

Premier Annastacia Palaszczuk declared that 'extraordinary times call for extraordinary measures'.[10] This was the first time since Queensland failed to keep out the Spanish flu that it closed its border with New South Wales. Showing little regard for the economic, health and social impacts on border-hugging cities running from the Gold Coast to Ballina, Palaszczuk warned people to 'stay in their own states and in their own suburbs'.

Despite the Sunshine State experiencing only a handful of Covid-19 cases, Queensland's premier would establish herself, alongside WA's Mark McGowan, as one of Australia's most militant leaders when it came to border closures and snap lockdowns.

In Canberra, the harsh verdict was that Palaszczuk and the state's chief health officer, Jeannette Young, were terrified that the Queensland public health system would not be able to cope with an outbreak. That Palaszczuk, seven months out from an election – Australia's first major pandemic poll – had seized a political opportunity to boost her profile and standing among nervous voters.

With other countries, including the US and UK, facing fierce and deadly Covid-19 waves, Australia's federal, state and territory leaders were publicly talking up a suppression strategy. Yet their actions were looking more and more like an elimination strategy.

Palaszczuk's border closures – enforced by Queensland and NSW police – stopped family and friends from seeing each other and made it difficult for residents and students working and studying either side of the border.

The sick in northern New South Wales were being blocked from accessing medical treatment in Brisbane and the Gold Coast, including people suffering life-threatening illnesses who were unable to consult their specialists.

Ugly brawls took place between Palaszczuk and New South Wales's Berejiklian, who was flabbergasted that the terminally ill and patients with serious health conditions were being forced to pay thousands of dollars to quarantine for 14 days before they could access treatment.

Queensland-based doctors and nurses working in northern New South Wales were also stymied, and some transplant recipients and mothers with high-risk pregnancies had to cancel potentially life-saving procedures. Later, during a hard lockdown Palaszczuk ordered on 5 August, one of the twin baby girls who a Ballina mum, Kimberley Brown, was carrying died in utero after Brown was forced to travel the 750 kilometres to Sydney for emergency treatment.

The public backlash – outside of Queensland – against Palaszczuk was fierce. Morrison and Frydenberg described the Queensland border arrangements as 'heartbreaking'[11] and 'cruel'.[12]

The rancour between the Commonwealth and Queensland reached its peak during a phone call between Morrison and Palaszczuk early on the morning of 10 September.

Morrison was becoming agitated by the mounting pile of hardship cases being raised with his office, asking for federal intervention.

He called Palaszczuk to ask her whether she would overturn a decision to prevent a young NSW woman, Sarah Caisip, from attending her father's funeral in Brisbane that day.

The Queensland premier was furious at what she claimed was political interference.

It wasn't her decision to make, she told Morrison in the first heated conversation between the two leaders.

'You are bullying me,' Palaszczuk accused him abruptly, before reminding the prime minister that it was R U OK? Day.

She then hung up on him.

Facing mounting pressure, Palaszczuk eventually amended the border rules to allow border passes for NSW residents who needed specialist health care in Queensland.

But otherwise, she was unrepentant. With Queensland largely containing the virus and keeping its internal economy open, and pandemic incumbency, she reaped the political rewards of her tough border and Covid-19 restrictions with a thumping 31 October re-election victory.[13]

Later, as the crisis abated, there was sober reflection on the economic and human cost of the border and quarantine restrictions. While they helped slow the spread of the deadly disease there were countless tragic stories of families prevented from spending time with fathers, mothers and grandparents before their deaths. At the same time, reports that celebrities and wealthy Australians were being granted quarantine exemptions were fanning public fury.

Morrison and Frydenberg, aware that border closures and quarantine restrictions were necessary, were increasingly frustrated with the states' disproportionate responses of mounting restrictions in the face of handfuls of Covid cases.

The AHPPC had never recommended state and territory border closures but no amount of arguing budged the state leaders. Given that the three-step plan to reopen the economy by late July depended on internal border restrictions being lifted, Morrison saw the future looking bleak.

In the midst of these political conflicts, colourful billionaire mining magnate Clive Palmer picked a fight with the WA government after McGowan, on 25 May, declared that WA's border to the eastern states would remain shut for months. 'It's a small inconvenience,' McGowan said, '... it won't be forever. Our hard borders with the east and our isolation have worked to our advantage and we must keep it that way for now.'[14]

Palmer made a request to travel to WA as an 'exempt traveller'. The very day he was refused, the former member for Fairfax and one-time adviser to Queensland premier Joh Bjelke-Petersen launched an action in the High Court, claiming that McGowan's hard border policy breached section 92 of the Constitution, the provision that guarantees 'absolutely free' movement between states.[15] WA countered that the border closures were necessary to stop Covid spreading into the state. Two weeks later, Morrison announced that the Commonwealth would intervene in the case.

Strong public disapproval that the federal government appeared to be siding with Palmer prompted Morrison by August to write to McGowan and tell him that the Commonwealth was withdrawing from the case:

'While taking our constitutional responsibilities seriously in seeking to respect established conventions, I also accept that recent events in the eastern states, especially Victoria, are creating real concerns to residents in other states less impacted,' he wrote in a letter dated 2 August.

'I do not wish to see these concerns further exacerbated in Western Australia.'[16]

Following months of legal wrangling, the High Court ruled in favour of the state government and ordered Palmer to pay costs. The judgement confirmed the Federal Court's judgment that if people were allowed to travel to WA while infectious, there was a 'high probability that the virus would be transmitted into the WA population and at least a moderate probability that there would be uncontrolled outbreaks. If there were uncontrolled outbreaks, the consequences would include the risk of death and hospitalisation, particularly for [vulnerable groups]. In a worst-case scenario, the health consequences could be "catastrophic".'[17]

UNSW constitutional law expert Professor George Williams claimed the federal government's hesitancy in opposing state border closures early on had weakened its power within the federation. In an opinion piece in *The Australian*,[18] he accused the government of being 'reluctant to assume responsibility prior to the next election for a tough decision involving significant risks to the community'.

He continued: 'It is also evidence of a realignment of power within the federation. The pandemic has seen the states step up to lead, with the commonwealth often taking a back seat.

'Prior to the pandemic, successive federal governments were all too willing to direct and even overturn state action, by intervening across a wide range of what were once considered state responsibilities, including health and education, in the name of asserting the "national interest".'

The judgement meant that Morrison didn't have the constitutional authority to tell the states what to do. The fact they demanded autonomy in their decision-making but would assume no responsibility for the economic consequences – which fell back on the Commonwealth – became a constant source of frustration for the PM.

*

With the pandemic taking on a deeply political dimension – and the term 'Covid incumbency' becoming common to explain the high approval ratings of those in power – Morrison backed off from fighting the border wars.

McGowan's parochial rhetoric, hardline policies and public brawling with Palmer were paying him political dividends in the west. The harder the premier went, the more his popularity grew.

WA Labor's election victory on 13 March 2021 would deliver McGowan an historic landslide win, securing 53 seats, and plunging the Liberal and National parties into disarray. In the wake of the electoral bloodbath, the Liberals were left with two seats and the Nationals four seats, technically stripping both of party status. Labor's dominance in Queensland following its re-election and in WA – the nation's major resources states – was a huge concern for Liberal and National strategists.

The federal opposition was talking up the resounding nature of the victories. ALP officials waxed lyrical about voters in regional seats returning to Labor. Albanese and deputy Richard Marles were even drawing inspiration from legendary British Labor leader Clement Attlee, who defeated World War II hero Winston Churchill at the 1945 UK general election.[19]

To claw back mainstream support, they'd dropped Labor's focus on climate change targets and ambitious social policies in favour of a smaller target agenda based on national reconstruction.

Their Attlee-inspired strategy focused on convincing Australian voters that Labor was better placed to lead the national post-pandemic recovery and implement social and economic reforms.

It was an approach deeply rooted in a belief that Morrison would make mistakes and that the only way federal Labor could stay in the game politically would be to steadily try to strip away at Morrison's personal approval ratings.

They would be aided in this venture by the parochialism of the Labor state premiers, who had used the national cabinet as a springboard to elevate their status and as a platform for attacking the Commonwealth.

CHAPTER 15

'Xi's Chernobyl moment'

B Y MID-YEAR, OTHER nations were beginning to pay attention to China's behaviour to Australia. It wasn't just because Morrison was conducting a marathon of phone calls with European and Asian leaders from the beginning of June 2020, it was also a result of the Europeans, in particular, taking stock of their own vulnerabilities to China. China's threats to impose national security laws on Hong Kong, threatening its democracy, were yet another factor.[1]

While the pretext for most of Morrison's calls was his advocacy for Cormann's secret bid to become the next director general of the OECD, these discussions would inevitably swing around to China.

Ironically, the pandemic had brought like-minded countries together in a way that may never have occurred otherwise. It was a classic middle power push among liberal-democratic powers, committed, at least in principle, to greater collaboration and cooperation.

With each new retaliatory measure from China – fresh tariffs and additional restrictions on key commodities – the Morrison government could do little publicly other than grin and bear it, while at the same time trying to keep back channels open through DFAT officials in Beijing.

However, China's diplomatic assaults against Australia were having unintended consequences.

The EU, Britain, US, Canada and other nations began looking at their own supply chains with China.

On 18 June, Morrison spoke again with Boris Johnson and,

among other topics, they shared their concern over what was happening in Hong Kong. There was a closeness and a candour between them. Australian political strategist Lynton Crosby was a mutual close friend. Crosby had worked on successive Conservative Party campaigns in the UK, as well as for the Liberal Party in Australia. On Hong Kong, Johnson's view was that the national security laws threatened by China would breach both the letter and spirit of Britain's historic agreement with China.

During the pandemic, Australian aged care homes, hospitals, parliaments, water plants, logistics, media, and food companies kept being hit by cyber-attacks, but suddenly the attacks moved to an industrial scale. By mid-June, hackers were targeting Australian governments, critical infrastructure operators and major businesses.

Morrison did not name China as the culprit when, on 19 June, he announced the country had come under cyber assault from a sophisticated 'state-based' actor.[2] While the Australian intelligence community had good evidence that China was perhaps the most aggressive player, due to the fact that the significant technological resources required to undertake widespread attacks was limited to just a few countries, Russia and North Korea were also heavily engaged in foreign interference and cyber hacks, whether malicious attempts to disrupt systems or attempts to steal secrets.

Morrison said at the time, 'We know it's a sophisticated state-based cyber actor because of the scale and nature of the targeting and the tradecraft used … Regrettably, this activity is not new. But the frequency has been increasing.'

This would lead to Morrison allocating a record $1.67 billion in the 2020–21 budget to strengthen Australia's cyber-security defences in response to the alarming rise in activity. The Home Affairs Department also developed legislation to broaden the definition of critical infrastructure and bolster the cyber defences of governments and companies, supported by the Australian Signals Directorate (ASD). But there would be more. Post the 2022 Russian attacks on Ukraine, the 2022–23 budget included a further ten-year 'investment in Australia's cyber preparedness' of $9.9 billion. [3]

Through June and July 2020, the almost weekly dressing-down of Australia by Beijing's Foreign Ministry continued, but these attacks, their subjects ranging from Australia's treatment of Indigenous Australians to the historic White Australian policy and offshore refugee processing, were having no effect on Morrison and his cabinet.

Tensions ratcheted up at the end of June, when Beijing delivered on its threat to Hong Kong and, in contravention of the 'one country, two systems' model agreed with Britain before China reclaimed Hong Kong precisely 23 years earlier, Xi imposed the new national security laws, which covered subversion, foreign interference and terrorism, bypassing the Hong Kong legislature.[4] Beijing's trampling of Hong Kong's democratic institutions and violation of arbitrary detention protections, triggered mass rallies and violence and attracted strong responses from democracies across the globe, which only served to bring them closer in the pushback against Xi. Hong Kong had become yet another flashpoint for China and the West.

On 29 June, the NSC met again to canvass changes to Australia's foreign relations laws, which Morrison believed could be useful in dealing with Chinese foreign interference. One of the triggers for his thinking was Victoria signing a Belt and Road Initiative memorandum of understanding with China in 2018. It made its way back into headlines on 24 May 2020, when America's secretary of state, Mike Pompeo, made an extraordinary intrusion into Australian domestic policy in an interview on *Sky News*, suggesting that the US could 'simply disconnect' its intelligence sharing through the Five Eyes network, on the basis that Chinese investment in telecommunications assets could present an unacceptable risk.[5]

Andrews was understandably annoyed. There had not been any suggestion that the type of Chinese investment Victoria hoped to attract would involve sensitive infrastructure.

Pompeo's comments prompted a quick walkback from the US ambassador to Australia, Arthur B. Culvahouse Jr, who released a statement the following day to set the record straight: 'The United States has absolute confidence in the Australian Government's ability to protect the security of its telecommunications networks and those of its Five Eyes [US, UK, Canada, Australia and NZ] partners.'[6]

Despite the effort at conciliation, Pompeo's intervention was enough to till the soil for Commonwealth intervention. Morrison told the NSC meeting that the Australian states and territories didn't run Australia's foreign policy and that he would not allow them, or the country's institutions, to be exploited. Once again, he insisted that his government was merely acting in response to Beijing. 'The government has no wish to escalate things,' he assured colleagues. 'We have set out clear lines for years on these issues. Nothing we have done had been to injure the relationship.'

The Foreign Relations Bill – eventually introduced in September 2020 – would empower the Commonwealth to review and tear up bilateral agreements deemed to not be in Australia's national interest, including those signed by universities, and local and state governments.

At a meeting of the NSC the following day, Morrison said that the only path for Australia was for Beijing to work out that its approach was flawed. 'But I'm not holding my breath,' he said. When Morrison used the new powers to tear up the Victorian BRI deal in April 2021, China indefinitely suspended the China–Australia strategic economic dialogue.

On 2 July, during another meeting of the First Movers, Austria's chancellor, Sebastian Kurz, told the group that during an interview with the Australian media he had been somewhat blindsided.

'I wasn't prepared for so many questions on China,' he told them.

China's actions against Australia were getting noticed. Leaders elsewhere were aware that if it could happen to Australia, it could happen to their countries.

Australia's response to Beijing's national security law for Hong Kong – followed by similar moves from the US and UK – was decisive, fast-tracking visa and residency processing for Hong Kong citizens, prioritising more than 10,000 skilled and graduate visa holders already in the country, and targeting investment into Australia from firms seeking to move out of the former British colony. In early July, Australia suspended its extradition treaty with Hong Kong, citing 'deep concerns' over Beijing's national security crackdown, and upgraded its travel advice, telling citizens not to travel to China because they could face 'arbitrary detention'.[7]

China countered this by slapping fresh tariffs on Australian beef and extending trade threats against other products, including seafood and timber.

The Europeans were starting to realise how reliant they were on China, including for the supply of PPE essential for dealing with the pandemic.

Beijing's blatant attempts to spread disinformation and undermine Australia were becoming routine, and its approach was also spreading to other western nations that challenged Xi's authority.

*

China plays dirty

Morrison worried that the premiers didn't understand the extent of Beijing's coercion: that there was much more to it than the well-publicised trade sanctions and increasingly volatile rhetoric. So, on 31 July 2020, he arranged for the national cabinet to receive a national security briefing from ASIO director-general Mike Burgess.

This was without precedent, but Morrison felt it was essential for the states and territories to understand what was really going on. Burgess was brought in to brief the leaders about the growing threat of China in relation to foreign interference and cyber security.

A noticeable absentee from that meeting was Andrews, who had excused himself on the basis that he was too busy dealing with the pandemic.

In a dramatic moment on 14 November 2020, the Chinese embassy in Canberra issued a list of 14 grievances against Australia.[8]

The hit list ranged from the ban on Huawei to claims Australia was leading multilateral alliances against China on Taiwan, Xinjiang and Hong Kong. The government was accused of trying to 'torpedo' Victoria's BRI deal and engineer 'unfriendly or antagonistic' reporting by media outlets against China. A nameless junior embassy official laid bare the intention behind the list: 'China is angry. If you make China the enemy, China will be the enemy.'[9]

The response of the Morrison government to the unprecedented intervention by China's Canberra-based diplomats was effectively to cut off the embassy. Inside the Chinese embassy at Yarralumla, senior Chinese officials were frustrated by what they described as an unsanctioned release of the so-called 14 grievances. In their eyes, the grievances list ran far longer than that.

By the end of November 2020, the relationship had sunk to new lows. Chinese Ministry of Foreign Affairs spokesman Zhao Lijian – a chief proponent of Beijing's 'wolf warrior diplomacy' – posted a fake image on Twitter of an Australian soldier slitting the throat of an Afghan child. Zhao had attempted to seize on the findings of the Afghanistan Inquiry Report led by Paul Brereton, a major-general in the Australian Army Reserve and a NSW Supreme Court judge, which outlined alleged war crimes by Australian soldiers.[10]

Morrison, newly returned from Japan, where he had met new prime minister Yoshihide Suga, was in quarantine and peddling the exercise bike at The Lodge when Louw brought the tweet to his attention. Furious, the PM ordered a snap virtual press conference to slam the 'repugnant' post.

'The only thing that has brought shame today is this appalling post by the Chinese government. The Chinese government should be totally ashamed of this post. It diminishes them in the world's eyes.'[11]

*

WHO runs interference

When the WHO announced an Independent Panel for Pandemic Preparedness and Response in July 2020 – led by former New Zealand prime minister Helen Clark – it pledged to 'evaluate the world's response to the Covid-19 pandemic'.[12]

Separately, the WHO convened a Review Committee on the Functioning of the International Health Regulations (2005) during the Covid-19 response, which had last been assessed following the Influenza A (H1N1) pandemic in 2009–10. Predictably, the review committee found that existing IHR measures had been insufficient in identifying and repelling Covid-19.

'Indeed, some of the countries that had seemed best prepared to detect and respond to a deadly virus turned out to be among the least able to prevent or control the spread of severe acute respiratory syndrome coronavirus 2 (SARS-CoV-2) nationally, internationally or both,' the committee's final report said.[13]

As multiple probes got underway, it was the work of the 13-person independent panel, co-chaired by Ms Clark and former Liberian prime minister Ellen Johnson Sirleaf, that remained a priority for world leaders. The panel began its investigation in September 2020 and was given until the 74th World Health Assembly in May 2021 to complete its final report. It was tasked with piecing together failings in the reporting of initial coronavirus cases in Wuhan by the WHO and China, delays which caused the virus to spread across the world, and the origins of Covid-19. The investigation was also supported by a team of foreign scientists, despatched to tour hospitals and key sites, including the seafood market linked to some of the first reported cases, in Wuhan.

During the IPPPR team's highly publicised visit to Wuhan, Chinese authorities restricted access to data and relevant sites which had been requested by the WHO experts. When the scientific report, prepared in conjunction with Chinese Communist Party scientists, was released by the WHO in March 2021, it suggested the virus was probably transmitted by animals. It nominated a species of bat as the 'most likely reservoir host' and hypothesised that the virus may have spread via frozen food. It stressed that a lab leak was 'extremely unlikely'.[14]

Many western powers were skeptical about the report's findings, suspecting that Beijing may have used its influence to interfere with the investigation and/or whitewash the final outcome. The overarching narrative that had come from health advice provided to Morrison and other world leaders in the early days of the pandemic was that the virus had likely spread via natural origins, potentially linked to the Huanan wet market in Wuhan.

China's attempts from the outset to withhold key data and information in relation to the virus had prompted the *Wall Street Journal* to conduct its own months-long investigation into the origins of Covid-19 and the bungling of global investigations.[15] It found the WHO-led team sent to China to investigate the origins of the virus had been confronted with obfuscation by Chinese authorities, leaving them with insufficient evidence.

The *WSJ* investigation also revealed Chinese authorities had refused to provide WHO investigators with 'raw data on confirmed and potential early Covid-19 cases that could help determine how and when the coronavirus first began to spread in China.

'For months before the WHO investigators arrived, Beijing declined to disclose information about samples authorities took in the first weeks of the pandemic from animals sold at the Wuhan market linked to many early cases,' the *WSJ* said. 'During their visit, the investigators found no proof of live mammals being sold at that market and quoted market authorities saying there was no illegal wildlife traded there.

'A study later suggested the Wuhan market was the site of widespread trading in illegal caged wildlife, providing evidence that the virus could have spread naturally from market animals to humans.'

For the US, Britain, Australia and others, the question of whether Covid-19 may have leaked from laboratories at the Wuhan Institute of Virology was not yet settled. The case for a lab leak began to grow, first under the Trump administration and later under US president Joe Biden, who ordered his intelligence chiefs to launch an official probe into the origins of Covid-19 on 26 May 2021. This was after some failed attempts to gain access to China to learn more about the virus.

Biden, too, came up short. In his follow-up statement[16] he said:

The failure to get our inspectors on the ground in those early months will always hamper any investigation into the origin of Covid-19.

Nevertheless, shortly after I became President, in March, I had my National Security Advisor task the Intelligence Community to prepare a report on their most up-to-date analysis of the origins of Covid-19, including whether it emerged from human contact with an infected animal or from a laboratory accident.

As of today, the US Intelligence Community (IC) has 'coalesced around two likely scenarios' but has not reached a definitive conclusion on this question.

Here is their current position: 'while two elements in the IC leans toward the former scenario and one leans more toward the latter – each with low or moderate confidence – the majority of elements do not believe there is sufficient information to assess one to be more likely than the other.'

With China retreating further from the US, Australia and western nations amid tremors in global geostrategic competition, the prospect of ever definitively linking the pandemic with natural origins or a lab leak remained unlikely.

After a group of leading scientists published an open letter suggesting the lab leak theory 'was plausible enough to merit serious consideration',[17] the *WSJ* reported that other scientists had sought information about the Wuhan Institute of Virology's role in investigating a 'mysterious respiratory illness that afflicted six people clearing bat guano from a mine in southwest China in 2012.

'Three of them died, and samples the WIV took from bats in the mine were later found to contain the closest known virus on earth to the one that causes Covid-19.

'Unanswered questions about the miners' illness, the viruses found at the site and the research done with them elevated into the mainstream an idea once dismissed as a conspiracy theory: that SARS-CoV-2, the virus that causes Covid-19, might have leaked from a lab in Wuhan. China denies that the virus came from the Wuhan Institute of Virology or any other Chinese laboratory.'[18]

The final IPPPR report – released in May 2021,[19] long after the scientific report – did not explicitly criticise China, but rather poured blame on the WHO for being too slow in declaring a public health emergency.

It read, 'After a stuttering start to the global response in January 2020 by the end of that month it was clear that a full-scale response would be needed. It is glaringly obvious to the Panel that February 2020 was a lost month, when steps could and should have been taken to curtail the epidemic and forestall the pandemic.'[20]

The report described Covid-19 as the '21st century's Chernobyl moment – not because a disease outbreak is like a nuclear accident, but because it has shown so clearly the gravity of the threat to our health and well-being'.[21]

CHAPTER 16

Re-enter the Quad

BY 17 JULY 2020, the last time Morrison spoke leader-to-leader with Donald Trump, the fierce US election campaign between Trump and 'sleepy' Joe Biden was in full swing.

The PM was in Canberra, using the secure room off the cabinet suite. Trump was in the Oval Office. The call was set up as part of a scheduled re-affirmation of the broad Australia–US alliance and was to cover a range of issues, but Trump kicked it off with an excoriating assessment of the deteriorating global situation and what he was now claiming to be China's role in it.

'It was a "disgrace",' Trump said. 'Look what they have done to the world. They have fucked the world.'

The US president's descriptive language surprised none of the staff who were listening in to the call. They had come to expect the unexpected when it came to Trump.

The last time Morrison had spoken to him was on 2 June 2020, the day Trump had threatened to deploy the military to quell riots fuelled by the death of African-American George Floyd in Minneapolis.[1]

On that occasion, several of Morrison's staff had been sitting around in Kirribilli House at around 9am, waiting for a secure call from the White House to come through to the PM. When it did, they were to pull him out of his daily Covid health and Treasury briefing.

With the TV on, the staffers were surprised to see the US president leave the White House – it was around 7pm Washington DC time – flanked by his daughter Ivanka, her husband Jared Kushner, and numerous administration officials.

Earlier that evening, and using pepper spray and tear gas, DC police, the National Guard and other law enforcement officials had cleared protesters from what would become Trump's route through Lafayette Park. The president stopped outside St John's Episcopal Church – its basement had been set alight the night before – and he held a Bible up to the cameras.

Given the chaos they'd been witnessing on TV,[2] Morrison's staffers were surprised that the call came through at all. And, when the phone rang around 10am in Sydney, they hadn't had time to brief him about the maelstrom surrounding Trump.

The US president dealt breezily with the business part of the call, which was to invite Morrison to attend the G7 summit at Camp David later in 2020: 'We are doing great,' said Trump. 'We'd love you to come to the G7.'

It was a demonstration of Australia's emerging position in the world that for the second year in a row, it would participate as a guest member in this gathering of the world's leading industrialised economies – the US, UK, France, Germany, Italy, Canada and Japan.

Morrison made the point that the 2019 G7 meeting in Biarritz, France, which he'd attended alongside Indian prime minister Narendra Modi, had been such a successful summit because it brought like-minded liberal democracies together in one room at a time when the world was facing increasing strategic challenges.

*

'Don't invite Putin'

Since the 2019 G7, Morrison had been quietly behind the scenes putting the case to the Americans that there was nothing remotely liberal or democratic about Russia. Trump had been saying publicly that it was 'common sense' for Russia to rejoin the group. (It was kicked out after its annexation of Ukraine's Crimea in 2014.)[3]

Morrison, on the 17 July call, directly questioned Trump's desire to have Putin return to the forum.

'I think you're a bit more optimistic than we are,' Morrison told Trump during that last official conversation the two leaders would conduct.

Morrison's strong reservations about Putin being admitted back into a forum founded on the principles of the international rules-based order were later vindicated in February 2022, when Russia invaded Ukraine.

Changing the subject, Trump asked how Australia was managing to do so well during the pandemic, before the conversation pivoted back to China. Morrison highlighted how important it was to Australia to receive support in the face of China's campaign of economic coercion

The two leaders touched again on the preparations for the G7 and, again, Morrison reminded Trump that Russia would struggle to fall into any definition of a liberal democracy. He said Trump shouldn't forget Russia's role in downing Malaysian Airlines flight MH17 in 2014. Of the 298 people on board who were killed, 38 were Australians.[4]

Trump appeared to listen but offered no reply to Morrison's prescient warnings about the Russian autocrat.

Morrison also pressed the case for Washington to bring its focus back to the Indo-Pacific. He talked Trump through the points he'd been canvassing with like-minded leaders, particularly the importance of building stronger partnerships with India, Singapore, Japan and others.

A feature of Morrison's discussions with Trump through the year had been the Quadrilateral Security Dialogue, a strategic alliance between the US, Australia, Japan and India, generally known as the Quad.

His thrust was the need to elevate the engagement to a leaders-level meeting. He would maintain that position in his ongoing conversations with Pompeo and, eventually, the new US president, Joe Biden.

Trump finished the call noting he was in the middle of an election campaign against someone who 'was not too good'. He had wanted an easy, quick victory. The economy had been 'so great', he said, until it got hit by the virus. Now, he added, he had to go out and win the old-fashioned way.

Morrison never got too hung up on his relationship with Trump, who had started it off by introducing Morrison to the private reception of G7 leaders in 2019 as the 'President of Australia'. He'd recall that a year and a half later, when Trump's successor, Joe Biden, called him 'that fella down under' at the press conference to announce the AUKUS trilateral security partnership between the US, UK and Australia.

Trump, for his part, seemed fascinated with Morrison's 2019 election win, drawing parallels with his own political success.

Morrison had two other main points of contact with the US administration. He touched base frequently with secretary of State and former Central Intelligence Agency director Mike Pompeo, and the two developed a close relationship. They spoke often about their shared concerns over China's behaviour, in the context of the US–China trade war on foot since July 2018, and the newer, unrelated retaliatory trade actions China was now taking against Australia.

The PM also kept in contact with Vice-President Mike Pence.

If he needed to escalate an issue, he would usually try one of them first.

To Morrison, Trump's approach seemed to lack a strategy and was rooted in grievance. Morrison's position, which was attracting the Europeans in his many conversations, was not to engender an anti-China sentiment but rather – through the lens of the pandemic – to start binding the liberal democracies of the world together and thereby further Australia's future strategic interests.

He was seeking to employ several longer-term strategic chess pieces. The Quad was one, pivotal to act as a counterweight to China in the Indo-Pacific. Another was to draw Europe into the issues facing the region.

While the UK, Germany and France had broadly different views as to the challenges China posed in the international system, they had been shifting from a fairly relaxed, open approach, borne out of getting as much trade with China as possible, to growing concern about strategic competition and coercion.

Their shifting perspectives were not down to Morrison, but his dialogues with the other leaders were giving the issues heightened prominence.

Australian officials were also hard at work behind the scenes and, for example, had some influence in the UK's reversal of its Huawei decision, when it removed the Chinese telco from its 5G rollout, in line with the other Five Eyes counterparts.

America would, of course, be crucial in this. While Trump was not able to bind the Europeans together on anything, having criticised most of them individually and collectively, Biden, a multilateralist, seemed to offer more potential.

With Europe's dim view of Australia's early reluctance to sign up to net zero 2050 targets, Morrison also used his calls to push Australia's case on climate change, namely that it was one of the few countries that had so far actually met its commitments under the international agreements.

Yet the Australia–China dynamic was a backdrop to many if not most of Morrison's conversations.

Australia was accustomed to being consistent and strong on what it believed its national interest to be and had a highly nuanced relationship with China. Many European countries had specific PPE supply chain issues with China and were timid in speaking up. If at first somewhat surprised by Australia's hawkish position on the coronavirus inquiry, the Europeans welcomed the fact that someone was prepared to express what they were thinking but weren't willing to say.

'I think that is what has opened up during the Covid crisis,' Morrison recalls. 'The opportunity for mid-tier relationships to provide resilience against strategic tension over trade, security, supply chains. And people talking to each other who had never really spent much time talking before.

'One of the great mis-analyses that had been taking place was that we had been following the Americans. Frankly, in many cases they affirmed our positions, not the other way around. And our reasons for doing what we are doing are often quite different than what America was doing. We are not engaged in some geostrategic competition with China. We are just protecting and advancing our own interests in this part of the world. That means there are a range of things we have to do.

'Now, the US will support many of those things, out of the alliance but also for other motivations. There is an assumption about how we act and what we do that is misplaced. We will do what we think is right; it just so happens the US agree with us a lot. And what is interesting is that a lot more people are agreeing with us.'

The US alliance was, had been and would always remain Australia's overriding strategic partnership – the Indo-Pacific the axis around which the country's future would spin – and China would remain one of its key economic relationships.

In terms of the US relationship, Morrison would frame it as two countries with a strategic alignment but tactical flexibility. He had discussed the approach with Mike Pence shortly after he became prime minister.

In other words, the alliance would work best if Australia ran its own tactical response to issues in the region, primarily China, without any need to inform the US.

*

Australia's defence pivot

China hadn't accounted for the possibility that Australia might take other countries with it in pushing back against the CCP's growing influence. Beijing, seeking to isolate Morrison, discovered that Australia had more agency than it expected. Once Germany, France, the UK and Canada started to shift, others in Europe followed.

As Morrison saw it, the shared values, peoples and an adherence to universal principles of freedom and democracy that won the allies two world wars were in play again.

'We fought with each other like cats and dogs in between those conflicts but you pick a fight with any one of us and we come together. China picked a fight with us.'

It was during this period of Europe's shifting view on China that on 1 July 2020, Morrison announced the government's 2020 Defence Strategic Update (DSU), a headline-grabbing $270 billion dollar program to be staged over ten years.[5]

The DSU had been a long time in the making. Morrison wanted the posture to reflect the changing strategic landscape, which for Australia was the Indo-Pacific. Since 9/11, Defence policy had focused on distant operations. He considered that it was time to refocus back on the country's region of 'immediate concern' and away from the main theatres in the Middle East, including Afghanistan. This would not see Australia saying a blanket 'no' to participating in any future US expeditionary exercises in the Middle East, for example, but would set the bar a lot higher for any Australian deployment. Morrison had no desire to spread Australian forces thin.

He had begun laying the foundations for a defence pivot earlier in 2020. On 21 February, he'd flown out to the Tindal RAAF base in the Northern Territory, becoming the first prime minister since Bob Hawke to do so. Tindal, near the town of Katherine, plays host to US B-52 strategic bombers and will serve as the main base for Australia's F-35 strike fighter squadron. The PM's next stop was the joint Australia–US intelligence facility at Pine Gap. Seeing Pine Gap for himself made a significant impression on Morrison. He was struck not only by the degree that Australian and American defence intelligence were integrated but also by the sheer sophistication of the set-up. It is fair to say that the visit helped sharpen his strategic thinking.

During several NSC meetings during March and April of 2020, there was rigorous discussion around the new regional dynamic, and the belief that Australia simply couldn't afford *not* to have its force structure geared to the region instead of elsewhere. This prompted debate back and forth about the likely US reaction. Would America see this as Australia pulling back?

Morrison held a 'deep dive' session of the NSC with just him and the defence strategists present. Nothing emerged to make him change his thinking.

Morrison was crystal clear that a tilt towards the Indo-Pacific was the right thing to do.

Kunkel observed that the PM had delivered no significant defence speeches during his term, so he pushed for Morrison to make the DSU announcement, rather than Defence minister Linda Reynolds. This would give him portfolio ownership over Defence.

In an interview with *The Australian* the day before the speech, Morrison said that the defence update would reflect how the world had changed.

'The world hasn't known a time of economic and strategic uncertainty like this since the '30s and '40s,' he said. 'This has required us to sharpen our focus on our region and enhance our capability. We need to hold our potential adversaries to a greater distance. Part of our repositioning is to hold them further away.'[6]

Kunkel and Shearer worked together on the speech. Morrison's reference to the World War II era also made it into the speech: the DSU, he said, 'will guide our nation through one of the most challenging times we have known since the 1930s and the early 1940s.

'We have been a favoured isle, with many natural advantages for many decades, but we have not seen the conflation of global, economic and strategic uncertainty now being experienced here in Australia in our region since the existential threat we faced when the global and regional order collapsed in the 1930s and 1940s. That is a sobering thought, and it's something I have reflected on quite a lot lately, as we've considered the dire economic circumstances we face.'[7]

*

The irony of China's sharp reaction to Australia's posture was that none of what Morrison was putting was inflammatory, and certainly not new, as seen in a couple of speeches he'd given almost a year earlier.

In a speech in Chicago, on 23 September 2019, he questioned China's right to maintain its World Trade Organization 'developing nation' status, and the concessions that afforded, such as generous trading terms and the right to restrict imports to protect its industries.[8]

In a speech he gave to the Lowy Institute in Sydney a week later, on 3 October 2019, he had three key foreign policy messages, all of which would be dramatically emphasised by the pandemic.[9]

They were that the world was more dangerous, the institutions that governed it were in disrepair and Australia was determined to have a greater say.

He also spoke about vulnerabilities in global supply chains – which would become so pronounced at the height of the virus – and announced that he had tasked DFAT with conducting an audit of global institutions and rule-making processes where Australia had most at stake, and where Australia could become more influential.

Morrison opened that speech with the words, 'We have entered a new era of strategic competition – a not unnatural result of shifting power dynamics in our modern, more multi-polar world and globalised economy ... A time when global supply chains have become integrated to an unprecedented degree, and more of our economies are dependent on global trade than at any other time, including the major economic powers of the United States, China, Japan and Europe.

'An era where pragmatic international engagement, based on the cooperation of sovereign nation states, is being challenged by a new variant of globalism that seeks to elevate global institutions above the authority of nation states to direct national policies.'

In that speech, Morrison's tone on China was relatively moderate. While the US remained Australia's most important ally, he rejected the 'binary narrative of their strategic competition' with China.

What caught most attention, and attracted criticism from some quarters, was the Australian PM's reference to 'negative globalism':

'The world works best when the character and distinctiveness of independent nations is preserved within a framework of mutual respect. This includes respecting electoral mandates of their constituencies. 'I'm determined for [sic] Australia will play a more active role in standards setting.'

Australia had been the first of the world's middle powers to resist China, and Morrison was intent on being outspoken about it.

China was effectively singling out Australia for punishment, largely because of its relationship with the US.

It also sent a message to other countries that alignment with America – and by inference, standing in opposition to China's development – would incur consequences.

The only way that resistance would work was if the rest of the world was made aware of it.

CHAPTER 17

The second wave

ON THE MORNING of 6 July 2020, it took Morrison under 20 minutes to be driven from Kirribilli House to Sydney Airport but that was more than enough time for him and NSW premier Gladys Berejiklian to make a decision that hadn't been contemplated for more than 100 years.

From the back seat of the bullet-proof white BMW 7 Series limousine, the official car used by the PM in Sydney, he dialled Berejiklian ahead of his 30-minute flight to Canberra.

Morrison was becoming increasingly concerned by rising case numbers in Melbourne, following an outbreak of the virus from two 'hot' hotels in the city used to quarantine travellers returning from overseas. 'You have to shut the border,' he told the premier.

'Thank goodness,' Berejiklian replied, then told him she had been about to call him to discuss the same thing.

'We'll need to get Dan [Andrews] to agree to this. We should call him,' said Morrison.

Neither leader wanted to shut such a large part of the country down. But they could see no alternative.

Morrison tried to call Andrews but didn't get through, so sent him a text:

'Have spoken to Gladys this morning and agree that given escalating situation, it is regrettably necessary now to take the next step and close the Vic/NSW border. Will both continue to provide our assistance with resources and support.'

Minutes later, he boarded the plane, and as soon as he was back in his Parliament House office he got on a three-way call with Berejikian and Andrews. And so it was agreed: for the first time since February 1919, the border between Australia's two most populous states would be closed.

Despite the historical significance of the decision, there was an almost palpable spirit of cooperation on that call, a sense of solidarity that would be tested throughout the course of what would become Australia's second wave. Privately, Andrews and Morrison would remain on good terms but not so publicly, when it appeared the federation was fracturing as Victorians had to endure the most draconian and prolonged social restrictions in Australia, if not the world.

*

Over the prior weeks Morrison and Andrews were in almost constant contact. Fears had surfaced in early May that a new wave might be starting following an outbreak of unknown origin at an abattoir in Melbourne's western suburbs, the Cedar Meats butchery. It produced a cluster of 111 cases in two weeks. By the end of May, it was contained, the source believed to be from hotel quarantine. At the same time, a second cluster was emerging.

Victoria's second wave – which by December 2020 accounted for 20,351 cases and 820 deaths – was linked to cases at two quarantine hotels, the Stamford Plaza in Melbourne's CBD and the Rydges Hotel in Carlton.

Victorian health officials had set up a 'cohorting' system where positive Covid-19 cases were sent to 'hot', or 'red', hotels located away from those who were not infectious. On 2 April, the Rydges was designated a 'hot hotel' after receiving large numbers of positive cases who became infectious on the cruise ship MV *Greg Mortimer* while stranded off Uruguay.

Concern that community transmission was again underway was heightened by mid-June, when a protester who had attended a Black Lives Matter rally in Melbourne's CBD tested positive, and daily case numbers began to rise to double digits.[1] Victoria's chief health officer, Professor Brett Sutton, admitted to being 'nervous' about what was happening.[2]

By then, Andrews was becoming worried that his health officials didn't have a handle on the situation, and ordered a surge in Covid testing to find out how far it was going.

By 23 June, Victoria had recorded a week of double-digit daily cases, and Morrison considered it likely that Australia could, like other countries, suffer a second Covid wave.

What was not being made public at the time was that some of the cases were showing up as a variant that health experts suspected was a precursor to the highly transmissible strain that had forced Britain into a second hard lockdown.

From the outset, Morrison's stance was that three things were essential to managing the spread of the virus: testing, tracing and containing localised outbreaks.

His view was being reinforced by comments he was receiving from other world leaders such as Netanyahu, Abe and Korean prime minister Moon Jae-in.

Abe described how once an infection was detected in a Japanese suburb, rapid response cluster groups immediately went in and locked it down.

This rang a bell with Morrison. His preference from the outset had been to use the ADF to ringfence suburbs where there were clusters. But at national cabinet, when he proposed trying this during the early outbreaks in northwest Sydney, he got no support. The states were concerned about the optics of having 'khaki' on the streets.

At 9pm on 23 June, Morrison texted Andrews and offered the Commonwealth's support for whatever was needed. The PM then spoke to ADF chief Angus Campbell in case Andrews would ask for assistance.

On 25 June, Andrews replied that a request was being sent to the PM's office that afternoon.[3]

Morrison wrote again to Andrews on 29 June: 'Have been updated on your numbers today obviously concerning but not surprising with the broader testing. Are they all in the hotspots? Obviously you can have whatever you need. I assume you're now considering full hotspot lockdowns. Let's talk later today about what you need.'

Andrews replied and told him that he would call later that day with his then next steps. Everything was on the table, Andrews told him.

In a follow-up text, he said that his top public servant, the Victorian secretary of the Department of Premier and Cabinet, Chris Eccles, was talking about ADF support to the secretary of PM&C, Phil Gaetjens.

In spite of the acrimony that would play out publicly through the course of the second wave and beyond, Morrison and Andrews privately maintained a deep level of cooperation. In fact, they were in contact almost daily and often several times a day.

While the prime minister could see a lot of merit in imposing hard border lockdowns on individual suburbs and having the ADF stand guard in affected areas, he respected that there were sensitivities on the Victorian side, especially around uniformed officers patrolling some of the multicultural areas. A number of religious festivals were occurring at the time, and Andrews was trying to delicately find a way through.

Morrison had similar discussions with Indian prime minister Narendra Modi and Indonesian president Joko Widodo about the challenges they had faced in navigating religious festivals at the height of outbreaks.

'It would be good for us to have a shared road map on what's next and what is needed for what's next,' Morrison wrote to Andrews. 'The most extreme step is obviously total isolation and lockdown of the affected areas, which could be soon. Obviously the fed biosecurity powers could be used to support a complete lockdown.

'For now, it would seem necessary to reimpose no home visits and only leaving home for essentials, two-person rule, cafes pubs etc all closed.

'Would prefer if employment be restricted to places of work in hot zones. Obviously, these are your calls. We want to be supportive and do this by sticking together. I'm not offering any public or private commentary that is anything other than support but would express our preference for moving to stronger lockdowns sooner to sustain and bolster confidence.'

Andrews replied that he was grateful for the support and would make further announcements that day.

With his own officials, Morrison was canvassing the possibility of getting access to ATO data to know where people were working so as to be ready to deal with employers, and find out where people were travelling to work. The theory was that if people were all working in the outbreak zones, the whole place could be locked down.

When national cabinet met on 26 June and the topic of Covid suppression versus elimination came up, the three most strongly opposed to an elimination strategy were Morrison, Andrews and Berejiklian. All were clear-sighted about the economic consequences of such a policy.

At that meeting, Berejiklian pointed out that aside from New South Wales and Victoria, none of the other states were accepting many – if any – of the returning travellers into quarantine. Between them, New South Wales and Victoria were bearing the brunt, taking 90 per cent, and New South Wales was taking the majority of that. To make the point that New South Wales and Victoria were doing the heavy lifting, Berejiklian suggested that residents of other states who were coming into Sydney from overseas could simply transfer onto flights to their home states and quarantine there.

The response from the other leaders was an observable silence.

*

ADF amnesia

By the end of July 2020, a judicial inquiry[4] Andrews had commissioned to investigate the failure of Victoria's hotel quarantine program – headed by former Family Court justice Jennifer Coate – had begun to gather evidence. There were plenty of theories as to how the virus escaped, including sensational tales that the private security contractors were intimate with infected travellers. A separate parliamentary inquiry into Victoria's response to the pandemic would trigger a public brawl between the Commonwealth and the Andrews government over whether the ADF had ever been offered and for what purpose.

On 11 August, Andrews told the Victorian Parliament's Public Accounts and Estimates Committee – which was scrutinising the Victorian government's pandemic response – that while ADF support had been provided for transportation between airports and hotels in 'very limited circumstances in New South Wales', he did not assume that involved security. 'I think it is fundamentally incorrect to assert that there were hundreds of ADF staff on offer and somehow someone said no. That is just not in my judgement accurate.'[5]

Andrews' recollections prompted a swift response from Defence minister Linda Reynolds, who issued a statement later that day disputing any suggestion that the ADF assistance had not been offered.[6]

Reynolds made the point that Defence had agreed to requests for support for quarantine compliance from Queensland and New South Wales in March.

'On 24 June 2020, Defence agreed to a Victorian Government request for 850 ADF personnel to assist with hotel quarantine compliance,' Reynolds went on to say. 'The request was withdrawn by the Victorian Government the following day. The decision to withdraw the request is a matter for the Victorian Government.'

Justice Coate's report – published just before Christmas that year – would deliver seemingly contradictory findings: that everybody was to blame but no one was to blame.[7]

It cited the lack of any pandemic planning at a Commonwealth or state level for the employment of a large-scale hotel quarantine program.

Its findings, nonetheless, at least provided a copybook on how to not operate one.

The report said 'systemic governmental failings' rather than security guard breaches had led to poor infection control measures at hotel quarantine sites, which triggered Victoria's 112-day lockdown.[8]

*

By 7 July, the daily case numbers across the country hit 300, the majority in Victoria. Under the agreement between Victoria and New South Wales, movement between those two states had ceased and Victoria was largely isolated.

Andrews that day announced that the Stage 3 lockdown he'd put 12 suburbs in was being extended to the whole of Melbourne and it would be for six weeks. International flights into Melbourne were diverted.[9]

Morrison sent Andrews a friendly text: 'Hang in there Dan.'

National cabinet met the next day, 10 July. While the press conference that followed gave a positive picture of cooperation, behind the scenes parochialism was rife. The premiers had turned back into premiers.

Morrison was getting frustrated with the provincialism which he believed was being driven by politics. His position was that they had to contain the outbreaks where they were occurring. In places where there were no outbreaks, as much interaction in the economy as possible should be allowed.

The proposition put to the room was that when an outbreak occurred, it would be defined, with a line drawn around it and no one allowed to leave their own state, city or suburb. The Commonwealth would designate 'hotspots', which could be locally or regionally contained without the need to shut down entire states or territories. The premiers were reluctant to agree.

What was troubling Morrison was that the initial commitment by the premiers and chief ministers to doing what was right for the country had diminished and, with limited exceptions, he was facing increasing insularism. Berejiklian and the Northern Territory's Gunner were the exceptions. Morrison believed that Andrews would have been onside with them too had he not been dealing with his own crisis.

Published polling showed the premiers riding a wave of unprecedented approval among voters, serving to reinforce decision-making that ignored the broader national interest.

Even so, Morrison remained committed to the national cabinet process. In his view, there was no alternative model.

Morrison had told the premiers and chief ministers at the end of the national cabinet meeting that he'd be off for a week's break with his family. He was 'buggered', he said, and had seen little of his wife Jenny and their two daughters.

But, after the spotlight of attention the last time he went on vacation – to Hawaii during the bushfires – all he told the media was that he was having a break somewhere in Sydney. Because this time he wasn't leaving the country, he would not need to appoint anyone as acting prime minister.

Long before the second wave had broken, he had booked a rental property at Berowra Waters in Sydney's north.

But Morrison's weekend was mired in controversy. Between the meeting on Friday and the Sunday when he got in his car and drove to Berowra Waters, he was again taken to task by the media. In apparent insensitivity to Victorians, now in lockdown, he'd attended a football game at Sydney's Kogarah Oval, where his beloved Cronulla Sharks took on the Penrith Panthers. He'd even drunk a beer.

While he'd been looking forward to a break before the economic statement due to be handed down on 23 July, Morrison was now very conscious that the daily coronavirus cases kept heading upwards. Even so, at the sight of Berowra Creek valley, set into heavily wooded hills, the PM found himself breathing a little easier.

Access to the holiday property was only by water, and while the Australian Federal Police were concerned about the security around the property, he was happy with his choice and, against their well-meaning objections, insisted on taking his two daughters out on a tinny for a fishing expedition.

The Covid crisis didn't abate for his holiday and he was constantly on the phone speaking to Andrews and Berejiklian.

Over the course of his week away, the army was finally deployed to Victoria. Royal Australian Navy rear admiral Mark Hill was leading Operation COVID-19 Assist, the ADF contribution to the whole-of-government response.[10] Hill was now tasked with making a quick assessment of the testing and tracing systems in place to deal with the escalating case numbers. It did not take him long to report back that Victoria was effectively running blind on the data.

Unlike New South Wales, the state was still using paper-based rather than digital information systems.

*

With other countries relaxing quarantine measures, and combining rapid antigen tests with shorter isolation times, Morrison and the national cabinet came under pressure to get stranded Australians home sooner. This number would peak at almost 50,000 by mid-October 2021.[11]

In Britain, the government launched a red, amber, green system for visitors, based on where the traveller had been in the ten days before their arrival. Those who'd been in green destinations only required Covid-19 tests, but no quarantine. Those from amber destinations who had not been vaccinated in the UK were also tested but allowed to quarantine at home for ten days. Arrivals from red destinations had to quarantine in a managed quarantine hotels for ten days.

Singapore, Hong Kong and other Asian destinations were early adopters of rapid antigen testing. New arrivals were to be tested at the airport and required to wait for their result.

Morrison was open to a traffic light model. As early as 2020, federal government officials had begun working with counterparts in NZ, Singapore, Japan and Korea to harmonise border and health controls ahead of a gradual resumption of two-way travel with Australia. Morrison wanted the infrastructure in place but was cognisant of the political fallout if strict 14-day hotel quarantine arrangements were relaxed too soon. The state and territory governments had little appetite for moving quickly.

He also viewed a vaccination program, with multiple trials underway globally showing promising signs, as the new key to avoiding prolonged international and domestic border closures and Australians being caught up by harsh restrictions imposed by the states and territories.

His argument, which the states initially railed against, was that if a person in Australia was vaccinated, they should be offered more freedom of movement.

Australia remaining shut off to the world for several years was not an option that Morrison wanted to countenance. While the domestic economy had performed well – when Covid-19 lockdowns and restrictions were avoided – all levels of government knew migration and tourism had to be reactivated to plug skills and jobs gaps and support the long-term viability of the tourism and university sectors. Not to mention the worker shortages in the agricultural and hospitality sectors.

Meanwhile, a federal review of the hotel quarantine system got underway. Covid-19 Commission member Jane Halton – who had previously headed both the federal Finance and Health departments, and was heavily involved with the international COVAX vaccine facility as co-chair of the Coalition for Epidemic Preparedness Innovations (CEPI)[12] – formally launched at Davos in 2017 – was tapped by Morrison and the national cabinet to lead it.[13]

Halton's review, separate to the Victorian Hotel Quarantine Inquiry led by Justice Coate, addressed the logistical, mental health and virus breach pressures associated with operating one of the world's toughest quarantine regimes.

From day one, the quarantine debate sparked friction between state and federal governments over stand-alone facilities and jurisdictional responsibilities in sharing the burden of getting Australians home. The Labor states and Albanese used hotel quarantine breaches and the vaccine rollout to shift blame on to Morrison for new outbreaks, lockdowns and abandoning Australians stranded overseas.

As demand for hotel quarantine grew, Halton's review called for an expansion of national facilities – in addition to the Howard Springs Accommodation Village located near Darwin – after initial plans to use the Christmas Island immigration facility for quarantine were shelved.[14]

*

The issue of quarantine would become one of the most politically contested issues of the pandemic until delays in the vaccination rollout and shortages of rapid antigen tests would emerge. On one level, Australia's quarantine performance was overwhelmingly successful, with only a handful of breaches out of hundreds of thousands of returned travellers. The pressing issue for health professionals like Murphy was how to best manage a breach once the virus broke through, which they knew it inevitably would.

What the second wave had exposed in Victoria was a massive failing of the state's public health response. The Victorian government had been slow to lock down, which meant its Health department's inadequate contact tracing systems were unable to cope.

Morrison believed that Andrews was being let down badly by his officials.

*

'Victoria may have buggered up the entire country'

As July neared its end, the situation was getting more serious by the day. On the 30th, 723 new cases were reported, the highest national tally during the second wave. The total so far was over 16,000, and there had been 189 deaths.[15]

Morrison was on his morning call with Murphy when the CMO warned that Victoria would have to go further with restrictions if the outbreak was to get under control.

'I'm looking at this data. I know it's a big call, but they aren't on top of this. It's not getting better,' Murphy told the prime minister. 'The initial restrictions are not going to do the job. They are going to have to go further.'

'That's going to have a massive impact. That is serious,' Morrison replied. 'My problem with you telling me that, Brendan, is that you don't know everything about what's going on in the Victorian system.'

Never before through the pandemic had Morrison seen Murphy so rattled. It was clear the CMO was anxious and believed Victoria had been too slow to act

Murphy had been telling him for weeks that he was having difficulty getting accurate information and data out of Victoria. Yet, as always, Morrison wanted to interrogate the data before the AHPPC recommended that Victoria go into hard lockdown, then known as Stage 4 restrictions.

'I need you to know the things that you don't know, and if you tell them then that it needs to happen, then sure,' Morrison told him. 'You're probably right but I'm not hitting that button unless there is complete agreement between Victoria and the Commonwealth. I need you in the data room.'

Morrison was frustrated rather than angry. He was simply saying that such a serious step needed to be made on the best available information, and it appeared no one had that information.

That evening, Morrison had invited Indigenous Affairs minister Ken Wyatt to The Lodge for dinner, after announcing new national targets for Closing the Gap.

At one point, the PM apologised and excused himself to take a call he had arranged with Andrews. He left the dining room to take the call in the small office adjoining the lounge room. He told

Andrews that he wanted Victoria's health bureaucrats to share their Covid tracing data with Murphy, so the Commonwealth could get a handle on exactly what was going on.

Morrison wanted his people to know everything that Andrews' people did. There was a concern that walls had gone up around Sutton's team. Rear Admiral Hill was also struggling to get access to everything he needed to run the Covid-19 Assist operation.

Andrews gave his word that he would make it happen.

The next morning, Murphy received an email from the Victorian Health department with a completely different read-out of the conversation: agreeing to simply copy in Murphy on emails and correspondence. After considerable to and fro, it was eventually sorted out, thanks to Andrews' involvement.

Once Murphy had access to a fuller picture of the situation in Melbourne, he was alarmed. Later that same morning, he called the prime minister to give him the grim news.

'It is as bad as they said it was,' Murphy told Morrison.

'I'm afraid Victoria may have buggered up the entire country.'

Morrison once again found himself infuriated.

*

Victoria wasn't the only frustration for Morrison. He was of the firm belief that Australians should be wearing masks. To him it was an obvious measure. But he was having a hard time convincing health officials.

'I would go in to meeting after meeting and talk about masks … the AHPPC would push back,' Morrison recalls.

'I said, "Know at some point you will change your mind."'

Supply wasn't the problem: the national medical stockpile – the nation's strategic reserve of drugs and medical equipment – had purchased more than enough. At the beginning of the crisis, in March, Morrison announced an investment of an additional $1.1 billion to purchase PPE as part of a broader health package.[16] The problem was that people did not want to wear them.

Determined to change public perception, Hunt finished a press conference by urging Australians to adopt the simple but effective precaution. He then proceeded to fumble as he tried to put his own mask on.

Fuelling the public's hesitancy over mask-wearing was medical advice. Many in the health field questioned if they were necessary, and some suggested they might be counterproductive. The concern was that masks might give people a false sense of security and compromise the social distancing rules then believed to be more effective in stopping the spread.

*

Victorian lockdowns cost $1 billion a week

On 2 August, Andrews announced that Stage 4 lockdowns would apply from six o'clock that night across metropolitan Melbourne. People would only be allowed to go out for necessary supplies and then only within a 5-kilometre radius of their homes. Distribution centres would be limited to a workforce of 33 per cent. Outdoor exercise would be restricted to one hour per day. And curfews would apply from 8pm to 5am. He warned that police would be out in large numbers to enforce the restrictions.

It was obvious that, beyond the social hardship, the economic impacts from this – not only for Victoria but for the national economy – would be severe.

Paul Grigson, Home Affairs deputy secretary, and Phil Gaetjens, secretary of PM&C, were feeding in all the advice from the Commonwealth end from the National Covid Commission and the National Coordination Mechanism, a feedback loop integrating economic, health and business issues in as close to real time as possible.

What was immediately apparent was that the 33 per cent limit on distribution centre workforces would create havoc. By Wednesday 5 August, Morrison was hearing that supermarkets were having significant problems getting food. The critical message from business groups – including Woolworths and Coles, whose CEOs contacted Morrison directly – was that there would be no food on Victorian shelves by Friday, and there would be knock-on effects for the rest of the country.

Frydenberg was getting call after call from CEOs pleading for intervention. They felt they were being frozen out by Victorian Treasurer Tim Pallas. That afternoon he organised an emergency Zoom meeting with the industry lobby groups and their members, including the Australian Chamber of Commerce and Industry, the Business Council of Australia, the Australian Industry Group and the Victorian Chamber of Commerce and Industry. Grigson was also on the call. Frydenberg was given a very clear signal that a potential disaster was on the cards. He took a moment to calm himself and then phoned Pallas. 'You need to ring these people!' Frydenberg told him.

Unlike Victoria, the NSW government was having weekly calls with business groups to keep them in the loop, and the federal government was speaking to CEOs on an almost daily basis. But with Victoria there was no real linkage between the political and bureaucratic leadership and the private sector that underpinned its economy.

Andrews changed the restrictions and averted a potential food shortage crisis.

On 6 August, at a meeting of the Expenditure Review Committee to consider the work that was underway to shape the federal budget, Frydenberg sounded a warning: the country would be paying an economic price for the Victorian lockdowns.

Frydenberg told the meeting that the price could be in the vicinity of $1 billion a week in lost economic activity.

Morrison could barely believe what he was hearing. The successes the nation had posted early on in the pandemic were about to be undone.

CHAPTER 18

Aged care in crisis

WHEN ADF PERSONNEL arrived at the Epping Gardens aged care facility in Melbourne's northern suburbs on 27 July 2020, the Covid-19-ravaged nursing home resembled a scene worse than anything they had witnessed outside of combat.[1]

Despite their training and experience, they were not prepared for the civilian 'Armageddon' they walked into.

With aged care workers told to vacate the facility, military medical staff found nursing home residents walking around aimlessly, some only partly clothed and others in fits of hysterical dementia. Two nurses were posted to care for 110 elderly patients, some of whom had been left to die alone in their beds and others with limited treatment or access to food.[2]

The situation was without precedent, and it began three weeks earlier, on 9 July 2020, the second day of the Andrews government's lockdown, one that would last 112 days, when the manager of another Melbourne nursing home, St Basil's Home for the Aged in Fawkner, contacted Victoria's public health unit to report a staff member had tested positive.

Six days later, when Melbourne Pathology tested the 213 St Basil's residents and staff 33 Covid cases were detected. By 19 July, amid a chaotic response at the north Melbourne nursing home, the number of Covid-19 cases had blown out to 65.

Within 24 hours, on 20 July, a parallel story was emerging at the Heritage Care-operated Epping Gardens nursing home, about 13 kilometres north. A worker informed her general manager she had tested positive overnight. The aged care home also learned that a resident they had transferred to the Royal Melbourne

Hospital – who died three days later – had recorded a positive Covid-19 test.

Victoria's public health unit instructed Epping Gardens to immediately isolate its residents, as it had done with St Basil's, shutting them off from care and contact with family and friends. But testing delays and staff shortages set the facility on the same course as St Basil's and eventually 103 residents and 86 staff tested positive, and 38 died.

'It wasn't a sleeper but the pressure was building and then one day it just went pop,' Morrison recalls. 'We had responsibilities. I wasn't happy. I raised questions and was given assurances that aged care was under control. I had been raising it. But at that stage no one had rung alarm bells around me.

'While we were responsible for regulating aged care, we don't run aged care facilities. They are run by private operators and not-for-profits, state governments. We regulated it and funded it.'

On 24 July, following a meeting of the national cabinet, a team of senior nurses and health experts from Epworth Hospital, tasked with overseeing the immediate transfer of residents, visited St Basil's.

Epworth's chief medical officer, Luis Prado, later told the independent review being conducted into the outbreaks at St Basil's and Epping Gardens that he was shocked by the confusion, infection prevention and control breaches, and condition of residents: 'I've never seen anything as appalling as this in Australia ... in terms of health care provided to Australians.'[3]

By the end of the St Basil's outbreak, 94 of 117 residents and 94 of 120 staff members had been infected with Covid-19. Australia's deadliest aged care breach during the pandemic would claim the lives of 45 residents. But it didn't end there.

With question marks over the Victorian public health unit's contact tracing and testing regime, the collapse in control meant that an infected staff member in an aged care facility, even in the best of worlds, could infect the whole facility before they were even tested or the Commonwealth even knew.

And often the federal government would not find out until it was too late.

With 217 residential aged care facilities reporting outbreaks up to mid-September, and over 4000 residents and staff testing positive,[4] the publicity around the worst cases was intense.

Post-mortems examining those outbreaks – headlined in Victoria with St Basil's and Epping Gardens, and in New South Wales with Newmarch House and Dorothy Henderson Lodge – would shine a light on bureaucratic, administrative and public health failings that left Australia's most vulnerable highly exposed.

At its basic level, Victoria's initial problem arose when health authorities walked into the facilities and ordered staff to leave but would not transfer infected elderly patients to hospitals. The decisions, abandoning what appeared to be basic principles of patients' human rights, seemed incomprehensible.

'It was horrific. Those facilities went to hell,' Morrison would recall.

During the Newmarch House outbreak, New South Wales similarly insisted on keeping patients inside the facilities, but with a key difference: they didn't stand down the entire workforce. No state had ever done that before, and no one, not least the federal government, had any idea Victoria was going to do that.

'Here we are, there is no one there, no staff, so you can imagine what happens in that situation,' Morrison recalls.

*

'I was shitty it wasn't elevated to us'

On Monday 27 July – a week into the unfolding tragedy – Morrison was in the Sydney Commonwealth Parliament Offices preparing a series of announcements, including the appointment of former union leader Paul Howes to the Covid Commission. The PM's schedule was packed: he was set to fly the following day to Queensland's Sunshine Coast for a series of events.

Australia had hit a new record high in reported Covid cases the previous day, with 532 in Victoria and 17 in New South Wales.

From a statement put out by Janet Anderson, the Aged Care Quality and Safety Commissioner, in response to the St Basil's outbreak it was clear to Morrison the situation was deteriorating rapidly.[5]

Meanwhile, Lieutenant General John Frewen, a veteran army officer seconded from the Australian Signals Directorate in March to command the Defence Covid-19 Taskforce, phoned through to the PMO for his daily check-in.

Frewen reported to Morrison that ADF personnel had witnessed appalling scenes after arriving at Epping Gardens over the weekend, following desperate pleas from the aged care home's operator. Frewen said three ADF had turned up at the facility the previous night to try to help and there was only one staff member there: 'People were dying in their beds; there was no food'.

On 28 July, as Morrison headed to the airport to fly to Queensland for a three-day visit, he was on the phone for the daily morning health briefing, and received further updates from Murphy and Frewen.

He was still listening to the grim details of what was unfolding as he walked onto the plane and sat down next to his media director, Andrew Carswell. As the plane was taking off, he said, 'I think we are going to have to turn around.'

He then called Nico Louw, asking him to start cancelling his meetings while he was in the air. Louw was in isolation in Sydney after dining the previous week at a Potts Point restaurant that had been designated a hotspot.

By the time Morrison landed, the three-day Queensland trip had been cut back to a little more than three hours, a visit to a local fishmonger and one other event, and he headed back to the airport.

'I was shitty about how it wasn't elevated to us. We only got a sense of how serious it was on the Tuesday morning,' Morrison said later.

*

To avoid repeats of the St Basil's and Epping Gardens outbreaks, the federal government moved quickly to deploy ADF and AUSMAT (the Australian Medical Assistance Team) into aged care facilities across Victoria.

Morrison told Aged Care minister Richard Colbeck to focus on communications with the families of patients who, understandably, were losing confidence.

A few days earlier, on 25 July, Murphy had told the PM that Victoria would again have to shut down elective surgery to free up hospital beds for the anticipated surge in Covid patients.

Morrison raised this directly with Andrews in a text on 27 July:

> I have been on call this morning re aged care. Maximising transfers is a high priority, are you ceasing elective surgery today to free up private hospitals for aged care transfers?
>
> Ending elective surgery will also assist in recruiting nursing staff in other states to assist in aged care where as you know the workforce has been depleted. Compliance with infection control practices in facilities is also a high priority.

Andrews was chairing a state cabinet meeting at the time and texted Morrison back back to tell him that if the Commonwealth needed any assistance in the private aged care facilities, then it only need ask.

Later, Morrison texted back:

> Have just been advised on a situation at Epping Gardens and a further 100 staff being isolated. The Nursing pool is running dry. To attract additional staff and free up beds for transfers we need you to shut down elective surgery in Victoria. Do you have any update on this position, both Hunt and Colbeck have raised the same with counterparts.

Morrison's rising sense of alarm followed a briefing that morning from Murphy. As well as highlighting the urgency of elective surgery closures, he was concerned that Victoria's Public Health was mandating, for reasons of infection control, that all or a significant part of the aged-care workforce isolate immediately. Entire staffing contingents were being told not to turn up to work the next day.

This, he told Morrison, would have the dangerous effect of abandoning aged-care homes and the patients in them.

Meanwhile, the Commonwealth was working on bringing in staff from interstate to assist Victoria, with South Australia expressing a preparedness to provide support. However, that picture changed, with Premier Steven Marshall reluctant to send in staff while Victoria was still continuing with elective surgery.

As the aged care outbreaks intensified, Morrison messaged Andrews again to reiterate that Commonwealth health officials would continue working closely with their Victorian counterparts. But he raised a second item of concern. Some public hospital officials were resisting the transfer of Covid-positive patients from residential facilities.

Morrison asked Andrews to ensure all public hospitals in Victoria understood the critical importance of receiving Covid-positive patients where it was necessary for the patient's safety and health needs.

On 28 July, with more aged-care horror stories emerging by the hour, Andrews inflamed the situation at a press conference, claiming the facilities were so substandard as to be uninhabitable.

'I would not let my mum be in some of these places, I just wouldn't,' Andrews said.[6]

Hunt, whose father had been in an aged-care facility, was incensed. While Morrison wasn't willing to engage publicly with Andrews, he wasn't going to stop Hunt, a Victorian, from hitting back.

Hunt told reporters, 'My father lived in one, yes. It's a difficult decision for any family and it's a difficult time. My father lived in one and we knew that that meant he was in the latest stages of his life.

'I cannot imagine better care that my family and my father could have got and I speak, I think, for hundreds of thousands of families around the country.

'So, yes. The idea that our carers, that our nurses are not providing that care, I think, is a dangerous statement to make. They are wonderful human beings and I will not hear a word against them.'[7]

Morrison sought to calm the situation and sent Andrews a text:

Am standing up shortly, I assure you my tone will be very supportive, you'll note Greg's tone this morning was very supportive, let's speak later today/this evening. All good. There is nothing to be gained by personalising the challenges we both face.

Andrews replied:

Agreed

As they had done before when tensions were high, Andrews and Morrison reset the relationship.

On the morning of Thursday 30 July, Morrison texted Andrews again:

The latest data our team has looked at, they are now likely to advise further restrictions both in metro and balance of state. I will share this advice with you when you're available.

As Morrison sought to deal with the crisis, he drafted in Joe Buffone, director-general of Emergency Management Australia, in a bid to tackle the crisis from a different angle.

Buffone, a former head of the Victorian Country Fire Authority and former Victorian Deputy Emergency Services Commissioner, was leading the new Victorian Aged Care Response Centre,[8] which had been set up by Murphy.

Morrison recalls, 'We put an emergency management person in charge of the response. It was a completely different perspective. He understood that it is a workforce issue and moving people from one place to another. From one building to another. He was looking at the problem from a logistics perspective.

'We developed a system of acute watch lists, watch list, and facilities. We did a status update on PPE. Hunt had put more PPE into the system but we were getting stories of people turning up at aged care facilities with inadequate protection or weren't wearing it properly despite having had the training'.

Morrison, however, was fuming about the failure of his own officials to pass information up the chain in those early days of the aged care crisis. And it was on this issue that he used his strongest language during the pandemic.

'St Basil's cannot happen again,' he told Murphy and others during a rare dressing-down of his health bureaucrats. 'We will completely lose the public and we will completely lose control of this if this situation happens again. So, whatever you do, this does not happen again.'

Murphy, however, was already on the case. Largely under the radar, he was making direct contact with several local public hospitals in Victoria, leaning on his vast network of contacts from his time as CEO of Austin Hospital in Melbourne. Taking the same approach as when he'd brought in a surge workforce to Victoria, Murphy effectively bypassed Victoria's public health unit and put in place a team to independently conduct contact tracing.

He was deeply concerned about aged-care facilities. They were not hospitals. Within 24 hours he established a response unit, headed by Terry Symonds, a deputy secretary from within the Victorian Department of Health.

He said to Symonds, 'Give me six of your best people and we will set up this new model.'

Hunt would later privately credit Murphy, telling him directly, that he had personally saved hundreds of lives in Victoria through his actions.

From day one of the pandemic, health experts had made clear that elderly Australians were most at risk.

*

Alarm bells

The first alarm bells over the vulnerability of aged-care facilities to a pandemic were ringing as early as 3 March at the Dorothy Henderson Lodge, a BaptistCare facility in Sydney's northwest. Within two days of an assistant nurse testing positive, four residents and two employees were infected.[9]

A similar outbreak occurred at Newmarch House, an aged care home in the western Sydney suburb of Kingswood. It began on 11 April and ended on 15 June, and left 71 residents and staff battling the virus. It too was sparked by a staff member testing positive for Covid-19.

The first page of the independent review into the Newmarch House outbreak, led by Professor Lyn Gilbert and Adjunct Professor Alan Lilly, prominently featured quotes from frontline staff and family members, impressing how unprepared the aged care sector, public health officials and governments were in dealing with Covid-19 nursing home breaches.[10]

An Aspen Medical staff member said: 'I couldn't believe this was happening in my country.'

A specialist at the Nepean Hospital said: 'Although we were preparing, I thought we were prepared. Nothing prepared us for what was to come.'

Of the 37 Newmarch House residents infected, 19 would lose their lives, including 17 whose deaths were directly attributed to Covid-19.[11]

It begged the question as to how it could have been allowed to happen again, this time in Victoria.

Of 907 deaths from Covid-19 in Australia up until 12 November 2020, 685 (or 75 per cent) were among residents of aged care facilities, and of those 655 were in Victoria.[12]

*

The final report of the Royal Commission into Aged Care Quality and Safety, which Morrison established in October 2018 soon after becoming prime minister, released on 1 March 2021, found that the Australian aged care system 'has been under prolonged stress and has reached crisis point'.[13]

Covid-19, while proving deadly for residents, also exposed fundamental and systemic failures already apparent in the sector. Chiefly, that no single agency or jurisdiction appeared to be in charge despite all having a responsibility.

The irony was that the GPs had only a year earlier been sounding the alarm over lack of coordination or policy to deal with flu outbreaks which had occurred across 360 facilities in 2019, killing hundreds of elderly residents.[14]

Again, lessons of history were there to be learned but it appeared no one in government had been paying attention.

CHAPTER 19

The way out

MORRISON MET JENNY Warren at a church group while both were still at school. They married when he was 21 and she was 22. Though Jenny had always been an astute observer of politics, she rarely offered advice to her husband. In late July 2020, she made a rare exception.

Twice in the past week, Frydenberg had publicly pointed to Ronald Reagan and Margaret Thatcher as inspirations. The first was in a Q&A after a National Press Club speech when the Treasurer invoked the economic principles the two conservative former leaders had shared as a touchstone for managing the supply-side challenges of the post-pandemic economic recovery.[1] The second was two days later when journalist David Speers pushed him on it on ABC TV's *Insiders* program.[2]

Unable to resist an ideological skirmish, Labor seized on the reference. It was a short-lived and trivial affair, but it made Morrison wince, though he didn't haul Frydenberg over the coals for it. After all, the economic story of the pandemic he was trying to weave was an Australian one and not an ideological facsimile of a bygone era.

What Jenny Morrison said gave her husband pause. 'People don't care who Ronald Reagan is; they sort of all get that you guys like him and Thatcher, and that's all fine. But they don't want you to do what Ronald Reagan did; they want you to do what they need you to do.'

For the PM, with Australians lurching from the hope of a miracle recovery into the gloom of what Victoria's lockdown might bring, his wife's remark captured the national mood. That his job was about helping Australians survive the crisis, not about conforming to ideology, and that was precisely how he and Frydenberg had approached the introduction of JobKeeper.

But one of the most important economic questions that now faced them was when and how to turn it off without hurting a jobs recovery. Morrison described it as the most complex problem his cabinet would face.

Suggestions were floating around that, with a Treasury review pending, they might end JobKeeper sooner than its planned six-month duration. And Andrews, looking into a lockdown abyss in Victoria, was anxious to know what the federal government was planning.

The official data from Treasury and the Australian Bureau of Statistics for March through to April was dire.[3] In the March quarter, GDP had slipped 0.3 per cent, with 66 per cent of businesses reporting a fall in turnover amid a 64 per cent reduction in demand. By April, underemployment reached an historic high of 13.8 per cent, with youth unemployment hitting 23.6 per cent. By May, 870,000 people had lost their jobs.

While the official June quarter figures wouldn't be known until the national accounts were released in September, they would record a further decline in GDP of 7 per cent, confirming the depth of the recession.

Though Morrison was awaiting a Treasury review of the scheme, he saw JobKeeper as of inestimable value, providing Australians with certainty and stability in extraordinary times. He knew some businesses would do well out of it, getting a boost they might not truly need; however, the impact on the government's credibility in dealing honestly with people would have been deeply impaired were they to cut the program short.

Working out the next phase of economic assistance was no easy matter for a Coalition government – it wasn't just about the preservation of jobs through JobKeeper, it was also about income support delivered through JobSeeker.[4] Both programs had to be in sync.

Morrison knew, even then, that the government would have to consider a permanent increase to the JobSeeker welfare payment. Given rises in living standards and wages growth, it was at an historically low rate in real terms. Even among more conservative MPs, and despite the structural cost to the budget, he faced little internal party resistance to lifting it, which he did in February 2021, with a $50 per fortnight increase.[5] Had it not been for the pandemic, that was yet another decision that would have been thought improbable at best for the Liberal Party.

By the end of June though, and despite the depressing numbers the ABS had been posting for March and April, anecdotal evidence coming into the government through the business liaison unit and Treasury was that the economy was on the way out of the crisis. Data indicated, for example, that people on JobKeeper were taking just hours to get back into work. But Morrison and Frydenberg were not at that stage willing to make assumptions that this was an economy-wide trend, not yet.

On the day of the Eden-Monaro by-election, which Labor won by the slimmest of margins following a swing to the Coalition, Cormann confirmed he would retire from politics after the October budget. Morrison had known this moment was coming for six months. The country's longest serving and most highly regarded Finance minister, Cormann had successfully led the Coalition's ambitions to return the budget to balance before the coronavirus crisis struck.

Cormann had been pivotal in steering the ERC through the gravest policy decisions a government had had to make in 70 years. When asked at a press conference how the government would deal with the soaring debt and deficit levels incurred by the policy response to the pandemic, the minister would famously remark, 'What was the alternative? You tell me.'[6]

Treasury secretary Kennedy had been telling Morrison that the scheme was doing its job and was having a positive impact on stabilising the labour market. Even so, with the economic recovery fragile, maintaining industrial relations flexibility was important.

But there was a competing view within the ERC: the government needed to remove the disincentive to work and also to feed labour mobility. In other words, to help get the unemployed back on a path to getting a job.

Cabinet colleagues were leaning towards extending JobKeeper and JobSeeker beyond the September deadline. Morrison knew the band-aid had to be ripped off at some stage but instead of giving a short, sharp shock, he knew he needed to develop a transition path.

Part of a 6 July cabinet discussion centred around so-called 'zombie businesses' – firms that were marginal before the pandemic but thrown a temporary lifeline through JobKeeper. No one wanted JobKeeper or JobSeeker to artificially keep people connected to businesses that would not survive and were never going to re-employ them.

It was also the case that large firms, such as Qantas, could not take all their workers back. Part of the thinking was that for workers who were not going to be brought back on, giving them a false sense of security would not encourage them to retrain or make educated decisions about their future.

Labor's argument, that by dumping JobKeeper workers would be forced onto the dole, was at the same time both blindingly obvious and counterintuitive. The opposition began to stigmatise the dole whereas the government was arguing that it was the better vehicle for moving people into training and re-employment if their employers were never going to bring them back on.

The hardest aspect of the pending decision was that no one could predict what the end of September was going to look like economically and, crucially, how Victoria's problems would play out. Yet they knew business needed to have some sense of what was coming: firms couldn't be deactivated and reactivated at the flick of a switch.

There was discussion in the ERC about extending the schemes to December or even to March. Morrison agonised over the decision – not only the timeframe but fixing integrity issues that had arisen, particularly with sole traders.

The problems with keeping it going too long were, according to Treasury, the distortions it created in the labour market, the dampening of incentives to work and the propping up of inviable businesses.

Morrison, Frydenberg and Cormann landed on a decision to extend the JobSeeker payment through to December and JobKeeper until March the following year, but they would tighten up the eligibility rules.

During these discussions, Morrison and Frydenberg were keeping a close eye on Victoria.

Morrison was preparing to return to Canberra after his stay at Berowra Waters when his phone pinged. It was Frydenberg. While the pair agreed on a lot, they didn't always agree, and this was one of those occasions.

Treasury had advised, based on its concerns around compliance, that the eligibility rules be tightened for JobKeeper, including cutting 1.5 million sole trader businesses out of the program. Morrison as a former Treasurer agreed, but with all that was happening with Victoria, Frydenberg was concerned about the impact on small business. That if they didn't revise the scaling back of the scheme, then hundreds of thousands of businesses would suffer as a consequence.

'Maybe we should reconsider this,' Frydenberg told the PM. 'The situation has changed.'

Morrison, while reticent, deferred to his Treasurer's judgement.

*

On 10 July, national cabinet met again to agree on a skills and training reform package. Originally, Morrison was going to put down $250 million but then realised it would not create enough places. Consequently, he went into the meeting and put $500 million on the table. All the states and territories said yes, with the exception of WA.

Kunkel would make the point that the Commonwealth could apply the same efficient pricing mechanism that applied to its funding of the state hospital systems to drive reform in the skills and training sector.

Under traditional structures such as COAG, a reform like that could take years. But using the new national cabinet framework such a reform could be achieved within weeks.

On 16 July the new package was announced, along with a $1.5 billion apprenticeship scheme dubbed JobTrainer.[7]

Morrison regarded the training places as the key transition mechanism for bolstering the labour force.

On the same day, the jobs numbers came out, confirming unemployment had peaked at 7.4 per cent. The official numbers from the Bureau of Statistics revealed that the jobless rate had reached a 20-year high.[8]

Frydenberg would claim that the numbers – the effective unemployment rate – would have been twice as high if not for JobKeeper keeping workers tied to their jobs, even though many hadn't worked a single hour.

On 23 July – a week before Andrews would declare a State of Disaster for the whole of Victoria for the first time in the state's history – Frydenberg released a fiscal and economic update that revealed the scale of the crisis the country was facing.[9] The deficit was predicted to exceed $270 billion for the two financial years 2019–2021. And the unemployment rate was expected to peak at 9.25 per cent.

'The economic and fiscal outlook remains highly uncertain,' Frydenberg said.

Over the course of 2020, the economy was expected to contract by 3.75 per cent.

All of this of course sounded, and was, grim. But by international standards, the Australian economy was holding up better than almost all other comparable nations.

*

Although the budget was still months away, early work had begun on the fundamentals of a document that both Morrison and Frydenberg knew would post one of the largest deficits in Australia's economic history. Framing it would prove monumentally difficult, particularly in light of the economic drag that the Victorian lockdowns would inflict.

Equally challenging was getting the budget messaging right so people could digest what the country was facing. With the nation still in the grip of the pandemic, Frydenberg and his team had to bear in mind that many people were struggling to think more than a week ahead, let alone to the future.

As well, it was essential that the budget provided hope: that there was a way out and that people could see that their government was planning for what the economy would look like on the other side.

What message did Australians want to hear? Survive or thrive, or something in between? Morrison saw it as a battle between those who wanted to fix the 'now' and those not too worried about 'tomorrow'.

Morrison, not unlike Joseph Lyons before him, believed that a business-led recovery rather than a state-fuelled one was called for, but one that would nevertheless require more leveraging of the budget balance sheet to drive investment.

So he needed a comprehensive plan, one to restore the confidence the pandemic had shattered while still meeting the policy and political needs of a typical budget. Simply pumping out money and looking back in 12 months and seeing where it landed didn't wash.

As part of looking forward, he brought Productivity Commission chair Michael Brennan in to brief the national cabinet on the need for reform, particularly around industrial relations and regulation.

If the economy was to bounce back, Brennan maintained, it needed a more flexible environment. Aggregate demand stimulus – putting money into consumers' pockets – was not enduring.

Morrison knew it had its place but he was worried it could be a temporary sugar hit with a downer afterwards. Unless the labour market and infrastructure were reformed, the economic recovery would be slowed.

*

Morrison was finding the situation with Victoria increasingly exasperating. Watching the economic fallout of the long lockdown was hard enough but a social crisis was also unfolding: job losses, mental health issues, educational disruption, and communities divided over whether Andrews was a saint or a sinner. The middle ground on that question had disappeared.

The PM asked RBA governor Lowe to brief the premiers. Lowe suggested that they'd need to contribute in excess of $40 billion from their budgets. And while the states did open up their balance sheets, they didn't match what the Commonwealth expected from them.

The media were having a field day with the Commonwealth versus the states narrative. It was undeniable that there were areas of conflict.

Morrison did not have the constitutional authority to tell the states what to do. But there was an expectation they could make autonomous decisions while bearing no responsibility for the economic consequences that fell back on the Commonwealth.

Morrison made a strategic decision that as prime minister he needed to try to stay above the politics. But he also needed to speak to the concerns of Victorians, who were fast becoming the most locked-down citizens in the world, and Frydenberg was the perfect vessel to vent the Commonwealth's frustrations. He was Treasurer, and he was Victorian.

On 27 October, Frydenberg let loose in a speech to the parliament:[10]

The Victorian people have been magnificent. The Victorian people's dedication and their commitment to adhering to the rules have seen the number of daily cases reduced to zero yesterday and today, and it is their victory and no-one else's victory. The Victorian people have suffered so much – the pain, the cost, and the loss of Victorian people. It should never ever have come to this.

My children are the same as the children of everyone else from Victoria in this place – six months lost from schooling; six months that they will never, ever get back.

I am so happy to join with all those in this place in celebrating the fact that the numbers have come down, but do not pretend there has not been a price.

*

Here comes Alpha

By the end of November, Victoria had recorded its 28th consecutive day of no new cases, no deaths, and no active cases. By an epidemiological definition, it had effectively suppressed the virus, but there was no doubt that the state had dragged down the nation's economic recovery.

The number of 'for lease' signs on small business shopfronts across Melbourne told the story. And it wasn't unexpected: the World Bank had been warning that more economies would go into recession, or near recession, than at any time since the Long Depression of the 1870s.

Fortunately, the national economy showed remarkable resilience. According to the 3 November minutes of that day's RBA board meeting[11], even with the Victorian outbreak, Australia's recovery was well underway.

By the first quarter of 2021, Australia was the first of the major advanced economies to see employment return to above pre-Covid levels and the first economy to emerge larger than it was before the crisis.

The health outcome was no less impressive, even if the federal government would eventually become the political victim of a collective success.

Spot outbreaks in Sydney, Brisbane, Perth and Adelaide would be contained, which underscored the possibility that a Covid-zero world was attainable. This notion was adopted by the states.

Australia seemed to be out of the worst of it. There was no doubt the nation had done remarkably well: the mortality rate was the second lowest of any of the OECD countries. The nation appeared to be heading into a golden period.

But neither Morrison, Hunt nor Murphy believed it was over.

Overseas, a second wave had begun in December 2020. Across the UK and the US, a variant of the virus – the UK, or Alpha strain – had taken hold. While the original strain was the dominant factor in Victoria's second wave, Murphy shared with government his conviction that there was every chance a more contagious strain would emerge in Australia.

CHAPTER 20

The race for a cure

HUNT WAS REMINDED of his wife's dark divination of a looming pandemic when in January 2021, the winner of the inaugural Best Minister in the World award[1] struck a problem he'd been worrying about since the previous July – vaccine nationalism.

A vaccine export ban by Europe was threatening to derail the first shipments to Australia.[2] That would leave the country hopelessly exposed until it could ramp up domestic production. Many European countries were experiencing shortages and, with much of the world's production located there, Brussels was giving a green light to member states to block batches leaving the continent.

Australia needed a contingency plan.

Hunt raised his concerns with Morrison, who got on the phone to Boris Johnson while Hunt called the UK Health minister, Matt Hancock. Essentially, they were asking if Britain could help Australia get around the Europeans.

The answer from both was a yes, with a proviso. The deal had to be a cloak and dagger exercise. With Britain also in the grip of the pandemic, the UK politicians didn't want any controversy for potentially favouring Australians over their own population. They also didn't want to unecessarily annoy the Europeans.

Hunt and Morrison then hatched a plan with the UK government and the head of AstraZeneca, Pascal Soriot, to secretly fly a load of pallets containing 700,000 British-manufactured vaccine doses out of the UK and into Sydney.[3]

The vaccine wars had begun. And so had the race – although Morrison would later come to regret his initial insistence that it wasn't a race at all.[4]

*

For most of history, infectious diseases have ranked alongside war and famine as the greatest people killers. In the past 100 years there have been five flu pandemics. Between World War II and the turn of the century, several hundred lethal infectious diseases emerged that were either entirely new to humans or were pre-existing but had expanded their range and ability to cause harm.

This was relatively common knowledge, yet for the vast majority Covid-19 was somehow a surprise, something shocking and existential despite its inevitability. Our age of hi-tech medicine had cultivated a widespread assumption that modern society was invulnerable to the kinds of cataclysms that had afflicted previous generations.

What was without scientific or medical precedent was the scale and pace of the global search for a Covid-19 vaccine.

And everyone wanted to be first, including the US military which, for over a decade, had been funding research into messenger-RNA vaccine technology in its pursuit of a way to respond rapidly to pandemic-scale pathogens.[5]

As hospitalisations of Covid patients across the world reached breaking point and horrific images emerged of bodies piling up in crematoriums and makeshift gravesites, the WHO focused on a program dubbed the 'Solidarity Trial'[6] – combining international clinical trials using various treatments to determine the most effective in managing Covid.

The trials, which began in March 2020, investigated a range of medications, including hydroxychloroquine, remdesivir, lopinavir and interferon regimens.

Despite Trump calling hydroxychloroquine, an anti-malarial drug, a 'game changer' in March,[7] the WHO had halted its use by June after trials showed it was not reducing mortality for hospitalised patients.[8]

Separate work was being overseen by the WHO in fast-tracking the development of a vaccine. In April 2020, it published a draft landscape of 76 leading Covid vaccine candidates[9] and released a statement alongside 130 of the world's leading scientists, funders and manufacturers committing to speed up the process.[10]

By 15 October 2020, the WHO knocked out most of the trialled treatments for having minimal or no effect.[11]

The pandemic's early days were dominated by news of medical trials and theories about how to treat or slow down Covid-19, which led to a spread of a different kind: misinformation – like that from Trump – and its darker cousin, disinformation.

*

Moonshot moment

It was clear even early on in the pandemic that vaccination would be the only pathway to the reopening of international borders and to bringing an end to the lockdowns and other restrictions.

This presented a dual political challenge for Morrison. Putting hope into the hands of bio-tech companies and setting a timetable for a rollout left the government vulnerable to unforeseen delays.

There was an assumption that around 10 per cent of a population would be opposed to getting vaccinated. Politicians knew that this risked creating two classes of citizens when some would rebel against the kinds of restrictions state or federal governments might impose: vaccine passports, mandatory vaccinations across some workforce sectors, and restrictions on the unvaccinated entering pubs and clubs.

Pauline Hanson's One Nation Party, Clive Palmer's United Australia Party, anti-vaxxers, the anti-lockdown movement and a handful of conservative MPs tapped into and fuelled pockets of dissident.

Morrison was forced to personally deal with rogue government backbenchers led by the unpredictable Sydney Liberal MP Craig Kelly, who was using social media and press interviews to openly question vaccines and Covid-19 treatments.

Kelly, who would eventually resign from the Liberal Party to join Palmer's UAP, pursued his oppositional campaign against vaccines, appearing at rallies and stoking a potent anti-government movement.

Yet in spite of this, Australia would reach an adult vaccination rate of more than 95 per cent,[12] among the highest in the world.

When the search for a vaccine began in 2020, messenger RNA (mRNA) vaccines like that made by Pfizer/BioNTech were, Morrison later said, 'almost science fiction' such was the infancy of their development when the pandemic hit.[13]

The US Centers for Disease Control and Prevention explains mRNA vaccines as teaching 'our cells how to make a protein – or even just a piece of a protein – that triggers an immune response inside our bodies. That immune response, which produces antibodies, is what protects us from getting infected if the real virus enters our bodies.'[14] With traditional vaccines, a weakened or inactive germ is put into the body to trigger an immune response.

From early on, the health advice was clear – Covid-19 was here to stay and would need to be managed in a similar way to influenza to ensure Australia was not permanently shut off to the world.

If, as Scott Morrison later described it, the search for a vaccine was the 'moonshot' moment, getting access to the proven vaccines was as tricky as obtaining a piece of lunar rock. The pressure was on the PM to put Australia at the front of the pack.

*

One of Australia's first vaccine investments came in February 2020: a $2 million package to support the development of vaccines, funded via the $20 billion Medical Research Future Fund.[15] It complemented work already underway at Melbourne's Doherty Institute, the CSIRO and University of Queensland (UQ) to find, manufacture and deploy vaccines as soon as possible.

Murphy, Hunt and Morrison decided that Australia, unlike the UK and the US, wouldn't go for emergency use of vaccines.

They would instead require the full approval process through the Therapeutic Goods Administration (TGA), Australia's peak body for assessing the safety, efficacy and administration of medicines, as well as the Australian Technical Advisory Group on Immunisation (ATAGI).

An expert panel was appointed to make purchases, and the preference was for proven technologies.

In the early phase, three classes of vaccine technologies were under trial, with the government leaning towards a protein-based vaccine being developed by Novavax and UQ's innovative molecular clamp technology.

At that stage, the mRNA models of Pfizer-BioNTech and Moderna were not yet proven. The government knew that if it purchased those, it would have to wait for TGA approval. Also showing promise was the viral vector technology being developed by AstraZeneca.

Murphy had advised early on, and Hunt agreed, that they would need a portfolio of vaccine types and should keep an open mind. Hunt entered talks with Pfizer in July 2020. Both were concerned, however, that the US government would limit the export of vaccines from their plants.

Hunt saw the potential for the same thing to happen out of Europe. This raised doubts about the level of confidence the Australian government could have in international supply lines.

For most of July 2020, Victoria was in lockdown and Hunt was quarantined in his Canberra residence. With little else to distract him, he dedicated himself to understanding the different vaccine protocols and tracking the progress of the research.

The early lab data coming out of UQ was promising but Hunt's attention had turned heavily towards AstraZeneca (AZ) and brokering a marriage with CSL.

Neither company believed they needed Australian vaccine production. CSL saw such a prospect as a massive disruption to its normal business operations. The Melbourne-based company, despite having pioneered the first attempts at inoculation during the Spanish flu, was reluctant to turn over a large part of its facilities to produce AZ's vaccine.

For its part, AZ was simultaneously saying it could supply Australia from Europe.

But early on Saturday 11 July, Greg Hunt had an epiphany. While he trusted AZ, he didn't trust the Europeans to maintain supply lines. He raised the issue with Morrison, predicting even back then there could eventually be the potential for export bans on vaccines.

Hunt's assessment was that local vaccine production was going to be vital to Australian management of the pandemic.

The Health minister got on the phone to AstraZeneca's CEO, Pascal Soriot, and CSL's US-based CEO, Paul Perreault. He told them both that the government believed it was critical that they had onshore manufacturing capability for AZ.

The French-born Soriot had been splitting his time between Australia and Europe since the early '90s. Early on in Hunt's term as Health minister, he had assisted Soriot in securing permanent residency, giving a verbal reference to the Department of Immigration on the basis that having a CEO of one of the largest bio-tech companies in the world based in Australia could only be a good thing.

Employing classic shuttle diplomacy, albeit by phone – including an exhaustive round of calls with CSL's Perreault and its Melbourne-based chairman, Brian McNamee – Hunt sealed a deal between the two firms and established Australia as the first AZ manufacturing hub outside the UK and Europe.

But the arrangement came at a cost: Hunt agreed that the Australian government would fund the capital works to adapt CSL's Melbourne facilities for coronavirus vaccine production. Mindful of AZ's deal with Oxford University, Hunt agreed to pay the standard vaccine price.

That ensured Australia would have a base supply.

At the same time, and in what seemed a major breakthrough, the Coalition for Epidemic Preparedness Innovations (CEPI) – a global partnership between public, private, philanthropic and civic organisations dedicated to effective management of pandemic threats – and UQ entered into an agreement with CSL, to 'support the clinical development and industrial-scale manufacturing to allow initial production in the order of 100 million doses' by the end of 2020. Under the arrangement, CSL would manufacture and distribute UQ's Covid-19 vaccine, which was expected to be available in 2021 pending successful clinical trials in Brisbane.[16]

In September 2020, CSL announced it had signed a head of agreement with the Morrison government for the supply of 51 million doses of the UQ vaccine candidate and a separate deal with AstraZeneca to manufacture 30 million doses of its Oxford candidate, with first doses ready by mid-2021.[17] As part of CSL's vaccine commitments, it also signed a funding deed with the federal government to prepare its facilities for the mass manufacturing of doses to support the domestic vaccine program.

A century on from its first attempt at producing a vaccine for the Spanish flu, CSL was being called upon once again.

At the same time, Hunt was still working out arrangements with Pfizer and Moderna. There was good early science on what was reliable and what wasn't. The advice he was getting was that with Pfizer the more reliable supplier, Moderna could be kept in reserve, and Novavax used as a back-up booster if and when needed.

Hunt maintains there was never any prospect of early access to large volumes of the Pfizer vaccine. The Biden administration would confirm this in its repeated refusals of Australian requests for supply.

To counter this, Hunt had been paving the way for AZ: which turned out to be the first vaccine that would be offered in Australia.

In October 2020, he announced the government was committed to investing $2.3 billion in supporting home-grown researchers and manufacturers to 'develop and produce a Covid-19 vaccine', while also engaging in international partnerships. Additional to the government's pledge to spend $1.7 billion pre-ordering

84.8 million doses of Astra Zeneca vaccines with CSL was a strategy to ramp up access to vaccines for developing nations under the COVAX initiative, a global partnership dedicated to pooled procurement and equitable distribution of Covid-19 vaccines to poorer nations.[18]

By November, Morrison had announced an extra $1.5 billion for sourcing more Pfizer and Novavax vaccines to bolster domestic supply.[19]

With Australia's economic recovery underway, the vaccine rollout also seemed on track.

*

Trouble

The first signs of trouble came in December 2020, two months after Morrison visited the UQ vaccine labs in Brisbane.[20] At an early morning press conference with Hunt and Murphy at Parliament House on 11 December 2020, Morrison announced UQ's candidate and Australia's most promising home-grown vaccine had been dumped. False-positive HIV results had been recorded during trials. It wasn't that the recipients were getting HIV but that an HIV protein used in the 'molecular clamp' technology triggered an antibody response picked up in HIV testing.[21]

While all that was required was a tweaking of the technology, the reputational damage had been done and the cost and time it would have taken to rectify it were not deemed worthwhile as other vaccines were beginning to come online.

*

Trouble struck again, however, only weeks out from the expected delivery of Australia's first shipments. This was what prompted Hunt and Morrison's secret negotiations with the UK.

On 6 January 2021, Australia had been given a guarantee that the 3.8 million first-release doses of AstraZeneca from Europe would arrive on time by the end of March. But early production was less than predicted. This threatened a global supply shock that would put timing back significantly.

At the same time, Morrison's chief of staff, John Kunkel, opened a dialogue with his 10 Downing Street counterpart, Boris Johnson's chief of staff Dan Rosenfield.

While Australia was in a better position than the UK in terms of the caseload and containment of the virus, Britain's vaccine rollout was up and running. Its government gave an emergency approval for AZ in late December.[22]

Johnson had appointed a former National Health Service executive, Emily Watson, to lead their vaccine rollout out of No 10. Kunkel, impressed by her, set up a dedicated regular call between Watson's health team and Australian health officials, including Murphy and Kelly, to swap notes and learn lessons. It became an invaluable line of communication, not just on vaccine rollout and how to get into hard-to-reach communities but on understanding the new variants of the virus.

By then, Hunt was pressing the issue again with Soriot, who was running AstraZeneca's global operations out of his home on Sydney's lower north shore as well as from an office next to its manufacturing plant in a Sydney business park. Prior to Christmas, Hunt had helped him get back into Australia, where his family was settled, after a successful appeal to the Department of Home Affairs.

*

Australia's first supply of 142,000 Pfizer doses arrived at Sydney Airport on 15 February, ahead of the planned first vaccine deliveries from 22 February.[23] The first 300,000 of Australia's order of 53.8 million AstraZeneca doses arrived 13 days later.[24]

On their arrival, Hunt announced that Australia had received the AZ vaccines through 'global supply chains' rather than reveal the actual source.

To a sharp-eyed observer – and there were none at the time – it should have been apparent where the doses came from. AZ's European plants were producing eight-dose vials while the UK plant was producing ten-dose vials. The Australian shipment contained ten-dose vials.

It required immense diplomatic effort to get around the European regulators, who were still blocking supply to Australia well into the second half of 2021. Hunt would claim that his back-door efforts got the country over the initial hurdle before the domestic production from the CSL factories in Melbourne came online.

Under the national vaccination program, the rollout would be delivered in five stages starting with up to 1.4 million doses for Phase 1a focused on aged care residents and frontline workers. It would move across the stages according to highest-risk workers, age groups and cultural backgrounds.

But Morrison and Hunt's initial spruiking of an October 2021 vaccine rollout completion date soon began unravelling.

Shifting deadlines, issues over vaccine complications, delays around inoculations of aged care residents and workforces and skirmishes with state governments over vaccine supply would keep the pressure on Morrison and Hunt through 2021.

Standing alongside Morrison at a press conference on 7 April, Murphy conceded 'the only thing that is limiting the rollout is vaccine supply', exposing concerns around Australia's pre-ordered doses.

Asked how many doses Australia had in stock at that time, Murphy replied, 'There are no doses that are in reserve.'[25]

*

Vaxx-mail

Vaccines would also become a pawn in the broader geopolitical chess game. China and Russia had also moved swiftly to develop and roll out their own vaccines at home and abroad. The vaccine race this set off intersected with geopolitical tensions that had been heightened during the pandemic.

As its case numbers kept climbing, the US was stockpiling vaccines to combat its own coronavirus infections. Meanwhile, the global demand for vaccines was also rising sharply.

When Vladimir Putin announced in August 2020 that Russia's Sputnik V had become the world's first approved Covid-19 vaccine, few trials of that drug had actually been completed. But the Russian product had met Putin's ambition to beat UK efforts in Europe to deliver the first major vaccine.

Questions around the efficacy of Beijing's Sinopharm and Sinovac vaccines would ultimately put at risk China's attempt to use them as a soft power measure to win trade and technological access to countries in Asia, South America, Africa and the South Pacific.

But the desperation of some nations to access vaccines meant the usual checks and balances were discarded.

By March 2021, more than 60 countries had approved the use of Chinese vaccines, including Chile, Brazil, Mongolia, the United Arab Emirates, Pakistan and Egypt.

Those countries desperate for relief from the health ravages of Covid-19 were quick to sign up to foreign vaccines, despite the risks and questions over efficacy and supply.

A key target for China was Latin America and the Caribbean, domains traditionally dominated by the US. Countries in Africa, the Middle East, South-East Asia and the South Pacific were also expressing strong interest in accessing China's Sinopharm and Sinovac vaccines.[26]

By the end of 2020, the Brazilian government had lost control of Covid-19, crippling its economy and iron ore output. The rates of Covid-19 infections and deaths in Brazil were jaw-dropping, but only the tip of the iceberg that was coming, given the country's size and poverty. As Brazil's economic gains slid amid a Covid-19 haze, with an estimated 12.8 per cent of the nation's population plunging below the poverty line after financial supports stopped at the end of 2020, President Jair Bolsonaro was under intense pressure to control the country's Covid-19 crisis.[27]

For Bolsonaro to secure help from China, however, he needed to resolve one contentious matter. Previously, Brazil – encouraged by Trump – had barred Chinese telecommunications giant Huawei from involvement in the country's upcoming 5G auction. The Brazilian government was being urged to backflip on its tough position in return for vaccines.

Beijing's vast supply of vaccines was now a bargaining chip used to leverage not only Brazil but other countries into major concessions on technological and trade access. It was a modus operandi China had used before, and would aggressively pursue throughout the course of the pandemic.

In February 2021, Brazil's Communications minister Fábio Faria travelled to Beijing to meet with Huawei executives and ask for vaccines. After softening its position on Huawei, Brazil's vaccine wish was granted.[28]

The Chilean government was another early mover on Chinese vaccines. But like Brazil, despite mass vaccinations, it continued to grapple with Covid-19 lockdowns and infections. The efficacy of Chinese vaccines remained under a cloud.

Repeated global cases indicating flaws in China's vaccines – including Pakistan prime minister Imran Khan testing positive for Covid-19 after receiving a Sinopharm jab – did little to stop Chinese doses flooding the global market.

Closer to home in the Indo-Pacific, Australia, the US, India and Japan – members of the Quadrilateral Security Dialogue – knew they had to disrupt China's vaccine diplomacy march through the region.

In the South Pacific, where China had spent the past decade ramping up its diplomatic and strategic presence, Australia's neighbours including Papua New Guinea, the Solomon Islands and Fiji signed up to vaccine deals with Beijing.

With Xi personally engaging with South Pacific leaders to pledge vaccine support, Morrison and Quad leaders had to make their presence felt.

Morrison's 'Pacific Step-Up', a foreign policy reset he considers one of his major achievements, came after successive governments allowed China's influence in the region to grow unfettered. The Chinese strategy was simple – throw cash at leaders and governments and build infrastructure projects for Pacific nations in return for access.

It didn't matter if the projects remained unfinished or turned out to be unusable. China's 'strings attached' approach, while unsophisticated, was highly effective in putting Australia on the back foot.

Morrison, who had worked closely with Britain, France, the US and Japan to increase their footprints in the region, described the South Pacific as Australia's 'first sphere of responsibility'.

'It's welcome so long as you are guests, and you're helping and you're enabling and you're respecting and you're supporting,' Morrison said.

'Sovereignty, improved governance, better outcomes for people. This is why I think we will always be the partner of choice in the Pacific because I think it's understood we're there because we're there and we're always there.

'That's why I deliberately have used the word "family" from the outset, because that's what it is.'

The one thing Morrison asks of South Pacific leaders is to provide Australia with the first opportunity to counter or beat offers of support from major powers outside the region.

Morrison was on high alert about China being on the ground with vaccines in the South Pacific before Australia. Beijing boasted diplomatic footholds and relationships across the region, which allowed Chinese officials to swiftly deliver their vaccines.

When PNG – Australia's closest neighbour – confronted a wave of coronavirus cases in March 2021, Morrison pledged PPE, logistical support and vaccines. Australia's Pacific strategy was based on offering support first and providing quality and delivery that could be relied upon.

The worsening Covid-19 situation in Indonesia – where local authorities battled unsuccessfully to contain outbreaks across the sprawling archipelago – was also of concern to Morrison.

India's Covid-19 outbreak, fanned by the fast-moving Delta variant, had also shaken global vaccine supply chains with the world's largest producer struggling to deliver stock.

The deteriorating situation in the Indo-Pacific handed China another opening to spruik its own vaccines.

In June, Singapore prime minister Lee Hsien Loong – an ASEAN statesman and conduit between Beijing and the West – bluntly said that 'countries will certainly use vaccines in order to win friends and influence people'.[29]

Whether it was India, China, Russia, the US or others with vaccine development capacity, the ultimate goal had to be vaccinating the globe, while understanding that using jabs as a diplomatic tool was 'to be expected and par for the course'.

CHAPTER 21

How Delta killed Covid-zero

ON 9 JUNE 2021, the evening before Morrison's second overseas trip since the pandemic struck, he paced around his Ritz-Carlton Perth suite, with its views across the Swan River, and contemplated the clear and present danger the coronavirus Delta variant posed to Australia's success in suppressing the virus.

Ahead of watching game one of the State of Origin rugby league match, in which New South Wales would thrash Queensland 50-6, Morrison and his advisers finalised the whirlwind trip – the G7 leaders 'plus' summit in Cornwall and state visits to 10 Downing Street in London, the Élysée Palace in Paris and Singapore's Istana, the president's residence.

Morrison also had weighty issues of trade and national security – especially to do with China – on his mind. But Delta was here and now.

Just a month earlier a Sydney couple tested positive to the variant, the first cases in the community, and on 6 June Victoria reported its first Delta infections, a west Melbourne family who had returned from New South Wales.[1]

It was a devastating blow to Australia after the jubilation; the nation had seemingly got on top of Covid-19.

Delta was first identified in India in October 2020, around the same time Victoria's 112-day lockdown ended on 26 October 2020 and the national cabinet finalised its Christmas 2020 target to resume 'Covid-normal life'. It was only on 10 May 2021, a month before Morrison's trip, that the WHO named it as a variant of concern.[2]

Morrison was told by Murphy that it would inevitably seep into Australia.

Countries with close ties to India, including Britain, Singapore, the US and Fiji, were hit with fresh waves of cases, hospitalisations and deaths. India staggered under the weight of its massive caseload and death toll. Across the world, people gaped at the horrific images beamed across TV screens and phones, bodies being burned on rooftops, makeshift crematoriums for the thousands of dead.

Murphy and Morrison would later concede that Delta 'changed the game', taking the world by surprise and rewriting the manual for dealing with Covid-19.

The path to freedom had been within touching distance after national cabinet released its three-stage reopening framework in November 2020, promising an end to lockdowns, border closures and social restrictions.[3] It was not to be.

*

Scandal-plagued

When the PM returned to parliament in February 2021, he had been buoyant. The vaccine rollout had begun and the economy was recovering faster than Treasury predicted.

But with community fears about the pandemic subsiding, the shifting political landscape was fertile ground for new issues to dominate. The government found it was ill-prepared to deal with other political crises, and its agenda was about to be derailed by rolling scandals alleging poor behaviour in parliament and a lack of support for sexual assault victims.

On 15 February Morrison was told by his media team that a story was about to be aired involving a young Liberal staffer, Brittany Higgins, who alleged that she had been raped in the office of then Defence Industry minister Linda Reynolds in early 2019. Higgins went public, telling her story to journalist Samantha Maiden at *news.com.au* and to *The Project*.[4] The following day, Morrison and Reynolds offered apologies in parliament and launched two reviews.

Then, on 26 February, ABC investigative journalist Louise Milligan published an article about a letter to the PM, alleging a historical (1988) rape by a senior cabinet minister.[5] Subsequently, Attorney-General Christian Porter went public, confirming he was the subject of the allegation, a claim he vehemently denied, and launched legal proceedings. On 8 March, ABC's *Four Corners* aired 'Bursting the Canberra Bubble', giving more details of the allegation.[6]

Community rage about these allegations was laid bare on 15 March, when more than 110,000 women and allies attended March4Justice rallies across the country, with thousands pouring onto the lawns in front of Parliament House. Higgins spoke to the crowd about her alleged experience and the need for cultural change.

Morrison, who offered to meet privately with the march organisers, was slammed when he clumsily invoked protests occurring in Myanmar, saying, 'Not far from here, such marches even now are being met with bullets, but not here in this country'.[7]

The Higgins allegation would see a former staffer, who had denied the claims, charged with one count of sexual intercourse without consent. It rocked the Coalition amid allegations of internal mishandling by senior government figures. Morrison ordered two internal reviews led by Kunkel and PMC chief Phil Gaetjens to test the validity of public accusations, but neither went far. Citing court proceedings and the AFP investigation, Gaetjens suspended his investigation into who in the PMO knew what and when.

By 29 March the scandal was at fever pitch and Morrison had no option but to reshuffle his cabinet. Porter and Reynolds were demoted. In Reynolds' case, revelations surfaced that she had referred to Higgins as a 'lying cow'.[8] Porter resigned from cabinet in September over mystery donations to a blind trust set up to support his defamation proceedings against the ABC – reported to come with a price tag of $1 million – which were ultimately settled out of court.[9]

Morrison used these cabinet changes to elevate women's economic security and safety into the ministry and announce the government would host a National Summit on Women's Safety in September.

While these issues did not go away, growing fear over the spread of Delta brought the pandemic back to reclaim the political terrain.

*

Biosecurity emergency extended

By April, arrivals from the Indian subcontinent to the Howard Springs quarantine facility near Darwin were showing an infection rate of 14 per cent, unacceptably high. On 29 April, the US told its citizens to leave India as soon as possible. That day, India reported almost 380,000 new infections, the world's highest single-day total.[10]

Hunt, in the early hours of the morning of Saturday 30 April, hoping to buy time and head off Delta's arrival, again executed his powers under the Biosecurity Act.[11] This time he temporarily blocked Australians returning from India, threatening fines and up to five years' jail if anyone broke the new rules. Against a backdrop of emotional stories of stranded children and families separated, this use of the biosecurity powers triggered public anger.

Meanwhile, the threat from Delta continued to escalate.

Health authorities and researchers studying the new strain found that the existing vaccines' power to combat it was diminished. Countries with high inoculation rates began reporting that the vaccinated were contracting and spreading the virus in worrying numbers.

Despite boasting world-leading vaccination rates, surges in infections and hospitalisations would lead Israel, Singapore and other countries to reimpose Covid-19 restrictions and bring forward vaccine boosters.

*

AUKUS is born in secret in Cornwall

One month before the G7 summit, Morrison and Johnson had secretly coined a working title for the landmark AUKUS (Australia, UK and US) nuclear submarine pact – 'Project Freedom'.

The historic military agreement – strengthening security cooperation between Australia, the UK and US – now only needed US president Joe Biden's seal of approval.

On the sidelines of the G7-plus summit at the picturesque Carbis Bay Hotel in Cornwall on England's south-west coast, Morrison held his first face-to-face meeting with Biden.

AUKUS – which would be announced three months later, in September[12] – was landed, in secret, during a 45-minute private meeting between Morrison, Biden and Johnson on 12 June in a small room overlooking the beach.

Biden is said to have done most of the talking.

Originally, the meeting was intended to be the first in-person talks between Morrison and Biden. But this changed when, amid a flurry of backroom negotiations between Australia–US–UK officials, Johnson invited Morrison to his poolside villa an hour before the talks. Johnson told Morrison AUKUS was a reality.

When travelling media were told at the last minute that Johnson would be joining Biden and the Australian PM, some interpreted it as Biden snubbing Morrison by not seeing him one-on-one.

What they didn't know was that the three leaders were formalising one of the most significant postwar agreements ever forged among allies. At the end of the meeting, which ran overtime, Biden stood up and shook hands with Morrison and Johnson on AUKUS. The US president's first overseas trip, headlined by the G7, NATO leaders' summit and a meeting with Russian president Vladimir Putin, promised a shift away from Trump's isolationism.

Biden's handlers kept him under wraps at the G7, limiting his contact with leaders. He was late to functions, often left early and was kept away from press conferences to avoid embarrassing slip-ups. British and Australian officials had wanted to hold a joint press conference following the trilateral meeting but were overruled.

For journalists, there was little to report on from the Biden meeting other than a three-line joint statement, which said the leaders had 'discussed a number of issues of mutual concern, including the Indo-Pacific region. They agreed that the strategic context in the Indo-Pacific was changing and there was a strong rationale for deepening cooperation between the three governments.'[13]

Astonished watchers would later pore over the words. Understatedly, they conveyed that Morrison had pulled off one of the most important security agreements in Australia's history.

In private sessions at the G7, Morrison had also stunned the other leaders with details of China's aggressive stance towards Australia. Jaws dropped when he began reading out the list of 14 grievances Beijing's embassy in Canberra had issued in November 2020.[14] The dossier – which included demands for Australia to reverse or amend actions, policies and key national security decisions in areas of foreign investment – had been sent to a Channel Nine journalist one day after Morrison announced a new defence treaty with Japan. Sources at the Chinese embassy claim the list was inadequate because it failed to address the 'full breadth of our grievances'. This extraordinary move by Beijing marked a significant escalation in China's diplomatic strong-arm tactics in trying to pressure Canberra. French president Emmanuel Macron would later present the list of grievances to his own cabinet to impress on it the threat posed by Chinese economic coercion.

*

European leaders' eyes opened to China

Morrison's pitch to the private G7 leaders' forum was extraordinary in itself.

It was a culmination of what he had been saying to them individually in conversations over the course of the pandemic.

In his estimation G7 was one of the most important international summits Australia would attend in decades, and it was imperative in Australia's national interests to go there and tell the other leaders what was really going on in the Indo-Pacific.

In the room were Biden, Johnson, Macron, German chancellor Angela Merkel, Italian prime minister Mario Draghi, Canadian prime minister Justin Trudeau, Japan's new prime minister Yoshihide Suga (who, three months later, would step down from the role), president of the European Commission Ursula von der Leyen and EU council president Charles Michel. South Korea's president Moon Jae-in and South Africa president Cyril Ramaphosa were also present as invitees to the summit. Indian prime minister Narendra Modi attended virtually.

Morrison put the document containing the 14 grievances issued by China against Australia on the table and made sure all the leaders had a copy in front of them.

'This is what they are doing, this is what we are dealing with. Which of you would be happy to give up any of those?' Morrison asked them.

'If we give up on any of them, they will be after you for yours.'

He told the room that Australia would not tolerate it.

Morrison had the floor both as the leader of a nation that had done well during the pandemic and also because of a dawning sense among other leaders that something broader was developing with the Indo-Pacific and China. There was trust that Australia would give an unvarnished account of what was happening in its own region.

Most of the leaders, including Biden, sat there in a semi-stunned silence as they digested the document in front of them.

Morrison's premise was that there had never been a greater need for closer defence cooperation, more economic integration, better supply chain security and the need to collaborate in international fora to ensure they maintained a liberal democratic philosophical base.

The final G7 communique named China only three times but the bulk of discussions in Cornwall and at the NATO summit in Brussels immediately after focused on efforts by Beijing and Moscow to undermine liberal democracies in the Indo-Pacific and Europe.

*

Morrison, Macron and the subs

After securing the UK–Australia free trade agreement with Johnson over late-night drinks at 10 Downing Street, Morrison flew to Paris. A business roundtable, which included Naval Group representatives, was first on the agenda. His second engagement on French soil was dinner with Macron at his Paris residence, the Élysée Palace.

Statements read by the leaders before the dinner, in lieu of a press conference, to avoid questions on submarines, suggested their discussions would focus on challenges in the Indo-Pacific, China, and Macron's commitment to protect democracy and freedom of navigation in the South Pacific.

But contrary to later claims by the French they had been blindsided by Australia's September 2021 announcement it was cancelling the submarine contract, Morrison had spoken frankly with Macron that evening.

He told the French president that, in his view, the conventional submarine platform no longer met Australia's strategic needs.

In plain terms, Morrison told Macron that while he couldn't go into the other options available to Australia, he made clear Australia had initiated them.

Morrison was at pains to ensure there was no misunderstanding down the track. While he could not yet name it, AUKUS had come about entirely at the behest of Australia – and not the US or the UK. He didn't want Macron to be angry with Australia's partners.

When Morrison held a press conference the following day on 16 June, mentioning 'contract gates',[15] it was an unambiguous message to French officials that Australia was laying the groundwork to exit the Naval Group contract.

The eight-day trip, which Morrison deemed a success, also attracted negative headlines after he made three side trips, including a visit to his family's ancestral village of St Keverne.[16] The first stop, the Jamaica Inn Restaurant in Launceston, came after his arrival into Brize Norton RAF base, west of London, after Cornish fog diverted his plane from Newquay Airport. This had meant a 4-hour drive, after the 30-hour flight, to get to the G7 venue. They needed to stop for lunch. Morrison's flying visits were revealed after images emerged on social media, showing him mingling with staff who had asked Morrison to pose for photos outside, where masks weren't required.

He later explained his visit to the Three Tuns pub, near Falmouth, included tours of the Bodmin Jail, which was on the way to the G7, and St Keverne parish church, retracing the steps of William Roberts, his fifth-great-grandfather.

Roberts, born in Cornwall in 1755, was tried for stealing 'five pound and a half weight of yarn' before being placed on the convict transport *Scarborough* – one of the 11 First Fleet ships that arrived at Sydney Cove in 1788. As the member for Cook, the Cronulla-based southern Sydney electorate named after Captain James Cook, Morrison had a personal affinity for First Fleet convicts.

Not unlike with his Hawaiian holiday during the 2019–2020 summer bushfires, some colleagues questioned the prime minister's judgement. If he wanted to retrace his family roots in between G7 commitments, they argued, he should have put it on the official itinerary.

*

ATAGI puts dagger into AstraZeneca

Despite hesitation in his inner circle about the prime minister leaving Australia during the pandemic, Morrison was hard-headed about the importance of engaging with leaders face-to-face amid unprecedented geostrategic competition, increasing Chinese aggression, and vaccine nationalism.

As his plane – RAAF KC-30A, a heavily modified Airbus A330 reconfigured to replace the ageing prime ministerial Boeing 737-700 – approached Australian air space on 17 June, Morrison received a call from Murphy. The news was disturbing.

ATAGI was changing its advice again. Because of rare blood clotting complications, the government's advisory body for the vaccination program was now recommending even more extreme restrictions on the distribution of the AstraZeneca vaccine.[17]

Morrison, who was sitting in the boardroom at the front of the plane adjoining his private suite decked out with two repurposed first-class lounges, expressed his displeasure to Murphy.

The damage done to confidence in the vaccination program the first time ATAGI changed its advice – only two months earlier[18] – was already considerable.

Several European countries had placed temporary bans on the AZ vaccine because of a risk of developing what was seen as an extremely rare side effect. That risk for the general population was four to six cases per million. People were more at risk of being hit by a car.

Despite that, ATAGI's advice to Murphy was to restrict AZ – up to then Australia's primary vaccine – to the over-50s, people with a higher benefit from vaccination, and to recommend Pfizer for those younger than 50.

Murphy's news about ATAGI's updated position, advising the government to restrict AZ even further, to the over-60s, left the PM stunned. He wanted the vaccine program done so the country could reopen.

Morrison cross-examined Murphy about ATAGI's advice but even though he believed it was being too conservative, he told Murphy he wouldn't break with his government's policy of following the expert health recommendations.

Once again, Morrison was a political hostage to the advice of the medical professionals.

After observing the success of the UK vaccine program – built on millions of AstraZeneca doses – Morrison worried that further blows to public confidence in AZ could derail the national vaccine rollout, put more lives at risk and increase pressure on the government.

The contrast with the UK was stark. After a year of extended hard lockdowns and world-leading death and infection rates, Boris Johnson was riding a wave of popularity off the back of a successful vaccine rollout underpinned by the Oxford University-developed AZ jab.

Johnson had been able to shake off a year from hell through a combination of vaccines, rapid antigen tests and a Covid-19 traffic light system, making it easier for residents and foreigners to travel to the UK and avoid harsh quarantine measures.

The accepted advice was that people who had recovered from Covid-19 were equipped with antibodies which, when combined with vaccination, meant they were largely protected from severe illness and death. As crowds poured back into events, including Wimbledon, Premier League football matches, the Tour De France, Formula 1 races and music festivals, all eyes in Australia were turning to the speed of the national vaccine rollout.

The Morrison government's vaccine plan hinged on millions of AZ doses, produced at the CSL manufacturing plant in Melbourne, being administered across Australia.

The new health advice further risked undermining confidence in AZ and compromising the Commonwealth's supply strategy.[19]

ATAGI had thrown a second curve ball at the nation's vaccine program.

CHAPTER 22

The Delta wave

AFTER TOUCHING DOWN in Canberra that evening of Thursday 17 June, Morrison went straight to The Lodge, where he would quarantine for 14 days.

Australia's vaccine rate was short of where it needed to be, given the imminent threat of Delta and the damage being done to public confidence by ATAGI and state health officials shifting the goalposts. The government was under political assault on multiple fronts: vaccine supply, failure to put in place domestic mRNA vaccine production capacity, the speed of the national rollout and bickering over quarantine arrangements.

The last thing Morrison needed at that time was a messy internal political problem. Barnaby Joyce, the maverick Nationals MP and former deputy prime minister, had other ideas. On 22 June, Joyce rolled Nationals leader Michael McCormack in a leadership spill.

Whereas Morrison found McCormack easy to work with, Joyce was a wildcard. The PM's senior advisers were anxious about his return. To them, the Nationals' internal machinations were an unwelcome distraction from the immediate problems facing the government's management of the Delta crisis.

Their worst fears were realised as New South Wales confronted a third outbreak – one that would end Australia's false COVID-zero dream.

Before Delta, there was a sense of public optimism that Australia had made it through the worst of the pandemic and that normal life would return, albeit with some restrictions.

But now plans to launch international pilot programs for students and expand travel bubbles with Covid-safe countries had to be put on ice. The priority shifted to vaccinating as many people as possible as quickly as possible.

*

Vaccine 'strollout'

By the time the PM exited quarantine on 1 July, outbreaks of the Delta strain had plunged Greater Sydney, the Blue Mountains, the Central Coast and Wollongong into lockdown. Australia's third Covid-19 wave had not only arrived but quickly spiralled.

Gladys Berejiklian had ordered a snap lockdown from 26 June after an unvaccinated limousine driver transporting airline crew sparked an outbreak in Bondi. [1]

Weeks before the deadly outbreak began, Berejiklian had been dubbed 'The Woman who Saved Australia' on the *Australian Financial Review Magazine's* cover, for avoiding draconian Covid-19 restrictions and keeping New South Wales open to the rest of the country.[2] The NSW premier, who would quit politics on 30 September after being linked to an Independent Commission Against Corruption probe into her ex-boyfriend and former Liberal MP Daryl Maguire, had surfed a wave of popularity through relative success in suppressing the virus. But Delta had caught everyone off guard with the speed of its transmission through the community.

In the early days of this eastern suburbs outbreak, Morrison was advised that the virus would be near impossible to contain, and knew pressure would shift back to him over vaccines and quarantine.

For a state proud of its record of containing the virus and keeping its businesses and borders open, Berejiklian's first instinct was to impose a weakly enforced lockdown.

Images and stories once again emerged of Sydneysiders gathering en masse at beaches, as they did a year earlier at the height of the first wave: NRL players holding house parties; long cafe lines; extended families catching up in homes; and retail outlets like Bunnings crammed with people.

Sydney's southwest quickly emerged as a new hotspot for the NSW outbreak, forcing the state government to impose suburb-specific curfews.

Eventually, Berejiklian found herself calling on the Commonwealth for ADF support to supplement NSW Police enforcement efforts.

The Delta variant kept moving at a frightening pace – across regional New South Wales, including through vulnerable Indigenous communities in the state's west, and into Victoria, Queensland and across the Tasman to New Zealand.

When the outbreak spread south into Victoria, Andrews plunged the state into its sixth lockdown. Covid-19 restrictions imposed on long-suffering Melburnians would see the Victorian capital claim the unwanted mantle of the world's most locked-down city during the Covid-19 pandemic.[3]

As New South Wales and Victoria tried and failed to contain the Delta outbreaks, pressure was now increasing on Morrison to accelerate the national vaccine rollout, which ACTU secretary Sally McManus in mid-May had dubbed on Twitter a 'strollout',[4] a word that was already working its way into the vernacular and which the Macquarie dictionary would choose, later that year, as its word of the year.[5]

Morrison turned to the Defence Covid-19 Taskforce and asked Lieutenant-General John Frewen to take charge.

*

High numbers of aged care and health care workers remained unvaccinated because states had baulked at imposing mandatory vaccine orders, and the vaccine rate among Indigenous Australians was stubbornly low. The speed of the tiered vaccine program was also locking out millions of younger Australian adults who, health experts warned, were most susceptible to the Delta strain. The stakes for Morrison were high as disturbing reports emerged of unvaccinated Sydneysiders in their 30s and 40s dying from the virus.

But rising hesitancy over the use of AZ put the government's strategy under pressure. Morrison's argument back in April was that Australia needed to make an early call on domestic production.[6] Soon after, on 21 May 2021, his government announced it had approached the market to set up onshore manufacturing of mRNA vaccines, acknowledging these pioneering vaccines could be vital in combating fast-evolving coronavirus strains.[7]

Morrison, Hunt, Murphy and Frewen could not wait for a tender process. Immediate action was required. Morrison, critical of 'hindsight heroes', took on the challenge: to bring forward vaccine orders, to source millions of new vaccines and to turn around the country's AZ hesitancy.

As well as ordering DFAT and health officials to leave no stone unturned in their search for additional doses to bolster the vaccine program, the PM leveraged his personal relationships with world leaders to organise vaccine swaps and purchase deals.

Pfizer and Moderna jabs, expected in the fourth quarter, were brought forward to help fast-track vaccine timelines.

Poland's prime minister Mateusz Morawiecki was the first to answer Morrison's vaccine SOS. For an undisclosed fee, the Polish government authorised the sale of 1 million Pfizer doses. Singapore was next, with Lee Hsien Loong approving a vaccine swap deal that saw 500,000 Pfizer doses sent to Australia. Boris Johnson again proved Morrison's saviour, agreeing to fly 4 million Pfizer vaccines to Australia under a swap arrangement.

Even the European Union, which had clashed with Australia over vaccine exports, provided a million Moderna doses to help vaccinate children aged 12 and over.

As supply pressures eased and vaccinations were offered to younger age groups, vaccine rates across the country surged.

Berejiklian and Andrews turned to the AstraZeneca vaccine to increase jab rates. Clinics allowing younger Australians to access AZ were set up and leading health experts came out in support of the jab, explaining that the Oxford University-developed drug posed no serious health effects.

By September, more than 10 million AZ doses had been administered in Australia.

Murphy bristles at the suggestion the vaccine rollout was 'bungled'.

'If we didn't have the thrombosis issues with AstraZeneca, we would have been as well vaccinated then as any country,' he recalls.

'The thing that upsets me most is the suggestion that it was somehow bungled. It hasn't been bungled, it has had some curve balls, and we have pivoted around them.'

But vaccines were only one part of the puzzle. If Delta could not be suppressed, Australia would need to unshackle itself from Covid-zero ambitions and join the rest of the world in living with the virus.

*

Old habits die hard

The deadly new front in Australia's coronavirus battle reopened old wounds inside national cabinet and ushered a return to lockdowns, border closures and squabbling – matters many had thought were in the rear-view mirror.

As Delta raged across the east coast, sniping among federal, state and territory governments resumed with ferocity. Only months after promising a return to Covid-normal life, the mood inside national cabinet fractured, with Palaszczuk, McGowan and Andrews blaming Berejiklian and Morrison for the unfolding crisis: Berejiklian for not locking New South Wales down fast enough and Morrison for what was perceived as the federal government's flawed handling of the vaccine rollout and quarantine.

Morrison found himself reliving the battles of a year ago, but with diminishing political capital. His approval ratings in the polls were beginning to fall markedly. He needed a strategy to end the impasse, to speed up vaccine delivery and map out a national plan to live with the virus.

Following a national cabinet meeting on 30 July, Morrison unveiled the four-phase national reopening plan in a late-afternoon press conference at The Lodge.[8] The strategy – informed by Treasury advice on economic forecasts and Doherty Institute analysis of epidemiological and health risks associated with the Delta strain – laid out how Australia would resume international travel, ease and eradicate restrictions and lockdowns, and provide exemptions for vaccinated people.

Central to the plan were two vaccine targets that would dominate the national psyche. Freedoms would be restored in two steps – the first easings on the achievement of full vaccination status by 70 per cent of Australians aged over 16, and the second at 80 per cent.

Morrison set himself a Christmas deadline to reach the targets which, based on drastically improved vaccination rates, was a realistic goal.[9]

The Doherty Institute modelling called for a revised vaccine strategy to fast-track jabs for under-40s, who were considered 'peak transmitters' of the Delta strain.[10] The research showed that Australia could reduce adverse outcomes a hundredfold if some social measures were kept in place and public health capacity was maintained. With 70 per cent of the population vaccinated, only 16 people would die in a breakout's first 180 days if effective tracing, testing and quarantine arrangements were in place. With ineffective arrangements, that would rise to nearly 2000 deaths.

In a repeat of 2020, Palaszczuk imposed strict border bans, not only on people travelling from Delta hotspots – which caused chaos for northern NSW and Gold Coast residents – but also on Queenslanders.

With health advice requiring returning residents to enter hotel quarantine, Palaszczuk was forced to 'temporarily pause' Queenslanders coming home. In a 25 August statement, Palaszczuk said, 'Our hotels are full.'"[11]

The move was met with public anger, especially as significant numbers of NRL and rugby union international players had been entering the state to play footy. Under attack from stranded residents and federal government ministers, Palaszczuk backflipped on 1 September and offered more hotel quarantine places for Queenslanders.

Partisanship and fierce parochialism re-emerged. Palaszczuk and McGowan were firing political salvos at the federal government and undermining the national plan, in part to deflect their own shortcomings, with their states reporting the lowest vaccine rates in the country.

Following a 27 August national cabinet meeting, McGowan signalled his reluctance to be led on the issue when his state had no Covid cases to speak of and highlighted that there would still be 1 million unvaccinated West Australians when the national 70 per cent target was reached.

'The idea that we just deliberately infect our citizens, if we have no Covid when we get to 70 per cent two-dose vaccination, I just can't do,' McGowan said. 'People would die and we would have huge dislocation. It's different for other states that have Covid-positive people.'[12]

Since the beginning of the pandemic, Victoria and New South Wales had significantly bolstered their public health and hospital capacity in preparation for worst-case scenarios, having learned the hard way during its second wave.

Western Australia and Queensland remained poorly prepared. The advice of health officials to McGowan and Palaszczuk was that their state hospital and health systems were not equipped to deal with outbreaks, which would occur when state borders reopened.

State and territory leaders also agitated for children to be included in the vaccination program and the national plan, despite existing vaccine targets being predicated on adults aged 16 and over.

After ATAGI approved vaccines for children aged 12–15 in late August, the national cabinet endorsed a plan to begin administrating jabs to all teenagers from 13 September. Inoculation rates for children would be included in public data but not incorporated in vaccine targets.

*

A billion-dollar-a-week curry

Shortly after the national plan was agreed on 30 July 2021, Frydenberg moved into Morrison's Covid war bunker at The Lodge.

ACT health restrictions dictated that he could travel only between The Lodge and his Parliament House office. Frydenberg was concerned that he would be stranded in Victoria. So the two decided to become flatmates as they plotted the economic response to the second crisis.

The day of Frydenberg's arrival at The Lodge, Morrison sent all the staff home early. He made a fire in the lounge room and went into the kitchen to make a curry for the two of them.

Over dinner, the pair worked through major economic rescue packages and began finalising the government's Covid-19 disaster payments, effectively a JobKeeper replacement, which was coming with a price tag of $1 billion a week.

In their downtime as temporary flatmates, they would watch action films and re-runs of *Yes Minister*, or play pool in a small room off the main dining room adorned with sporting memorabilia including a small table pasted with images of the Cronulla Sharks, handcrafted by one of Morrison's constituents.

With New South Wales, Victoria and the ACT in lockdown, Frydenberg was acutely aware of the looming economic and social crises if Australia could not unshackle itself from lockdowns and severe restrictions. His focus was fixed on avoiding a second Covid recession. He engaged business leaders and bosses of companies employing millions of Australians to support the national plan and vaccinate their staff. Achieving the reopening strategy's key milestones was critical to maintaining the economic recovery and would help paint a rosier picture in December's mid-year economic update.

By contrast, RBA governor Lowe was optimistic that the Delta outbreak would not plunge the nation back into recession. Lowe said while lockdowns would trigger a 'material' downturn in the September quarter, growth was 'expected to delay, but not derail, the recovery', and predicted the economy would be back on its pre-Delta path by the second half of 2022. After keeping interest rates at a record low of 0.1 per cent at the RBA's board meeting on 7 September, Dr Lowe said while the unemployment rate was expected to increase, 'this setback to the economic expansion is expected to be only temporary'.[13]

National accounts released by the Australian Bureau of Statistics in September revealed economic growth had slowed to 0.7 per cent in the June quarter. While the economy was 9.6 per cent larger in the June quarter when compared to the same period in 2020 – the biggest year-on-year increase on record – real GDP growth decelerated sharply from 1.8 per cent in the previous quarter. Treasury forecast the economy would fall by at least 2 per cent in the September quarter, dragged down by the NSW and Victorian lockdowns.

Frydenberg increased the pressure on wavering states and territories, warning them the Commonwealth couldn't subsidise the economy forever.

*

In late August, Morrison decided to end the nation's vain crusade to keep Covid out and began prosecuting the case for why Australians needed to learn to live with the virus.

Many Australians were fed up with constant disruption in their lives due to lockdowns and restrictions. They wanted to know when their kids could go back to school, when they could visit their relatives interstate or overseas, or even go back to the pub or a restaurant. Social unrest continued to rear its head, with freedom rallies and violent protests in Sydney, Melbourne and Brisbane.

Lockdowns were less effective in dealing with Delta, which was proving difficult to contain.

Morrison wanted states and territories to hit their vaccine targets, prepare hospitals for spikes in cases, adopt home quarantine and get systems in place to reopen businesses for vaccinated people.

The under-stress hotel quarantine system had never been intended to be a permanent fixture, and needed to work in tandem with shorter isolation periods at home to make international travel possible.

In a major reset, Morrison and his colleagues started taking a more active position in arguing for a transition out of lockdowns and restrictions.

Morrison needed to push back on the political war being waged against him but decided he couldn't be seen to be engaged in the politicking himself.

He was happy for senior ministers including Frydenberg, Joyce, Peter Dutton, Karen Andrews and David Littleproud to publicly defend the Commonwealth and begin attacking the state and territory leaders for what they would claim was a deliberate campaign of disinformation.[14]

Rejecting a proposal from Albanese to hand Australians $300 payments in return for getting vaccinated, Morrison, with the support of national cabinet, instead pursued 'freedom incentives' similar to those adopted in Europe and the US to bring up the vaccination rates.

Relaxing restrictions for vaccinated people, rather than financial incentives, had been identified as a successful tool for governments, with vaccination rates in France spiking after Macron on 12 July threatened to restrict access to public places for unvaccinated residents.

Morrison believed that Australia could not remain cut off from the rest of the world forever. Attracting skilled migrants, students and tourists back to Australia, and not slipping behind global competitors, was essential to the nation's future prosperity.

By October, with well over half the eligible population fully vaccinated, and on its way to the 80 per cent benchmark, Australia was behind only New Zealand in recording the fewest cumulative deaths per capita across all 38 OECD countries.

CHAPTER 23

A new world (dis)order

OUT OF THE calamity of Covid-19 arose a new world order which would forever change Australia's place in it. After Russia's invasion of Ukraine shocked the world in March 2022 – and China's subsequent failure to condemn it – this new paradigm could have easily fit the description of a new world disorder.

The growing assertiveness of China had not only driven liberal democracies to examine their consciences and their own strategic interests, it forced Australia to ask of itself fundamental and existential questions.

What role would it seek to play in helping to maintain stability and prosperity in the Indo-Pacific – the epicentre of the great power competition – and to what lengths would it go in the defence of the nation's sovereignty?

What emerged post Covid was a country that had adroitly – albeit with sacrifices by Australians – navigated an economic and health crisis, the likes of which the world hadn't experienced collectively for a century. It had also proven itself to be a nation more resilient than other countries may have anticipated.

Morrison's staunch defence of Australia's national interest in the face of Chinese coercion surprised many. He was determined to put Australia at the centre of a new coalition of middle powers striving to traverse the US–China nexus and drive a renewal of enthusiasm for the foundational principles of the postwar international rules-based order.

While the pandemic, and the economic, trade and strategic challenges it exposed, accelerated the evolution of an idea into a more concrete form, design as much as circumstances propelled that process.

The greatest expression of this came with the AUKUS agreement of September 2021 – an historic defence partnership between Australia, the US and the UK.[1] *The Australian*'s editor-at-large, Paul Kelly, hailed it at the time as the most 'significant strategic decision' since the ANZUS treaty of 1951.[2] 'This event is a turning point for Australia,' Kelly wrote. 'It locks Australia "forever" – to quote Morrison – into a compact with our traditional partners as distinct from any strategic option of working with China. That alternative option is now all but extinguished.'

*

Genesis of AUKUS

The genesis of AUKUS traced back to an informal conversation Morrison had with his defence adviser Jimmy Kiploks in late 2019, several weeks after Morrison's August visit to the French town of Biarritz for the G7 summit. He was interrogating Kiploks on the delivery of the myriad defence contracts that he inherited as prime minister.

Some of the contracts had significant challenges. None more so than the $90 billion French deal for twelve Attack-class subs, signed in 2016 by Malcolm Turnbull and then Defence Industry minister Christopher Pyne.[3]

Morrison wanted to reassure himself of the commercial rigour around the project, with all its delays, jostling and cost blowouts. Above all, he wanted to test whether it was still the right strategic decision.

The reassessment of China's gambit and Australia's need for a revised defence strategy that swung the force posture away from the multiple theatres of operation it had been engaged in for the past two decades, and towards a more potent Indo-Pacific focus, had hardened.

Morrison asked Kiploks to make some discreet technical enquiries of Defence. He wanted to know whether there was any prospect of a nuclear-powered option with the US. And if so, how that could happen.

That same question had been asked by Tony Abbott, who had raised the idea of buying US Virginia-class nuclear submarines during a 'deep dive' session of the National Security Committee in 2015.

Turnbull is understood to have also quietly sought Defence views about a nuclear option.

But Defence officials had discouraged both of Morrison's predecessors from pursuing it because at that point there was no confidence the US would ever share its nuclear technology.

The Defence secretary at the time, Dennis Richardson, later confirmed that he had approached US counterparts in the mid-2010s but had been told that 'without a nuclear industry, it would be very difficult for Australia to acquire a nuclear-powered submarine, and the [US] wouldn't be in a position to, in fact, provide one'.[4]

When Turnbull struck the French deal, the economic industrial imperative, and the importance of naval shipbuilding capability, was a big part of the equation. Sovereign capability was central to the vision.

But to Morrison, several years later, these considerations did not trump the strategic issues he saw that Australia was now facing. Circumstances had dramatically changed by the time he found himself posing these questions. Not only had the great power competition accelerated but technology had also changed. Morrison's primary concern was that the conventionally powered French submarine capability would be redundant by the time the vessels got wet.

Morrison had even more questions: what strategic benefits a nuclear-powered submarine platform would provide for Australia, and would Defence be prepared to have a good look at it?

Kiploks came back with an unexpected initial response: nuclear submarines were worth exploring. This was a significant shift in the space of only a few years and Morrison later admitted he'd been surprised to hear Defence's change of heart.

Surprise or not, the shift in thinking put in motion a series of secret negotiations that would crystallise Morrison's overarching strategy and set Australia on a new course.

A significant reason for the development was that a key technological and political barrier had been overcome: the new US nuclear reactor platforms required no servicing for the entire life of the boat. This meant that Australia could itself operate a nuclear-powered naval fleet without the need for a domestic nuclear industry.

While the French also had a nuclear boat to offer, Dutton, as Defence minister, would later simply dismiss it, claiming that the French nuclear option was 'not superior' to the US/UK options.[5]

The larger question was US willingness to share its tightly guarded nuclear propulsion technology. This had occurred only once before when, under the 1958 US–UK Mutual Defence Agreement, the US supplied a single nuclear submarine propulsion system to the UK under a broader nuclear-technology sharing pact.

*

It was time to look at options. Defence Department secretary Greg Moriarty was asked to form a top-secret technical group advised by experts including former chief scientist Alan Finkel. Before long, it reported back that a nuclear submarine option might be workable, and continued to sift through mountains of detail. At various stages throughout 2020, Morrison was briefed on progress.

It wasn't until the Biden administration that any serious discussions were engaged in at a political level. This was not something Morrison had ever discussed with Trump.

By early 2021, Kiploks and Morrison's international adviser, Michelle Chan, began a dialogue with US and UK officials: Kurt Campbell, White House coordinator for the Indo-Pacific; Joe Biden's National Security Adviser, Jake Sullivan; and the UK

Secretary of Defence, Stephen Lovegrove, who Johnson appointed as his national security adviser in March of that year.

AUKUS started taking shape for Morrison at the start of 2021, when it became clear that Australia should be looking at capabilities beyond just submarines.

This included precision-strike guided missiles, cruise missiles, hypersonic missile capability, cyber-warfare, undersea drones, space, artificial intelligence and quantum technology. Some of the missile technology on offer, including the Tomahawk cruise missiles, had been approved by the US more than a decade before but had fallen out of previous Defence white papers.

Morrison had come to the conclusion that Australia was now shopping for something broader than just submarines, even though there was a view within Defence that it should limit itself to upgrading the submarine capability.

Frustrated that the ADF top brass weren't seeing the bigger picture, he explained to Moriarty why he wanted to go wider: unless a new, revised submarine deal was done as part of a broader context, it wouldn't make as much sense.

Reflecting that it had taken a year just to resolve the submarine issue, Morrison wanted to avoid future Australian prime ministers being saddled with the same limitations every time they wanted to do something innovative or add a new technological capability.

This was about getting in on the ground floor and going beyond the concept of a treaty.

When Morrison had specifications drawn up and costed for his vision, the price tag was hefty: an annual Defence spend above 2.5 per cent of GDP. If it was passed, it would be the highest Defence spending in Australian history. Plus it would require an alignment across the defence forces and the defence establishment.

After the US indicated it might be prepared to offer Australia the 'holiest of holies', as Morrison described the US nuclear submarine technology, he met with the chief of the Defence Force, Angus Campbell and asked him bluntly, 'Should we do this?'

'Yes, Prime Minister, we should do this,' Campbell replied.

Once again, Morrison sequestered himself in his study to consider the relevant facts. Past assessments were that the French sub was the right sub, and the safest for Australian submariners: safety was always a major consideration.

Morrison, however, was now looking at Australia's defences from different angles and three questions arose: if Australia stuck with a conventionally powered submarine, could its navy deal with a situation beyond the Indonesian archipelago? Did Defence have options that didn't involve subs? And could the risk of armed conflict in the Indo-Pacific be managed without a strategic submarine capability?

The answers kept coming back to Morrison: 'No.'

Morrison knew his expanded vision would get a positive reaction from Johnson and was convinced that Biden would be amenable too. Thus began the pitch for a framework that would develop a cradle-to-nurse for not only the nuclear submarine project but other projects as well.

By the time Dutton had been appointed Defence minister in March 2021 – in the reshuffle of Morrison's cabinet that saw Reynolds moved out of the portfolio – much of the technical planning for the ambitious new project was already in place.

Morrison was then ready to formally take it to the National Security Committee, so as to brief other ministers on the plan and get approval to take the next step: to engage in the necessary political discussions with Johnson and Biden.

*

'I hear there is something exciting' – Johnson

Johnson had become aware of the plan through his own defence chiefs and had sent Morrison a cheeky text: 'I hear there is something exciting'.

But Morrison wouldn't engage in those high-level political discussions without the full knowledge of the NSC, which on 13 May met in a 'ministers only format', along with some key officials. The discussions, which began late afternoon, ran over time. Fresh from receiving approval to make the calls, Morrison and Frydenberg bolted across to the House of Representatives chamber, where Labor leader Anthony Albanese was on his feet delivering his budget-in-reply. The duo's late entry drew disapproving looks from members of the opposition.

A few days later, Morrison phoned Johnson for the formal discussion. The British prime minister was as supportive as Morrison anticipated. and would be pivotal in setting up an historic meeting with Biden in the weeks ahead, in which they would seal the deal.

*

French frustrations

While all three parties to the discussions regarding a nuclear option kept the French government in the dark, there were growing and very public frustrations over the submarine contract with Naval Group, a majority French state-controlled company, with deliverables already overdue.

An early clue that the ground was shifting in Australia's maritime defence arena came in early June. Moriarty revealed to a Senate Estimates Committee hearing that Defence had been working on other options in the event that the French project fell over.[6] He told the committee, 'It became clear to me we were having challenges with the Attack-class program over the last 15 to 12 months. So, of course, you do reasonably prudent thinking about what one of those options might be or what you might be able to if you are unable to proceed. The department is doing prudent contingency planning: a number of offices – not just the navy; other parts of the department – are involved from time-to-time in discussions.'

On a more basic level, Senate Estimates heard that the next contract gate for the French project was already overdue. The Royal Australian Navy's director-general of submarine capability, Commodore Timothy Brown, told them, 'Although my work is classified, I think in the broad you could say we're looking at the best options for Australia or defence to be able to counter future threats and making sure we understand the requirements.'[7]

The French had been given plenty of hints that there were serious concerns with the project and those concerns had been raised for some time.

Back in February 2019, Naval Group had asked for a 15-month delay in delivering submarine design. That had opened a window of opportunity for Morrison that might never have presented itself otherwise.

*

Biden's election was the game-changer

Morrison could not have envisaged Trump signing off on AUKUS and the nuclear submarine deal. The game-changer was Biden's election.

President Biden's international posture leaned heavily towards the Indo-Pacific, with his commitment to the pivot more concerted than Obama's. This was the impetus for reactivating the Quad. Morrison was mindful that the last time the US went passive in the region, China built installations in the South China Sea. No one had stopped them.

Biden's assessment was based on the US's national and strategic interest. Its most important strategic focus was no longer postwar Europe. It was no longer the Middle East. The US had formed the view it was now the Indo-Pacific. The US was also re-assessing what capabilities were required to address its interests there. Australia's role would be a critical element in that.

That involved the concept of 'integrated', or collective, deterrence in which the US saw increased military integration with allies or partners in the region to address the direct – as well as the grey-zone – threats posed by China.[8]

The attraction for the US in a submarine deal under AUKUS was the networked capability it added to its Indo-Pacific interests through its closest ally in the region.

At the same time, the UK was looking for partnerships post-Brexit. It had already been expressing more interest in this part of the world. Its joint ties with Australia were already well established. And Morrison believed that a third partner in the arrangement was vital.

By mid-June, the AUKUS deal was clinched after Morrison, Johnson and Biden met at the G7 summit in Cornwall. Three months later, it would be unveiled to the world.

*

'Quelle horreur!'

Morrison was prepared for a hostile reaction to the new defence initiative both from critics at home and from the French. For two days prior to the announcement of AUKUS on 16 September, the French president had refused to take his calls.

Eventually Morrison was left with no option but to text Macron, attaching a letter that explained the decision.

The reaction was both immediate and intense. France, incandescent with rage, recalled its ambassadors to Canberra and Washington DC.

When the Japanese had lost the original bid to the French, they too had been sorely disappointed but made no accusations of betrayal. Undoubtedly, losing the deal was a blow to French pride and would come with substantial commercial fallout for French interests. Weapons sales to other nations was a major plank of France's defence strategy: it had the double benefit of maintaining its sovereign defence manufacturing capability.

Morrison had balanced all this against Australia's ability to respond to an existential threat. To him there was no comparison. The argument that Australia should have not gone ahead with AUKUS to avoid upsetting France was naive.

It boiled down to the national strategic interest, and here Australia and France did not necessarily align. For Morrison, the French being unable to see why Australia needed to head in a different direction reflected their lack of clarity on what the issues in the Indo-Pacific actually were.

The first call Morrison made to international partners was to New Zealand prime minister Jacinda Ardern. He hoped New Zealand could help smooth things over among some of the South Pacific nations. Sensitivity to nuclear assets in the region lingered. Four decades of French nuclear testing on Pacific atolls only came to an end in the 1990s.[9]

Yet most of the Pacific Island nations were supportive.

Morrison also spoke to Indian prime minister Narendra Modi and outgoing Japanese prime minister Yoshihide Suga, who he would meet the following week in Washington for the first in-person leaders meeting of the Quad.

Apart from the European problem as a consequence of French anger, and the risk it presented in undoing the goodwill and influence Morrison had established with European leaders throughout the pandemic, Morrison's chief concern was ASEAN.

There were three components to Australia's broader Indo-Pacific strategy, which had the Quad – and now also AUKUS – as a central pillar. While Morrison and Turnbull had both elevated the Pacific Step-up as a strategic priority, the success of an Indo-Pacific strategy would ultimately stand or fall over which way South-East Asia decided to pivot.

The 2017 Foreign Policy White Paper warned that South-East Asia was the 'nexus' of the Indo-Pacific and that Australia needed to maintain its strong engagement at all levels, including economic, defence and security.[10] Morrison had announced a South-East Asia post-Covid recovery strategy in November 2020, which sought to head off China's growing influence. It had allocated $550 million to economic recovery projects aimed at reasserting Australia's presence.[11]

Yet he was concerned about the reaction of ASEAN – a ten-nation grouping of Singapore, Indonesia, Vietnam, Cambodia, Thailand, Brunei Darussalam, Myanmar (Burma), the Philippines, Malaysia and Laos.

Collectively, ASEAN was anxious about tensions in the region. Morrison knew he had to be extremely circumspect with his use of language. For countries such as Indonesia, it was paramount that an Australian nuclear submarine capability would not breach the nuclear non-proliferation treaty.

There was an irony, of course. No one was calling out China's military production as a threat to peace and stability in the region or as an escalation of tensions.

Morrison texted Widodo shortly before making the AUKUS announcement. Dutton and Marise Payne informed Indonesia's Defence minister, Prabowo Subianto, and Foreign Affairs minister, Retno Marsudi, the same day. Morrison spoke to other ASEAN leaders the next day.

Chinese officials were also offered a briefing.

On the eve of the announcement, the PM's last call was with the Japanese prime minister, Yoshihide Suga, who ended the conversation with 'Goodbye, Scomo, my forever friend,' a sign-off that stayed in Morrison's mind when he went to bed.

The next morning, he reprised Suga's words to describe the AUKUS agreement as a 'forever partnership'.[12] One that bound Australia to a strategy that would span generations.

*

Labor backed the agreement on conditions,[13] but they were conditions the government had already met. There was to be no nuclear weapon capability, no civil nuclear industry needed to service the boats and no clash with nuclear non-proliferation obligations.

Despite being from the Labor Left, Albanese was a staunch supporter of the Australia–US alliance. He recognised the political peril of opposing the submarine deal and AUKUS arrangement, conscious the ALP would inherit it in government. With an election due within six months, Albanese would not allow Labor to be wedged on national security, defence and China.

Not all in Labor were of the same opinion. Those such as former prime minister Paul Keating were aggressively opposed on the grounds that greater military integration represented a loss of Australian sovereignty. But even Labor wasn't onside with him, with Albanese saying 'China has changed ... Australia is right to stand up for our own values.'[14]

Morrison also countered, including assuring Australians that domestic political dynamics were not a consideration when he had embarked on the process. Nevertheless, he acknowledged that as well as solving difficulties, AUKUS had also presented new ones.

In a private moment with Attorney-General Michaelia Cash, he confided, 'Sometimes you have to decide whether there is a hill you are prepared to die on [politically].'

*

'Liar' ... 'Liar'

It was 28 October and, after a horror fortnight in parliament negotiating with the Nationals on a net zero emissions by 2050 target – to be Australia's key offering to Johnson at the upcoming UN climate change conference in Glasgow, COP26[15] – Morrison was preparing for the ten-minute drive to RAAF Base Fairbairn ahead of flying to the G20 summit in Rome.

At 6pm, following question time, with his car parked inside the prime minister's courtyard at Parliament House ready to take him to the airport, Morrison's phone rang. It was Macron.

The timing was exactly six weeks since the virtual joint press conference that unveiled AUKUS on 16 September.

Macron was still bitter after the pair had hugged and dined for hours at the Élysée Palace in June. Straight after the AUKUS announcement he'd recalled his ambassador from Canberra, his Defence minister had lashed Australia for the 'stab in the back'[16] and he had snubbed the letter, handwritten note and text Morrison had sent him in the days before AUKUS was revealed.

Seeking to project strength domestically, ahead of his April 2022 election, Macron's pre-G20 phone call was the first step in a plot to embarrass Morrison on the world stage.

As Morrison scrambled on to the government jet, which was running late for its 6.30pm departure, Macron's office released its take on the phone call. The Élysée statement,[17] said Macron, raised concerns with Morrison about the handling of the future submarine contract and Australia's climate change commitments.

'President Macron recalled that Australia's unilateral decision to scale back the French-Australian strategic partnership by putting an end to the ocean-class submarine programme in favour of another as-yet unspecified project broke the relationship of trust between our two countries. The situation of the French businesses and their subcontractors, including Australian companies, affected by this decision will be given our utmost attention,' the statement said.

'It is now up to the Australian government to propose tangible actions that embody the political will of Australia's highest authorities to redefine the basis of our bilateral relationship and continue joint action in the Indo-Pacific.'

Understanding the political heat he was facing on climate change, the French said Macron scolded Morrison for failing to adopt 'ambitious measures commensurate with the climate challenge' and called on Australia to phase out coal 'production and consumption'.

When Morrison stepped on to the plane, he spoke briefly with journalists and said, 'It's been a long day.' He made no mention of Macron's phone call. Unknown to him, Macron would get ahead of him in framing the narrative.

En route to Darwin, and discovering Macron's ruse, Morrison's team released a short statement on the 'ice breaker' phone call.[18]

'President Macron called the Prime Minister this evening, following a letter from the Prime Minister earlier this month,' a read-out of the call released by the PMO said.

'The Prime Minister was pleased to be able to speak with President Macron. They had a candid discussion on the bilateral relationship. The Prime Minister looks forward to future collaborations on our shared interests, particularly in the Indo-Pacific. The Prime Minister also took the opportunity to inform the President about Australia's commitment to deliver net zero emissions by 2050.'

The contrasts between the Australian and French read-outs were stark. Morrison's camp said Macron did not raise or comment on Australia's climate ambitions.

On the flight to Rome's Fiumicino Airport, via Darwin and Dubai, Morrison's advisers hatched a low-profile strategy for the G20 summit. Their main talking points focused on online trolling and securing support from world leaders on a unified approach targeting bullies, extremists and predators on digital platforms. They would later concede they underestimated the threat posed by Macron's revenge tactics and face-saving strategy to bolster his national security credentials ahead of the French election.

Coinciding with Morrison's Friday arrival, Macron invited Biden to La Villa Bonaparte, the French embassy to the Vatican in the heart of Rome.

With the cameras rolling, and Biden eager to soothe relations with Macron, the US president indirectly chided Australia over its handling of the French submarine contract, saying he had believed Canberra had kept Macron 'informed long before' about its intention to tear up the Naval deal.[19]

'I think what happened was, to use an English phrase, clumsy. It was not done with a lot of grace. I was under the impression certain things had happened that hadn't happened,' Biden said.

'I was under the impression that France had been informed long before that the deal was not going through. I, honest to God, did not know you had not been.'

Asked whether Biden had repaired the Franco–American alliance, Macron said they had 'clarified together what we had to clarify. The US was not the only party at stake.'

Morrison was stunned by Biden's intervention. Concerns were raised that Biden, who forgot Morrison's name during the AUKUS announcement and referenced him as 'that fella Down Under',[20] may have been kept in the dark by senior members of his administration about the AUKUS process. Australian negotiators said senior US officials were aware of both the concept of the military pact and the status of Australia's $90 billion contract with Naval.

As the Australian convoy drove to the La Nuvola Convention Center for the first day of the G20 summit, Morrison wanted to tackle the Macron problem head on. With Macron attending both the G20 and COP26 summits, Morrison was eager to clear the air.

Before the obligatory 'family photo', where leaders pose awkwardly on stage, Morrison approached Macron in the leaders' lounge on the Saturday morning.

As world leaders mingled, Morrison walked up to Macron, put his hand on his shoulder and said 'G'day.' The prime minister's photographer, Adam Taylor, was on hand to capture the fleeting handshake. The photo was distributed to the Australian press pack to display the leaders' 'warmth'.

It wasn't long before the proactive strategy fell in a heap.

When the G20 concluded on the Sunday evening, Morrison invited journalists from the media centre to La Nuvola for a final press conference before heading to Glasgow. He was huddled inside a small makeshift room on the convention centre ground floor with his senior advisers, who had been preparing for hostilities at COP26, not at the G20.

As journalists waited for the prime minister to emerge and wandered deeper into the convention centre, Morrison's press secretary, Andrew Carswell, walked out to chat with them.

About 50 metres from where Morrison was still gathering his thoughts, Macron was wrapping up a press conference with French reporters. When Macron left the glass-walled room, ABC political editor Andrew Probyn, *Sydney Morning Herald* Europe correspondent Bevan Shields and SBS political reporter Pablo Vinales made a beeline for the French president.

Probyn tasked Vinales with filming the exchange on his iPhone and the pair went for it.

Despite attempts by Macron's advisers to pull their leader away, he seized the opportunity.

'You have to respect allies and partners … and it was not the case with this deal. I think this is detrimental to the reputation of your country and your Prime Minister,' Macron said.

Asked by Shields whether Mr Morrison had lied to him about exiting the future submarines contract, the French president said: 'I don't think, I know.'

An official from the Department of Foreign Affairs and Trade who, mistakenly, believed the Australian journalists had been trying to get 'selfies' with Macron, relayed the false intelligence back to the prime minister's media team.

As journalists shared the video of Macron damning Morrison, Carswell's demeanour shifted from jovial to panicked. Without seeing the footage, he swiftly retreated into Morrison's room and informed him of the exchange.

Soon after, Morrison began his press conference. He accused journalists of 'getting selfies' with Macron and denied lying to the French president.

As journalists frantically filed the story before they all boarded the flight to Glasgow, the PMO shifted into damage control and disputed Macron's version of events.

The Macron bombshell broke early morning Australian time and dominated the news cycle. From Morrison's perspective, Macron had taken the gloves off and he had to hit back.

'Macron was told pretty clearly [about the Naval contract in June], but he just didn't want to hear it,' government sources briefed journalists.

A text exchange between Morrison and Macron was leaked,[22] in which the French leader said 'should I expect good or bad news for our joint submarine ambitions' at the same time Australia was trying to contact him two days before the AUKUS announcement.

With the Macron story still circulating in the Australian news cycle, a hastily organised early morning press conference was called at the BAE Systems shipyards in Glasgow. Following a tour of BAE's frigate operations in freezing conditions, Morrison delivered a lengthy defence of his dealings with the French, but did not deny the authenticity of the text, which refuted Macron's claims.[23]

Morrison, who expected more pain at the climate change summit, won a short reprieve after China, India and other developing nations thwarted Johnson and Biden's global plan to end coal-fired power and reduce methane emissions.

As a nation reliant on coal and agriculture, Australia could not entertain the ambitious climate targets pushed by the UK and US.

Nevertheless, Morrison was under intense pressure in the weeks leading up to the UN summit. He had put the Coalition on a climate change 'Road to Damascus' after railing against Bill Shorten in 2019 over Labor's 45 per cent emissions reduction by 2030 target.

Trying to shift the Coalition to a more moderate position on climate change had destroyed Turnbull's leadership. But the political capital Morrison had accrued during the early days of the pandemic had afforded him the authority that prior Liberal leaders had lacked.

Painstaking negotiations with Barnaby Joyce and the Nationals led to a last-minute deal on the net zero by 2050 emissions target, days before Morrison and Energy minister Angus Taylor flew to Europe. But winning the support of Nationals MPs, many resistant to the idea of climate change action after helping to destroy Labor's carbon tax, didn't come cheap.

With regional communities built on farming and mining, Joyce and Morrison secretly negotiated a 'net zero transition' deal worth more than $15 billion, to get the Nationals to support a position that would have been hitherto unthinkable.

As well as responding to pressure from Johnson and Biden, Morrison believed that the carbon neutral plan would provide the Coalition with a political shield to sandbag its inner-city metropolitan seats against a coordinated group of independents backed by the cashed-up Climate 200 movement.

The government had also pinned its hopes on Albanese politically overreaching on climate change policy.

Morrison believed he had escaped the climate change summit relatively unscathed, but on the final day of COP26 as Labor attacked him in Australia, Turnbull – who was close to Macron – made a cameo appearance at an 'impromptu' press conference in Glasgow. He used the media opportunity to label Morrison a 'liar'. It was an extraordinary claim for a former prime minister to make of a serving one.[24] But if creating more difficult headlines for Morrison was the intention, it had the desired effect.

Morrison arrived back in Australia hopeful the worst of the Delta variant would soon be over, grateful the trip was done and thankful that he would avoid another stint in quarantine at The Lodge.

CHAPTER 24

Where to from here?

IN THE AFTERMATH of Delta, Morrison reflected that Australia had faced three great challenges in the space of just 18 months. The health impacts of a one-in-100-year pandemic, the economic shock that came with it, and navigating the great power competition between China and the US, which forced Australia to challenge its providence in a changed world.

Morrison's thinking on the need for Australia to diversify its trade relationships as a hedge against reliance on China, to build a sovereign capability, and to draw the US and Europe back into Australia's strategic sphere had been developing before the pandemic. Covid-19 had merely accelerated it. It shone a new light on China at a time that the rest of the world was only beginning to look.

The Morrison government bore the brunt of China's response to the emerging pushback. But in the process, Australia in its steadfast response increased its influence among liberal democracies – notwithstanding the fallout with France – to emerge as a leading advocate for western democratic principles as an established and more assertive middle power.

Morrison advocated for the modernisation of multilateral organisations, which he had been critical of from the early days of his leadership, and became a warrior in the new battle of ideologies. He strove for the reactivation of the Quad, ultimately realised with Biden's election, while seeking to promote greater independence and sovereignty within ASEAN and the Pacific Island nations that were more robust against Chinese influence and hegemony. Engaging the US and Europe in the quest for a reawakening of what was at stake in the Indo-Pacific was fundamental to Morrison's proposition.

Critics would accuse him of megaphone diplomacy over his pursuit of answers to the origins of Covid. But to Morrison, the alternative would have been tantamount to appeasement. In his eyes, Australia had nothing to apologise for. And it was a strategy that had been months, if not years, in development.

Morrison had made an assessment that China's ambitions were now evident for the world to see. But this wasn't an anti-China approach. Australia was simply among the first to resist. Covid ignited a need for more durable alignment that promoted a longer period of peace based on reliable trading relationships and supply chains and more enduring strategic partnerships.

Domestically, Morrison had championed the notion of a post-Covid sovereignty around two themes: defence of the nation and an invigoration of the nation's productive capacity.

Internationally, Morrison had pushed the notion of sovereignty over nationalism as a theme to wed like-minded nations to a defence of democracy. It was this recalibration of Australia's resistance to coercion that enabled it to form alignments with countries sympathetic to its position.

There was no doubt that Australia was singled out as a target by China because of its relationship with the US.

But as important as the response to Covid was, Australia needed to influence the post-pandemic environment. Morrison saw that, coming out of Covid, there was an imperative for nations to work with those they could trust.

Several key themes or pillars emerged, and all were based on trying to refocus the world's attention, as well as realigning Australia's own defence and strategic interests. This was happening irrespective of Covid.

Morrison's defence speech a year earlier had signalled that Australia would reawaken in a post-Covid environment in which the developing world was poorer and strategic tensions more acute. In that setting, Australia was compelled to demonstrate a determination and resilience that appreciated China's ambitions.

This view wasn't universally shared.

An alternative analysis saw that Australia's role in the region could be advanced through an independent posture, one that was more disengaged from the US. Morrison's judgement, however, was that isolationism was fatal and that Australia's security and prosperity would only be achieved through diversification at one level, and a reinforcement of the old Anglosphere alliances at another, to provide the counterbalance required to secure Australia's future.

The key question was what Australia would look like on the other side of the pandemic.

'We have found ourselves ultimately in a position where we have had to be true to ourselves,' Morrison said of the great China question when reflecting on the challenges the nation would face long after the pandemic had faded.

'That is fundamentally what the choice was.

'Will we accept this and do nothing, seek to ameliorate it, live with it, adjust, or will we do something else?

'Has it harmed our relationships in Europe, which I had been building up to try and get awareness of this issue? Yes, that is true.

'But ensuring the more immediate need of having the partners that can help us deal with this situation here was more paramount.

'I think the others will come on and understand and work it out for themselves, that the steps we have taken on Covid, and everything else, that China picked the wrong country potentially to seek to marginalise.

'And why would anyone be surprised that we do this?

'I hope I am wrong. But I can't afford to be right if I don't do what I'm doing.'

CHAPTER 25

Omicron's curse

IT WAS JUST before 8pm on Monday 29 November 2021 when Morrison shot out of Parliament House for the quick drive up Adelaide Avenue to The Lodge. He was already late for the prime minister's annual pre-Christmas press gallery drinks.

A snap NSC meeting he'd had to call after news over the weekend that Australia had detected its first case of Omicron had run over time.

Until the prior Friday, Morrison had been cautiously optimistic about the threat of the new Covid-19 variant. Perhaps blindly so, as he, like most Australians, assumed that the peak of the pandemic might all be but over now that the Delta wave seemed to have run its course.

He well knew that his political fortunes were very much tied to the hopes of the community. After two years of incessant disruptions and fear, people were now clamouring to have a summer that was free of natural disaster or pestilence.

Well aware of that, Morrison knew he couldn't take anything for granted.

A call from Hunt two days earlier had changed everything. The health minister, in Melbourne, hooked CMO Paul Kelly into a teleconference so the two of them could brief the PM on troubling news coming out of South Africa.

Kelly had earlier briefed Hunt, late on the Friday, 26 November, over his concerns that the preliminary data he was seeing on the new strain would likely see the WHO declare it a variant of concern the following day.

'So Paul,' said Morrison, 'is it correct that this is likely to be more contagious, less severe and unknown in its potential for breakthrough infections?'

'Yes, prime minister,' said Kelly.

The three immediately agreed that they would need to pause the reopening of borders, extend existing pandemic measures – such as tele-health – and order a review of booster vaccines.

Back in early November, Australia had been one of the first countries in the world to offer a whole-of-nation booster program. But ATAGI's approval mandated a six-month window between a person getting their second dose of vaccine and getting a booster.

Hunt said that, given Omicron, Kelly might need to ask ATAGI to narrow that gap.

The early evidence was that while the variant appeared to be less lethal than its predecessors, it was more transmissible, and the three on the call were extremely concerned about the possibility of dramatically increased pressure on the country's hospital systems.

Only the week before, the federal government had announced the opening up of the border to allow more than 200,000 visa holders, migrant workers and tourists from Korea and Japan back into the country from 1 December.[1]

It was the latest data – on Omicron – that led Morrison to call the NSC together, and they had agreed to hit the pause button on those plans, delaying the opening-up until 15 December and reintroducing 14-day quarantine for anyone who'd been to any of eight southern African countries in the prior two weeks. The announcement was released later that evening.[2]

While Morrison put on his best face when he got to The Lodge, smiling and pressing the flesh with the press corps, almost 100 of them, who were gathered in the southern-facing courtyard adjacent the pool, he reflected on the ominous words his chief medical officer had used with the NSC only an hour earlier:

'No one can advise for now on Omicron's severity, or the efficacy of vaccines. We are not going to be able to stop it because it is already here.'

*

It's time to live with it

The following day, Morrison assembled the national cabinet a week earlier than planned to discuss Omicron or, as it was technically known, the B.1.1.529 variant.

The CMO took the premiers and chief ministers through the same briefing he had given to the NSC meeting on the Monday.

With no sense yet of how rapidly the new strain would spread, the decision taken was one of caution, that apart from the new quarantine rules endorsed by the NSC, the national cabinet would not yet alter the current settings in terms of testing and social restrictions.

But with parliament due to rise for the year in three days' time, the government appeared to be limping towards the end-of-year finish line.

Opinion polls were showing that Morrison had been personally damaged by the government's perceived failures on vaccine supply – the 'strollout' – and the brawls with state leaders over who was to blame for lockdowns during Delta.

He had other political headaches, too, such as very public internal party ill-discipline, with Coalition MPs crossing the floor of parliament over vaccine mandates, and threats by moderate Liberal MPs to scuttle the government's proposed religious freedoms legislation.

The PM was also forced that week to stand aside another minister. This time it was Education minister Alan Tudge, following allegations of ill-treatment raised by a former staffer with whom he had an affair. Tudge denied the allegations and, despite them not being proven in a subsequent inquiry, the optics fed into a narrative that the government had a problem with women, despite published polls suggesting otherwise.

Any notion that Covid incumbency – the proposition that governments derived a political dividend from crisis – would inoculate Morrison from the other events coming at him had long evaporated.

From the outside, the government had a 'last days of Rome' feel about it.

But Morrison was upbeat. He believed that if the government regrouped over the summer, it would eventually be rewarded by a more positive, forgiving electorate, with the people in a better frame of mind after reconnecting with family and friends over Christmas, liberated from lockdowns and optimistic about the future.

Morrison sought to tap into a vein of communal frustration with the deprivations of social liberties that Australians had been forced to endure over the past two years.

So he began to shift the political narrative: Australia had to 'live with the virus' and government needed to step back out of people's lives.

*

Hunt bows out

Hunt had tried to retire once before. Before the 2019 election he had gone to see Morrison and Frydenberg to tell them he was thinking about stepping down to spend more time with his family.

Morrison urged him to stay, as did Frydenberg, his closest friend.

'I don't think I can win without you,' Morrison told him.

Hunt was persuaded – he owed it to the team and he also felt he had unfinished business in the areas of rural health, the PBS, mental health and aged care.

But in November 2021, Hunt went to tell Morrison he was once again considering retiring. The PM held out a hope that Hunt would stay but believed there was probably little point trying to persuade him otherwise this time.

On Tuesday 30 November, in the last parliamentary sitting week of the year, Hunt went into Morrison's office and told him he had made up his mind.

'I won't even try to talk you out of it this time. I understand. You've played your part,' Morrison said.

Hunt simply said to Frydenberg: 'It's time, my friend.'

Hunt was a believer in the 'five Ds' that generally applied to the end of political careers: death, defeat, despair, disgrace or dignity. Hunt was aiming for option five.

On Thursday 2 December, Hunt formally announced he was retiring from parliament but would remain until the election, claiming it was 'time to come home'.[3]

After a 20-year political career that had robbed him of time with his teenage children, including the past two stressful years leading the nation's health response virtually day and night, he decided it was time to retire. Politicians often cite a need for family time as their reason for stepping down when it's actually a cover for a lack of support or a scandal. In Hunt's case it was genuine.

Even so, his job was far from done, and he knew it.

When Hunt made his announcement, few people appreciated the speed at which Omicron would take off, even though the preliminary data out of South Africa – where it originated – suggested its infection rate was way higher than all the previous strains.

Hunt had his concerns, however, and began pushing Murphy to lean on the regulators, for example, to bring forward booster shots and approve vaccines for 5–11-year-olds. For Hunt, if there was to be another wave, he saw it as vital that the population had as much protection as possible.

Once again, ATAGI was reluctant to act quickly, being used to operating in a high-data environment with the benefit of exhaustive clinical trials and testing. Forced by the urgency of the pandemic to work in a low-data environment, the expert panel was uncomfortable, and so was taking a more conservative approach.

For example, concerned about the potential side effects of paediatric vaccinations, and despite the community and political pressure, ATAGI wanted more data before giving the government the green light.

Then, on 3 December, when ATAGI rejected Hunt's call to shorten the gap for adult boosters, he pressed Murphy to try them again.

As a politician – even as Health minister – Hunt couldn't approach ATAGI directly himself. But Murphy, as secretary of the Health Department and chair of the scientific and technical advisory group, could.

By the end of that week, Murphy had moved them some of the way, pushing ATAGI to shorten the booster gap from six months to five.

Meanwhile, Hunt got yet another extension from the governor-general to keep the Human Biosecurity emergency measures in place until at least mid-February 2022.[4]

By then, daily case numbers were running at around 1700 a day. While high, it was a number Hunt and Murphy assessed would still allow the reopening of the country.

But within the space of three days, those numbers doubled.

And they continued to double every few days.

On 13 December, the day Queensland officially reopened its borders to the rest of the country, Morrison hosted the South Korean president Moon Jae-in and his wife at a state luncheon at Government House, Yarralumla, the governor-general's residence in Canberra. He then flew to Sydney to deliver what he hoped would be a landmark speech at the Sydney Institute's annual dinner.

The PM declared to great applause that after two years of significant social and economic intervention, it was 'now time for governments ... to step back. And let Australians step forward. To put Australians back in charge of their own lives.'[5]

He deliberately mingled with the crowd – which included several of his ministers, journalists, Liberal Party figures and a great many businesspeople – making a point about the restored freedoms he was championing in his speech.

What he and the organisers didn't know was that one of the guests was infected with Covid-19.

Early the following morning he flew to Melbourne for another significant announcement, one that had been months in the planning and kept to a tight circle of trust.

Since mid-2021 Hunt had been in secret talks with Moderna about building an mRNA manufacturing facility in Australia which would become the largest vaccine maker in the Southern Hemisphere.

Hunt and Energy minister Angus Taylor both knew Moderna president Stephen Hoge well, all three having once worked together at the global management consultancy McKinsey & Company.

Moderna's opening position was that if the federal government built a factory for them, they would manufacture the vaccines.

That proposal went through both the NSC and ERC but it wasn't viewed as viable, as too expensive for the government. Though Hunt wanted a global research centre and for Australia to become a South-East Asian vaccine hub, he wanted better terms. Moderna, he felt, was asking too much and not giving enough.

After bringing in commercial negotiators, an in-principle deal was struck and announced on 14 December. The final agreement, announced in March 2020, would see the Commonwealth and Andrews governments partnering with Moderna in a three-way project for a $2 billion investment over ten years to build the facility in Victoria.[6]

It was a major coup for Australia, with the promise of delivering one of the largest mRNA vaccine hubs outside of the US and Europe.

When Morrison landed back in Sydney that afternoon, he was alerted by staff that he was a casual contact from the previous night's event, and he called Kelly. In an hour he was due to have dinner at Kirribilli with the Korean president. Kelly consulted with President Moon's doctor and they agreed that the risk was low and allowed the event to proceed, albeit by then it had been pushed back by half an hour.

Three days later, 16 December, Morrison was in the PM's car, C1, on his way to the NSW central coast to make an announcement rejecting an offshore petroleum exploration project.

Louw wasn't travelling with him this time but called through to advise that, once again, Morrison had come in close contact with an infected case. That had apparently been three days before the Sydney Institute dinner, on 10 December, at a friend's private graduation ceremony that both Morrison and Jenny had attended.

Louw spoke to Morrison's senior media adviser Nick Creevey who was sitting in the back of the car with Morrison. The two decided that there was no way the PM could turn up to the event without having a test.

So Creevey, using Google Maps on his phone, found a pharmacy in Terrigal, a fairly upmarket seaside town, and called ahead to check if they had any rapid antigen tests (RATs), which they did.

The PM's driver pulled up where they'd be unseen, in a laneway around the corner from the pharmacy, and Creevey left to get a test kit.

When he returned, Morrison administered the nasal swab to himself in the back of the car but, in a comedic moment, burst into a fit of the sneezes.

All Creevey could think was, 'He'd better not have it. I'm supposed to be flying down to Melbourne tomorrow for Christmas.'

Just three days after the PM was lauding the opening up of the country, he was getting a real-time taste of Omicron's speed and the potential that 'living with Covid' could be thwarted almost as soon as it started.

While everyone in the PMO was on high alert, the health bureaucracies, state and federal, still seemed to be operating on a business-as-usual approach.

Such was the apparent lack of concern about Omicron among the state leaders and their chief health officers that national cabinet wasn't scheduled to meet again until February the following year.

Of course, it wasn't just Christmas that Morrison was worrying about. He was also turning his mind towards the federal election. It had to be held within the next six months.

After he and Frydenberg pencilled in an early budget, for 29 March 2022, they were all but confirming an election in May.

The PM was counting on his government's record in managing the pandemic as being a foundational piece of his re-election campaign.

But that was before Omicron, a development that would provide Albanese and the Labor opposition with yet another key weapon to undermine the government's management credentials.

*

RATs leaving the sinking ships

With Christmas holidays fast approaching, hundreds of thousands of interstate tourists were packing their bags for flights to Queensland.

It should have been smooth, especially after Kelly and Murphy's guidance to the 10 December national cabinet meeting that screening people crossing state borders for Covid-19 was no longer justifiable.

Premier Palaszczuk, however, ignored that advice. That same day, she imposed new restrictions, forcing travellers to provide evidence, at the border, of a negative PCR (polymerase chain reaction) test obtained in the 72 hours *before* arriving in the Sunshine State.[7]

A few days later, Palaszczuk and Morrison again came to blows when the Queensland government quarantined two planeloads of incoming passengers for 14 days as close contacts of a Covid case.[8]

Morrison took to Brisbane radio demanding they be released.

'Omicron is in Australia and we've got to live with it; we can't live in fear of it,' he said.[9]

Sensing that the public mood was against her, Palaszczuk backtracked and released the passengers.[10]

Hunt accused Queensland of 'breaking the system' by demanding testing for anyone entering the state.

Omicron or no Omicron, the sheer volume of testing demanded by the Queensland regime was unmanageable in the other states and was putting a major strain on the national system.

With the daily caseload having reached just shy of 4000, Morrison knew he needed to act to avert a Christmas disaster.

Covid testing sites, already overrun by Omicron outbreaks, were swelled with tourists who were neither infectious nor had symptoms. Across the east coast, wait times at test sites ballooned to between five and eight hours. Police were frequently being called out to quell scuffles in the lines between frustrated travellers.

The huge spike in the number of tests also triggered delays in the reporting of their results, which in turn forced families to cancel their holidays or anxiously stress over whether or not they'd be able to make it for long-delayed get-togethers over Christmas lunches.

As caseload numbers began exceeding the daily infection rates of previous waves of the virus, contact tracing teams were overwhelmed.

Lockdowns and border closures were clearly not going to be effective. Nor was there any community appetite to repeat the policies of the past.

On 20 December, Morrison decided to call the premiers and chief ministers back around the table to map a path through this.

Ahead of that meeting, he held a teleconference with his health officials to discuss how they could ramp up the booster rollout. Kelly's view was that, even at top speed and with interval changes by ATAGI, the booster program would not be able to keep up with the pace of Omicron's spread.

The pressure, Kelly told Morrison, had to be put back on to the states to reopen their vaccine clinics, many of which had been closed permanently.

By the time the national cabinet met, on 22 December, daily case numbers were approaching 6000. The Doherty Institute's latest modelling on Omicron was forecasting up to 190,000 cases a day by mid-January – and that was only if ATAGI agreed to bring the booster shots forward from a six-month to a three-month interval. If ATAGI didn't move on that, the daily case numbers could be as high as 250,000.

Up until then, most of the states had been clinging to the last vestiges of PCR testing, which, while more accurate than home testing kits, was beginning to buckle under the pressure imposed by some states, such as Queensland, in making them mandatory for travel.

At that time, rapid antigen tests, RATs, were still banned in South Australia and Western Australia. Victoria had only just sanctioned their use.

Morrison, sensing the national mood and appetite, took the idea of moving from PCR tests to RATs to the national cabinet.

At that time, there seemed to be no risk of a shortage of RATs. The TGA had approved dozens of tests for use, even more than had the US regulator, the Food and Drug Administration.

The Commonwealth had solid RAT supplies at that time, and was already providing them for use in the aged care setting.

Hunt, too, was pushing very hard through the AHPPC for the states to adopt RATs as the standard, but without success.

When the states did finally relent and switched from PCR to RATs, the pressure surge created a demand-side shock. Available RAT supplies were mopped up, and pharmacies and supermarkets were unable to restock quickly enough.

Australia was not alone in the world on this. In the US and UK, the daily newspapers were running similar headlines about their own countries' supply shortages.

The fact this was a global supply problem wasn't cutting it with the Australian public, and once again angry fingers were being pointed at Morrison.

The booster saga wasn't over either. By then, the modelling was warning that, without making boosters available faster, the country could face a million Covid cases in the space of a week.

On 12 December, ATAGI had reduced the six-month wait to five months.

But armed with the new data, within the space of 10 days ATAGI was ready to move again.

On the evening of 22 December, after national cabinet had finished, ATAGI informed the government it had decided after its meeting, also that day, that it would authorise another shortening of the booster vaccine interval from six to three months. They proposed to government that they would publicly announce the decision on Christmas Eve.

Already dealing with criticism over the RAT shortage, Morrison had to find out, and find out fast, what the knock-on effects of ATAGI's booster decision might be, especially since it could trigger a rush to be vaccinated over the Christmas break when supply logistics could be expected to be especially difficult.

He immediately called an emergency meeting for the next morning, 23 December, with Frewen and Kelly. The outcome was to stage the cut in the booster interval, not to go immediately to three months, but first to four.

There was no point telling the Australian people that they could get their boosters if the boosters weren't there in sufficient stocks to be given.

*

The Covid Brains Trust

In early 2020, Morrison had set up a private WhatsApp group. He'd called it the 'Covid Brains Trust'.

Originally a secret group for passing messages between Morrison, Hunt, Kunkel and Murphy, he had expanded it along the way to include others as roles changed, people like Kelly and Frewen.

On 27 December, Morrison messaged the group saying that work on the use of RATs needed to be accelerated along with the reclassification of close contacts, so he'd be prepared for the national cabinet meeting he'd scheduled for the following week.

He was concerned that serious supply chain issues would clearly arise from high caseloads if the quarantine rules around close contacts weren't relaxed and people like nurses, and workers crucial for staffing and stocking supermarkets, were forced to stay at home.

Kelly weighed in on the app, saying that AHPPC was working to wind back close contact rules and on ways to preserve PCR testing, but the states were split. Queensland was refusing to drop its PCR travel testing rules in favour of RATs.

Hunt messaged back that it was crucial to keep trying to accelerate both. 'But it is a decision for the states,' he once again was forced to add.

By Hunt's reckoning, the digital traffic coming into government, including WhatsApp, texts and email, was running at around 1000 a day, such was the intensity of activity every time there was an outbreak.

Two days later, on 29 December, the daily infection rate hit 18,243.[11]

At 8am, Morrison again messaged the Covid Brains Trust group.

'We have to bring NATCAB [national cabinet] forward to tomorrow,' he stressed. 'We need to action changes to RATs use and close contacts.'

By 9.30am, at the PM's latest health briefing, Kelly outlined a paper he was taking to the AHPPC that afternoon in which he'd be arguing for significant changes to isolation and testing rules and travel testing. Morrison also tasked Kelly with working up a plan to offer concessional access to RATs for pensioners and welfare recipients, due to a debate about whether RATs should be made free for everyone.

At 10am, the PM texted the premiers and chief ministers, calling them together for the following day so they could reconsider the rules around close contacts, testing regimes and testing supply. He told them he also wanted their views on surge planning for hospitals and booster rollouts.

In other words, he was pressing the states to get ready to re-open vaccine clinics over the holiday break so they could get boosters into people's arms.

He added that while it was New South Wales and Victoria that were currently experiencing soaring infections, it wouldn't be long before every state was in the same boat.

That afternoon, Victoria announced the purchase of 34 million RATs.

*

RATs nowhere to be found

Within the space of four days, when the daily case numbers almost doubled, Morrison decided to fly back to Canberra to work from the capital. On 4 January, he called a meeting of the ERC to discuss plans for a concessional RAT scheme.

The key problem was that with a worldwide shortage of RATs, the government couldn't subsidise something that wasn't available.

As Omicron cases exploded and vaccine rates surged in New South Wales, Victoria and ACT, the premiers and chief ministers were now being forced to accept it was time to live with Covid-19.

While Queensland had been stubbornly refusing to accept RAT results as an alternative to PCR tests, other states pleaded with their own residents to stay away from PCR testing venues and instead use home testing kits.

Like scenes from the dystopian Korean television series *Squid Game*, Australians were effectively being forced to beg, borrow and steal RATs from family and friends. Chemists didn't have them. Nobody had them. Pharmacies and supermarkets were even running out of thermometers and children's paracetamol.

As more and more Australians were struck down by the virus, people who could find RATs began stockpiling them, some even travelling to nearby cities and towns to hunt for supplies.

'Sorry, we don't have rapid antigen tests in stock' was becoming a very common sign around Australia outside pharmacies, supermarkets, service stations, and even toy stores.

It wasn't only RATs that were getting hoarded. So were groceries. Supply chains across the country were buckling.

Hospitals and aged care homes were also under pressure. As Omicron blanketed the country, the number of deaths and people in intensive care units continued to rise again.

Labor seized on the chaos, accusing Morrison and Hunt of being too slow to authorise RATs and to build a domestic manufacturing base to avoid the current shortages.

This was a political attack that would stick.

Over summer, community anger grew as governments everywhere were demanding people have tests at a time when no one could get them.

Morrison sought to start shifting some of the blame back to the states and territories but he was getting virtually no traction.

On top of that, another unexpected problem flew onto Morrison's centre court.

*

Grand slam

In a normal year, Australian prime ministers take a break over the Christmas–New Year–January period and the deputy PM steps in. But Morrison had already had one holiday debacle – when he was in Hawaii during the bushfires – and he wasn't about to have another.

At 11.55am on Wednesday 5 January, although Morrison was set to take a nine-day break with his family at a beach house on the NSW south coast, his first in more than a year, he called his deputy PM, Barnaby Joyce.

'Mate,' said Morrison, 'I won't be taking leave as planned. I need to be working on Omicron and the supply chain issues. So I won't need you to be acting PM.'

At best, Morrison hoped to squeeze in a couple of days with his wife and daughters. But first he had to ready himself for another national cabinet meeting.

The state leaders agreed to split the cost of a concessional RAT scheme and to further scale back their onerous testing requirements. Except for Queensland and Tasmania, which were still refusing to drop RATs as a prerequisite for travel.

Close to midnight that night, on top of the mess Morrison was already dealing with, the world's number one tennis player Novak Djokovic arrived unvaccinated at Melbourne Airport for the Australian Open and was refused entry. The next day his visa was cancelled. [12]

From the get-go, Morrison was adamant that the tennis star would not be allowed into the country. Out of fairness to Australians who had suffered under border and travel restrictions, he was hardly inclined to make an exception for a sports star.

Morrison believed that he had the law, and the weight of public opinion, on his side.

But it wasn't that simple.

The courts would hear, following an appeal by Djokovic, how the Australian Border Force had bungled the process in detaining the tennis ace, who claimed to have a certificate of exemption from Tennis Australia.

A political dispute erupted between Tennis Australia and the Victorian and Commonwealth governments about how he had been granted an exemption, and indeed a visa, in the first place.

What should have been a simple process turned into a week-long saga over whether he would be allowed to stay and play.

The politics, which were with Morrison at the beginning, began to turn.

Even so, on the evening of Monday 10 January, Morrison drove to the NSW south coast so he could at least spend two nights with his family and work remotely.

By Wednesday 12 January, he was back in his office at Parliament House, preparing for yet another national cabinet meeting as the fallout from the Djokovic affair deepened.

To top it off, on 7 January, he had received a call from Frydenberg, who was holidaying at Lorne on Victoria's south-west coast. Having woken with a sore throat and a headache after a feverish night in bed, he later that day tested positive for Covid-19. The Treasurer had to excuse himself from a virtual NSC meeting held that afternoon, and he was out of action for the best part of a week.

Eventually, on 16 January, a full bench of the Federal Court of Australia unanimously dismissed Djokovic's application to review the government's cancellation of his visa.[13]

The decision fell the right way for the government, but in the end it had lost the optics. The public perception was the process had been mismanaged.

It became just another episode in an accumulation of issues, on the top of RATs and people's Christmas travel being disrupted, that fed into a feeling of general frustration with the government. It was fodder for the federal Labor opposition's narrative that the government was losing control of Covid management.

*

Mea culpa

As Liberal Party strategists tracked electoral polling over summer, it was clear Morrison's personal standing had taken a significant hit.

Hence none were surprised when the Coalition plumbed new depths in the first Newspoll of the election year. The stratospheric levels of approval Morrison had garnered at the height of the pandemic's first wave in 2020 had sunk into negative territory.

Morrison's team weren't panicking yet, but they had become deeply worried about the government's electoral prospects.

Politically, the prime minister had fallen victim to the longevity of the plague, the elevation of hostile Labor premiers to a national platform, the inevitable mistakes that would be made the longer it persisted, and an impatient and cranky public.

Irrespective of the strong story that Morrison believed his government had to tell, his own MPs were getting desperate for him to fix what they viewed as the government's mistakes.

In late January, Morrison was putting the finishing touches on what he hoped would be a pre-election headland speech at the National Press Club. The PMO was agonising over every word, and struggling how to frame an apology to Australians without accepting total blame for the RATs calamity over summer.

Despite many other options – like rolling out major defence, energy, manufacturing, resources and other headline-grabbing announcements – Morrison and his advisers landed on a speech that, when he delivered it on 1 February, centred on a *mea culpa* of sorts.[14]

Morrison conceded he had been too optimistic about threats posed by the Omicron variant. From the NPC lectern, in front of senior cabinet ministers and public servants, staffers, lobbyists and journalists, Morrison said he hadn't got 'everything right and I'll take my fair share of the criticism and the blame.'

In his answers to questions, he went further.[15] 'As we went into this summer ... I was optimistic. We were all desperately looking forward to a great summer ... I think in raising those expectations about the summer, that we heightened the great sense of disappointment that people felt,' he added.

No matter how heartfelt and genuine, the public wasn't buying it.

CHAPTER 26

New threats emerge

BY MID-TO-LATE FEBRUARY 2022, most Australians on the east coast were moving on from Covid-19. Many had contracted the virus, or by then knew people who had. The number of people who contracted the virus in Australia had surpassed three million.[1]

Booster shots were available, and those eligible and craving a return to normal life were lining up for their shots in record numbers.

After two years dealing with schools opening and shutting, and parents struggling with homeschooling pressures, the national cabinet agreed that children would permanently return to their classrooms.

With RAT shortages also largely resolved, including schools stocking up on tests to send home, another great social experiment was underway.

Children under the age of 12 were sent back to school not fully vaccinated. Large numbers of them would come back home with Covid, leaving parents anxious and forcing many back into home quarantine.

Morrison's message that government needed to step back, out of people's lives, resonated with many but jarred with those who had concerns about sending their kids to school without the vaccine protection they had been afforded themselves.

On the fringes, where some remained deeply unhappy with the governments' interventions, large anti-vax and anti-government protest convoys descended on Canberra when parliament resumed in February.

When, on 18 February, Western Australia finally announced,[2] after almost 700 days as the 'hermit state', that its borders would reopen on 3 March, unity and freedom were finally being restored to the federation.

Almost as quickly as it arrived, Covid-19 began to recede as the issue dominating public discussion and concerns.

However, a new global threat was emerging, and a new domestic one.

*

Putin invades Ukraine

It was just after 4pm on Thursday 24 February, as Morrison was midway through a five-hour marathon meeting of cabinet's Expenditure Review Committee, when Louw came in and handed him a note:

> 'Putin has announced invasion of Ukraine and attacks are already starting.'

Louw had spent the day up to then ducking in and out of the room to bring in the latest updates, with high expectations that war was expected within 24 hours.

His last exit was less than 30 seconds earlier, and now he returned to give the prime minister the latest.

Morrison read out the note to his colleagues, and they sat in silence to digest what was unfolding.

Australia's condemnation was swift, and consistent with the US and Europe.

'I will call it what it is: the Russian government launched a brutal invasion, unprovoked, on Ukraine and should be condemned for doing so,' Mr Morrison said, issuing a statement following the ERC meeting.[3]

On 18 February, Australia and Russia had clashed in a closed-door meeting of G20 finance ministers and central bank officials in Jakarta, when Frydenberg had warned Russian deputy finance minister Timur Maksimov that an invasion would not only have unforgivable human consequences but send a second economic global shock on top of Covid-19.

Morrison himself wasn't caught by surprise.

In January, amid the bedlam of Omicron, he had received a secret intelligence briefing from the Office of National Intelligence about the likelihood that Russian president Vladimir Putin would mount an invasion of Ukraine. Shearer, as head of ONI and the nation's chief intelligence official, had briefed him on the latest assessments, which were that an invasion was looking 'probable'.

Morrison was among the first leaders to draw China into a nexus of Russian aggression with Beijing's refusal to condemn the invasion. His prior warnings about the emerging threats to global democracy were realised with the sound of cannon fire and missile strikes over Eastern Europe.

More than two years earlier, he had cautioned that western democracies and the freedoms they upheld were being challenged in a way that had not been experienced since the Cold War. He had informed G7 leaders about China's behaviour and he had warned Trump personally against a détente with Putin.

This was yet another cataclysmic event, a hot-war in a cold-war context, with global repercussions. There were the human dimensions of war of course. But there were the international economic and strategic consequences for a world that was only just emerging from the worst ravages of the pandemic.

There was also the domestic political dimension. Morrison drew Australia quickly and demonstrably into the conflict, with more than $120 million in military aide to Ukraine, including missiles and armoured vehicles, on top of economic sanctions and medical equipment.

This would all feed into the government's narrative as a federal election approached, that the world had just become an even more uncertain and dangerous place, and now would not be the time for voters to change horses.

*

Floods

On Sunday morning, 27 February 2022, Morrison woke early at home to prepare for a church service in his electorate. He planned to lead prayers dedicated to Ukraine. With the family in tow, he was also scheduled to attend a service later that morning at St Andrew's Ukrainian Catholic church at Lidcombe, in Sydney's western suburbs.

When one of his daughters got up feeling sick, he tested himself and his family for Covid, just to be safe.

They all returned negative results.

Feeling fine himself, he didn't give it a second thought when later that afternoon he headed off to the airport to fly to Brisbane. He was set to deliver a national security speech the following day to the Queensland Media Club.

But within minutes of boarding the plane, Louw leaned across from an adjoining seat to tell him he had just cancelled all his Brisbane events, including a series of party fundraisers.

'I've got a speech to deliver tomorrow,' Morrison told him.

'We've cancelled that too,' said Louw.

'Well, what am I doing in Brisbane then?'

Morrison was insisting that he would be giving the speech until Louw told him about the rapidly unfolding weather event, and how the Queensland Media Club could well be underwater by the following day.

It was only just then becoming apparent how bad the floods in south-east Queensland and northern New South Wales could get.

The trip to Queensland changed instantly, becoming a series of emergency briefings and site visits related to the unfolding flood disaster.

By Monday, as the flood situation worsened and spread to northern New South Wales, he headed back to Canberra, where the first item on his agenda was another flood briefing.

Back in his office, he confided in Louw that he wasn't feeling the best. 'I'm not feeling well,' he told his executive officer. 'Don't worry, I don't have Covid, I've done a test.'

To shake off whatever ailment he thought he had, Morrison returned to The Lodge and went for a swim.

The following morning, Tuesday, the PM was still feeling crook. He gave himself another test, which again returned a negative result, and then held a three-hour meeting of the national security committee, with Defence minister Peter Dutton, Home Affairs minister Karen Andrews, Josh Frydenberg and Ben Morton all attending in person. Morton would test positive the following day.

The meeting was to finalise Australia's initial military and humanitarian support package for Ukraine.

With Morrison spluttering his way through a press conference held in his courtyard later that day, Carswell, realising his boss was struggling, carried out a small table with a glass of water on it.

Morrison assumed he had a non-Covid bug and carried on. After the press conference, he flew to Sydney for a series of meetings including more updates on the flood disaster, which was worsening by the hour.

By late afternoon, his condition worsened. Louw walked in to find his boss bent over at his desk, coughing uncontrollably. Morrison was about to leave to drive back to Kirribilli and prepare for an event that evening at the Sydney Opera House, the building set to be illuminated in the colours of the Ukrainian flag.

'I really don't feel well at all,' Morrison told him.

'Sorry, but it really seems like you have Covid,' Louw told him. 'You should probably consider having another test when you get home.'

At home, he called for a nurse to conduct a PCR test under the service contracted for all parliamentarians.

At 7.36pm, the Canberra press gallery received a message via WhatsApp: the PM was no longer attending the Opera House event.

At 11.24pm, his office issued a media release confirming that Morrison had indeed contracted the virus.[4]

Meanwhile, unprecedented rains deluged south-east Queensland and northern New South Wales. No one could have predicted this 1-in-500-year flood event that would take 24 lives, destroy the livelihoods of thousands of people and wipe $10 billion from economic activity in just the first quarter of 2022.

When Morrison finally emerged from quarantine and headed to the flood zone, the spectre of the summer bushfires of 2019/2020 followed him up to Lismore in northern New South Wales.

Floods, war and plague.

It was if the world was going to hell in a handbasket.

*

Looking back

Morrison has reflected on all that had happened over those past two and a half years. A period that began with the domestic mega-fires of 2019/2020, got hit with a global one-in-100-year pandemic, then ended with an international geopolitical crisis and a domestic one-in-500-year flood disaster.

He described it the way he says people would come up and describe it to him:

'They would say,' he recalls, 'we can't remember a time when a government or a prime minister has had to deal with so many rolling crises whether it's pandemic, bushfires, floods, cyclones, and they throw in mice plague, and now we have Japanese encephalitis and lumpy skin disease and there are the ones you don't know about that I deal with on a daily basis.'

And there was the ever-present strategic threat posed by China's increasingly aggressive posture in the region and what that meant for Australia's security. Not to mention the outbreak of war in Eastern Europe.

Having taken a decision early onto try to stay above the fray of normal political combat and govern as the manager of a crisis, he had sacrificed his only defence to federal Labor's campaign to portray the government as incompetent, despite the successes the government had achieved when its record is put against that of most other developed nations.

Morrison quoted Bill Gates, Microsoft co-founder and one of the world's largest health philanthropists. At the annual Munich Security Conference in February 2022, Gates was asked if it was possible to prevent the next pandemic. He answered that, 'If every country does what Australia did [during the Covid crisis], then you wouldn't be calling it a pandemic.'[5]

Gates described the Australian response as the 'gold standard'.

'There were things to learn along the way,' Morrison readily admits. 'But when you go to the big markers, 40,000 people less dead, an economy with 250,000 more people employed in it, with an unemployment rate heading toward having a 3 in front of it, an economy that outperformed all the major advanced economies in the world, both on employment and growth, plus the vaccination rates where they are ... among the highest in the world ... when you bring all that together, it's hard to prosecute the case against the government.

'The only thing I can observe is that our critics are seeking absolute perfection and anything less than that is a failure, and that means the whole world failed.

'There is a view that the market, capitalism and business-led growth and entrepreneurialism, which has been able to produce the most amazing period of prosperity the world has even seen, is not capable of dealing with the pandemic and the recovery.

'We don't have that view. We want to get back to business-led growth.

'We have to get back to growing our economies in this way. If we think government is going to do it, if we think government will solve it all, we are kidding ourselves.

'My ability to prosecute the political case has been zero, because there have been too many more important things to do.'

*

Since the Morrison government's election in May 2019, there had been three enduring themes. Natural disasters, the pandemic and the great strategic challenge of the century, the arc of autocracy, as he described it.

The pandemic was not only bookended by disasters but punctuated by them. And the consistent theme that overshadowed all of it was China and later Russia, and the upheaval of the global strategic architecture.

For Morrison this was a greater and more enduring existential threat than anything else.

'We have been the most clear-eyed liberal democracy in the world. That is on show now. People were surprised that Russia invaded Ukraine, I wasn't. People were surprised that China has been working with them, and thrown them a lifeline, I'm not.

'Yet others are surprised.

'I hope that it has been a wake-up call for the world. I'm not sure it has woken up, I hope it has, but I'm not really sure it has.'

*

The Morrison government's tenure was that of an administration propelled into crisis from its infancy.

Any independent external observation could only conclude that it served the nation well, having presided over among the lowest per capita death rates in the world, highest vaccination rates and acted as steward of an economy that had bounced back stronger compared to all the major advanced economies.

It had also navigated, and at times led, the response to the global and regional strategic challenges that had emerged. Morrison had been right about Putin and he'd been right about Xi.

Putin's invasion of Ukraine had sent a tectonic shock through an already fragile geopolitical design, which not only vindicated Morrison's forewarnings about the rise of autocracy but justified

Australia's emboldened policy approach to the alteration of the strategic situation.

It not only brought Europe into the equation but broadened the divide between the West and the two dominant autocratic superpowers.

The new clash of political ideologies and the overt challenge to the postwar rules-based order, and Australia's early and decisive response to it, would be one of Morrison's enduring legacies.

Still, he had and has many and vocal critics. The government had doubtless made mistakes during the pandemic but set against what standards, Morrison would ask. There had been no guidebook.

Morrison's record would ultimately be judged against a broader range of domestic issues beyond the pandemic. Society's changed expectations and the decline of confidence in the two-party system weighed heavily against him.

When, on 10 April 2022, Morrison called the federal election for 21 May, he was optimistic that his government would be rewarded for leaving Australia in a stronger economic position than it was prior to the pandemic.

Despite having risen to record-high approval ratings for a prime minister at the start of the pandemic, by the time of the election he had become a deeply unpopular leader.

When voters finally delivered their verdict on three years of the Morrison government, it was a crushing defeat for the Coalition. Just as the pandemic had rewritten the rulebooks, the election result reframed Australia's political future, with voters lining up behind minor parties and independents in record numbers.

Morrison ultimately became a casualty of his own political failures. Nevertheless, along with Frydenberg and Hunt, he could still legitimately lay claim to steering the nation through the most extreme period of adversity for generations.

ENDNOTES

CHAPTER 1 • We've been here before

1. Barry JM. *The Great Influenza: the Epic Story of the Deadliest Plague in History*. New York. Viking, 2004. Also see: "The site of origin of the 1918 influenza pandemic and its public health implications", JM Barry, *Journal of Transnational Medicine*, 20 January 2004: https://www.ncbi.nlm.nih.gov/pmc/articles/PMC340389/
2. Centers for Disease Control and Prevention, "1918 Pandemic Influenza Historic Timeline", https://www.cdc.gov/flu/pandemic-resources/1918-commemoration/pandemic-timeline-1918.htm
3. *USA Today*, 23 March 2020, "Fact check: Why is the 1918 influenza virus called 'Spanish flu'?" https://www.usatoday.com/story/news/factcheck/2020/03/23/fact-check-how-did-1918-pandemic-get-name-spanish-flu/2895617001/
4. Humphrey McQueen, *The 'Spanish' Influenza Pandemic in Australia*, 1912-19, https://labourhistorycanberra.org/2018/06/the-spanish-influenza-pandemic-in-australia-1912-19/ (Originally published in *Social Policy in Australia – Some Perspectives 1901-1975*. Edited by Jill Roe. Cassell Australia, 1976.
5. NSW Department of Public Health leaflet issued in Sydney, April 1919, https://www.records.nsw.gov.au/sites/default/files/Exhibitions/WWI/NRS905%20[5_8097]%2019_57573.jpg
6. NSW State Archives & Records, see "Pneumonic Influenza (Spanish Flu), 1919", https://www.records.nsw.gov.au/archives/collections-and-research/guides-and-indexes/galleries/spanish-flu-1919
7. John Anderson and Geoffrey Searle, "Watt, William Alexander (1871–1946)", *Australian Dictionary of Biography*, National Centre of Biography, Australian National University, Volume 12, 1990, published online 2021, https://adb.anu.edu.au/biography/watt-william-alexander-9011/text15869, accessed online 11 November 2021.
8. Ibid.
9. National Museum of Australia, "Defining Moments, Influenza Pandemic", https://www.nma.gov.au/defining-moments/resources/influenza-pandemic
10. National Archives of Australia. "Influenza Epidemic. Border Regulations", NAA: A2, 1919/482 PART 2, page 22 of 57. Telegram from Acting Prime Minister to Premiers. 28 November 1918. https://recordsearch.naa.gov.au/SearchNRetrieve/Interface/ViewImage.aspx?B=48607
11. National Archives of Australia. "Influenza Epidemic. Border Regulations", NAA: A2, 1919/482 PART 2, page 31 of 57. Commonwealth and States of Australia Influenza Conference, November 1918 Resolutions. https://recordsearch.naa.gov.au/SearchNRetrieve/Interface/ViewImage.aspx?B=48607
12. National Museum of Australia, op. cit.
13. Curson, P. and McCracken, K. (2006). "An Australian perspective of the 1918-1919 influenza pandemic." *NSW Public Health Bulletin*, 17 (7-8), 103-107. https://www.phrp.com.au/wp-content/uploads/2014/10/NB06025.pdf
14. National Museum of Australia, op. cit.
15. NSW Parliamentary Papers, 1920, Volume 1, "Outbreak of Pneumonic Influenza in New South Wales in 1919", Section V, Part I, p. 158.
16. National Archives of Australia. "Influenza Epidemic. Border Regulations", NAA: A2, 1919/482 PART 1, p.8 of 14. Telegram from Tasmanian Premier to Acting

Prime Minister, 14 January 1919. https://recordsearch.naa.gov.au/SearchNRetrieve/Interface/ViewImage.aspx?B=48606
17. Ibid, pp. 2 and 7 of 14.
18. NSW Government Gazette, 28 January 1919
19. NSW State Archives and Records, "Pneumonic Influenza (Spanish Flu), 1919" https://www.records.nsw.gov.au/archives/collections-and-research/guides-and-indexes/galleries/spanish-flu-1919
20. "To the people of New South Wales", The *Sydney Morning Herald*, 3 February 1919, p.5, https://trove.nla.gov.au/newspaper/article/15823213/1256670 Accessed 23 February 2022.
21. McQueen, op. cit.
22. National Archives, op.cit., telegram from Watt to Lawson, 6 February 1919.
23. McQueen, op. cit.
24. National Archives, op. cit. Telegram from Watt to Theodore, 30 January 1919.
25. Ibid, telegram from Hunter to Watt, 1 February 1919.
26. Ibid, telegram from Watt to Hunter, 3 February 1919.
27. Ibid, advice from Macandie to Watt.
28. Ibid, telegram from Hunter to Watt, 5 February 1919.
29. Ibid, telegram from Cumpston to Watt, 29 January 1919.
30. Ibid, telegrams between Postmaster-General's Department and Secretary of Prime Minister's Department. 18 February 1919.
31. Ibid.
32. Ibid, Memorandum from Commonwealth Quarantine Service, 12 February 1919.
33. "Report of the Director-General of Public Health [Robert T. Paton] to the Honourable the Minister of Public Health", 27 April 1920, https://webarchive.nla.gov.au/awa/20080410052741/http://pandora.nla.gov.au/pan/83132/20080410-1521/influenza_report_full_3-5.pdf
34. Ibid.
35. NSW State Archives and Records, op.cit.
36. Curson and McCracken, op. cit.

CHAPTER 2 • A day from hell

1. Commonwealth Parliamentary Library, "COVID-19: a chronology of Australian Government announcements (up until 30 June 2020)", 23 June 2021. https://www.aph.gov.au/About_Parliament/Parliamentary_Departments/Parliamentary_Library/pubs/rp/rp2021/Chronologies/COVID-19AustralianGovernmentAnnouncements
2. Nicholas Christakis. *Apollo's Arrow*. Hachette Book Group 2020, p. 39.
3. Ibid, p.38.
4. Centers for Disease Control and Prevention (CDC), press release, "First Travel-related Case of 2019 Novel Coronavirus Detected in United States" 21 January 2020. https://www.cdc.gov/media/releases/2020/p0121-novel-coronavirus-travel-case.html
5. *The Coming Plague: Newly Emerging Diseases in a World Out of Balance*, Laurie Garrett. Farrar Straus & Giroux, 1994.
6. Commonwealth Parliamentary Library, "COVID-19: a chronology of Australian Government announcements (up until 30 June 2020)", 23 June 2021. Op. cit.
7. Prime Minister's Press Conference, Canberra, 23 January 2020. https://www.pm.gov.au/media/press-conference-parliament-house-0
8. Minister for Health, Greg Hunt, media release, 25 January 2020: "First confirmed case of novel coronavirus in Australia" https://www.health.gov.au/ministers/the-hon-greg-hunt-mp/media/first-confirmed-case-of-novel-coronavirus-in-australia

CHAPTER 3 • The twilight zone

1. *Sydney Morning Herald, Good Weekend*, Deborah Snow, 11 September 2020. "'I was getting about 1000 messages a day": why Greg Hunt gave up running for a while: https://www.smh.com.au/politics/federal/i-was-getting-about-1000-messages-a-day-why-greg-hunt-gave-up-running-for-a-while-20200806-p55j9s.html
2. Statement on the second meeting of the International Health Regulations (2005) Emergency Committee regarding the outbreak of novel coronavirus (2019-nCoV), 30 January 2020. https://www.who.int/news/item/30-01-2020-statement-on-the-second-meeting-of-the-international-health-regulations-(2005)-emergency-committee-regarding-the-outbreak-of-novel-coronavirus-(2019-ncov)
3. Prime Minister's Press Conference, Canberra, 27 February 2020. https://www.pm.gov.au/media/press-conference-australian-parliament-house-4

4. Department of Home Affairs, Parliamentary Inquiry, Written Question on Notice, Select Committee on COVID-19. QoN Number: CV19-56. May 2020. https://www.aph.gov.au/DocumentStore.ashx?id=c6cac43a-f480-49dd-acfc-d15d648a95cb

CHAPTER 4 • 'Forget about the surplus'

1. Prime Minister's Press Conference, Canberra, 3 March 2020: https://www.pm.gov.au/media/press-conference-australian-parliament-house-act-6
2. Minutes of the Monetary Policy Meeting of the Reserve Bank Board, 3 March 2020, https://www.rba.gov.au/monetary-policy/rba-board-minutes/2020/2020-03-03.html
3. Prime Minister's speech to *AFR* Business Summit, 10 March 2020. https://www.pm.gov.au/media/speech-afr-business-summit-sydney-nsw
4. Prime Minister's Press Conference, Canberra, 12 March 2020, announcing JobSeeker: https://www.pm.gov.au/media/press-conference-parliament-house-4
5. Prime Minister's Address to the Nation, 12 March 2020. https://www.pm.gov.au/media/address-nation

CHAPTER 5 • Covid kills COAG

1. Press conference with prime minister, premiers and chief ministers: Parramatta, NSW: 13 March 2020. https://www.pm.gov.au/media/press-conference-premiers-and-chief-ministers-parramatta-nsw
2. Media statement, "Minister for Home Affairs, Coronavirus update", 13 March 2020. https://www.pm.gov.au/media/statement-minister-home-affairs-coronavirus-update
3. Sky News Afternoon Agenda, 16 March 2020. Interview with Anthony Albanese. https://anthonyalbanese.com.au/anthony-albanese-transcript-television-interview-sky-news-afternoon-agenda-monday-16-march-2020
4. *Sunday Herald Sun*, 15 March 2020. "Coronavirus crisis: Eight new cases of COVID-19 in Victoria", Tamsin Rose, Nick D'Urbano and Mandy Squires. https://www.heraldsun.com.au/news/victoria/coronavirus-chaos-daily-life-grinds-to-a-halt-as-footy-events-and-school-cancelled/news-story/f02e58c0133b3959f28e6db8909a8576
5. ABC News, "Online sales halted, supermarket shelves stripped bare as shoppers prepare for coronavirus quarantine", Elise Kinsella, 16 March 2020. https://www.abc.net.au/news/2020-03-16/coronavirus-shopping-strips-supermarket-shelves-bare/12057924

CHAPTER 6 • Outbreaks on land and at sea

1. "Statement from the Australian Health Protection Principal Committee (AHPPC) about coronavirus (COVID-19)", 6 March 2020. https://www.health.gov.au/news/australian-health-protection-principal-committee-ahppc-coronavirus-covid-19-statement-on-4-march-2020-0
2. Report of the NSW Special Commission of Inquiry into the *Ruby Princess*, Brett Walker SC, 14 August 2020, p.110. https://www.dpc.nsw.gov.au/assets/dpc-nsw-gov-au/publications/The-Special-Commission-of-Inquiry-into-the-Ruby-Princess-Listing-1628/Report-of-the-Special-Commission-of-Inquiry-into-the-Ruby-Princess.pdf
3. Ibid, p.112.
4. Latest statement on coronavirus (COVID-19) from the Prime Minister. "Prime Minister, the Hon. Scott Morrison MP, announced new measures and restrictions to protect the Australian community from the spread of coronavirus (COVID-19)". 18 March 2020. https://www.health.gov.au/news/latest-statement-on-coronavirus-covid-19-from-the-prime-minister
5. Report of the NSW Special Commission of Inquiry into the *Ruby Princess*, op. cit. p. 147.
6. ABC News, "How the coronavirus pandemic would look in Australia if Ruby Princess had never docked", Paige Cockburn 23 April 2020. https://www.abc.net.au/news/2020-04-23/coronavirus-across-australia-if-ruby-princess-never-docked/12172314
7. NSW Special Commission of Inquiry into the *Ruby Princess*, established on 15 April 2020. https://www.rubyprincessinquiry.nsw.gov.au/ Report op.cit.
8. Report of the NSW Special Commission of Inquiry into the *Ruby Princess*, op.cit. p.196.
9. Ibid, p.263.

10. Ibid.
11. Ibid, p.197.
12. Ibid, p.34.
13. Ibid, p.115.
14. Ibid, p.115-116.
15. "Coronavirus Australia: Gladys Berejiklian issues 'unreserved apology' over Ruby debacle", *The Australian*, 17 August 2020, Yoni Bashan. https://www.theaustralian.com.au/nation/coronavirus-australia-gladys-berejiklian-issues-unreserved-apology-over-ruby-debacle/news-story/f1219b1e00018f05036e605933dfee34
16. Prime Minister's interview on *Today*, 14 April 2020. https://www.pm.gov.au/media/interview-today-1

CHAPTER 7 • Things get serious

1. "Australians could be detained or forced into treatment to prevent the spread of coronavirus. Here's how", *ABC News*, 3 March 2020. Matthew Doran. https://www.abc.net.au/news/2020-03-03/coronavirus-ag-flags-rarely-used-biosecurity-powers/12020034
2. "COVID-19 Legislative response—Human Biosecurity Emergency Declaration Explainer", Australian Parliamentary Library, 19 March 2020. https://www.aph.gov.au/About_Parliament/Parliamentary_Departments/Parliamentary_Library/FlagPost/2020/March/COVID-19_Biosecurity_Emergency_Declaration The emergency period, commencing on 18 March 2020, was extended numerous times, eg Health minister's media release, "Pandemic emergency measures extended to April 2022", 11 February 2022. https://www.health.gov.au/ministers/the-hon-greg-hunt-mp/media/pandemic-emergency-measures-extended-to-april.
3.. "Stop hoarding or risk supermarket rationing, Scott Morrison tells shoppers", *The Australian*, 18 March 2020, Elias Visontay. https://www.theaustralian.com.au/nation/politics/stop-hoarding-or-risk-supermarket-rationing-scott-morrison-tells-shoppers/news-story/648e170de4e89ea4c7186dc02742d0c7.
4. Prime Minister's Press Conference, Canberra, 22 March 2020. https://www.pm.gov.au/media/press-conference-australian-parliament-house-act-22march.
5. Tasmanian Premier's Press Release, "Nation Leading Border Restrictions to Protect Tasmanians", 19 March 2020. https://www.premier.tas.gov.au/releases/nation_leading_border_restrictions_to_protect_tasmanians.
6. "Berejiklian to push for a full lockdown of non essential services in NSW", *Sydney Morning Herald*, 22 March 2020, Alexandra Smith. https://www.smh.com.au/national/nsw/berejiklian-to-push-for-a-full-lock-down-of-non-essential-services-in-nsw-20200322-p54cph.html.
7. Statement from the Premier of Victoria, 22 March 2020. https://www.premier.vic.gov.au/statement-premier-61.
8. Senate Select Committee on Covid-19, First Interim Report, December 2020. Interim Finding 7.1, in Chapter 7, https://www.aph.gov.au/Parliamentary_Business/Committees/Senate/COVID-19/COVID19/Interim_Report
9. Ibid.
10. "Explainer: what is the national cabinet and is it democratic?" *The Conversation*, 31 March 2020, Jennifer Menzies. https://theconversation.com/explainer-what-is-the-national-cabinet-and-is-it-democratic-135036
11. Statement from the Premier of Victoria, op.cit.
12. Prime Minister's Media Statement, 22 March 2020. https://www.pm.gov.au/media/update-coronavirus-measures-220320
13. Prime Minister's Speech to Parliament, 23 March 2020. https://www.pm.gov.au/media/statement-covid-19-0

CHAPTER 8 • Hibernation

1. "Supporting Australian workers and business", Joint media release by Prime Minister Morrison and Treasurer Frydenberg, 22 March 2020. https://ministers.treasury.gov.au/ministers/josh-frydenberg-2018/media-releases/supporting-australian-workers-and-business
2. "Economic Stimulus Package" 12 March 2020, https://www.pm.gov.au/media/economic-stimulus-package
3. "RBA slashes interest rates to 0.25pc in emergency cut amid coronavirus pandemic", ABC News, 19 March 2020, Nassim Khadem. https://www.abc.net.au/news/2020-03-19/rba-cuts-interest-rates-coronavirus-covid-19/12070494

4. "Government's $66 billion coronavirus stimulus package seeks to keep businesses afloat and workers employed", *ABC News*, 22 March 2020, Brett Worthington. https://www.abc.net.au/news/2020-03-22/coronavirus-second-stimulus-economy-federal-government/12078982
5. "2020-21 Budget announcement", Joint Media Release, Finance Minister Cormann and Treasurer Frydenberg, 20 March 2020. https://www.financeminister.gov.au/media-release/2020/03/20/2020-21-budget-announcement
6. Prime Minister's Press Conference, Canberra, 20 March 2020. https://www.pm.gov.au/media/press-conference-australian-parliament-house-act-20march
7. Prime Minister's Media Release, "$130 billion JobKeeper payment to keep Australians in a job", 30 March 2020. https://www.pm.gov.au/media/130-billion-jobkeeper-payment-keep-australians-job
8. "Coronavirus: PM redefines 'Whatever it takes' with $130bn wage subsidy", *The Australian*, 31 March 2020, Paul Kelly. https://www.theaustralian.com.au/nation/politics/coronavirus-pm-redefines-whatever-it-takes-with-130bn-wage-subsidy/news-story/c4aee610c935475b1585e9fd95567bd5

CHAPTER 9 • Flattening the curve

1. Prime Minister's Press Conference, Canberra, 2 April 2020. https://www.pm.gov.au/media/press-conference-australian-parliament-house-act-020420
2. Ibid.
3. "A Journal of the Plague Year: An Archive of COVID-19", led by researchers from Arizona State University. https://covid-19archive.org
4. Prime Minister's Press Conference, Canberra, 2 April 2020. Op. cit.
5. Speech by Assistant Minister to the Prime Minister for Mental Health and Suicide Prevention, David Coleman MP, to Members Policy Forum, Mental Health Australia, Canberra, 9 December 2021. https://ministers.pmc.gov.au/coleman/2021/members-policy-forum-mental-health-australia-old-parliament-house
6. Prime Minister's Press Conference, Canberra, 3 April 2020. https://www.pm.gov.au/media/press-conference-australian-parliament-house-act-030420
7. Ibid.
8. "Virgin Australia forced into voluntary administration, as Deloitte says 'there are no plans to make redundancies'", *ABC News*, Nassim Khadem, 21 April 2020. https://www.abc.net.au/news/2020-04-21/virgin-australia-goes-into-voluntary-administration-coronavirus/12167814
9. "World Economic Outlook, April 2020: The Great Lockdown", IMF, 14 April 2020. https://www.imf.org/en/Publications/WEO/Issues/2020/04/14/World-Economic-Outlook-April-2020-The-Great-Lockdown-49306

CHAPTER 10 • The Middle Kingdom

1. Address by President Xi Jinping of the People's Republic of China to the Australian Parliament, 17 November 2014. https://parlinfo.aph.gov.au/parlInfo/search/display/display.w3p;query=Id:%22chamber/hansardr/35c9c2cf-9347-4a82-be89-20df5f76529b/0005%22
2. *Lee Kuan Yew: The Grand Master's Insights on China, the United States and the World*, Graham Allison, Robert Blackwill, Ali Wyne. MIT Press, 2013, p.54.
3. Ibid.
4. "Xi Jinping heralds 'new era' of Chinese power at Communist party congress", *The Guardian*, 18 October 2017, Tom Phillips. https://www.theguardian.com/world/2017/oct/18/xi-jinping-speech-new-era-chinese-power-party-congress
5. "Xi Jinping: The Backlash." Richard McGregor. A Lowy Institute Paper. Penguin. 2019. p.10.
6. Ibid.
7. Ibid, p.13
8. "The Long Game: China's Grand Strategy to Displace American Order", Rush Doshi. Oxford University Press. 2021.
9. "Senior Defence official raises security concerns over Darwin port lease to Chinese-owned company Landbridge", *ABC News*, Chris Uhlmann and Jane Norman. 15 October 2015. https://www.abc.net.au/news/2015-10-15/adf-concerned-over-darwin-port-sale-to-chinese-owned-company/6855182
10. "Operation Fox Hunt: Melbourne grandmother Zhou Shiqin prosecuted after return to China", *Sydney Morning Herald*, Philip Wen, 26 October 2016. https://

www.smh.com.au/world/operation-fox-hunt-melbourne-grandmother-zhou-shiqin-prosecuted-after-return-to-china-20161026-gsalul.html

11. "No hiding the blunder as limits to China ties exposed", *The Australian*, 28 March 2017, Paul Kelly. https://www.theaustralian.com.au/nation/politics/no-hiding-the-blunder-aslimits-to-china-ties-exposed/news-story/90c026535f38a04e27d8e96ac73e0ff2

12. Foreign Policy White Paper 2017, Australian Government, November 2017. https://www.dfat.gov.au/publications/minisite/2017-foreign-policy-white-paper/fpwhitepaper/foreign-policy-white-paper.html

13. "Doorstop with John Alexander OAM, Liberal candidate for Bennelong" Prime Minister Malcolm Turnbull, 9 December 2017. https://www.malcolmturnbull.com.au/media/doorstop-with-john-alexander-oam-liberal-candidate-for-bennelong-9-december

14. "Launch of Australia's Cyber Security Strategy", Prime Minister Malcolm Turnbull, 21 April 2016. https://www.malcolmturnbull.com.au/media/launch-of-australias-cyber-security-strategy

15. "Sam Dastyari defended China's policy in South China Sea in defiance of Labor policy, secret recording reveals", *ABC News*, Quentin McDermott, 29 November 2017. https://www.abc.net.au/news/2017-11-29/sam-dastyari-secret-south-china-sea-recordings/9198044?nw=0&r=HtmlFragment

16. "Australia-China rift spills into customs delays for Treasury Wine exports", Reuters, Byron Kaye, Colin Packham, 17 May 2018. https://www.reuters.com/article/us-australia-china-treasury-wine-idUSKCN1II08N

17. "Huawei banned from 5G mobile infrastructure rollout in Australia", *ABC News*, Michael Slezak and Ariel Bogle, 23 August 2018. https://www.abc.net.au/news/2018-08-23/huawei-banned-from-providing-5g-mobile-technology-australia/10155438

18. Joint Release, Acting Home Affairs minister Scott Morrison and Communications minister Mitch Fifield, "Government provides 5G security guidance to Australian carriers", 23 August 2018. https://www.mitchfifield.com/2018/08/joint-release-treasurer-government-provides-5g-security-guidance-to-australian-carriers/

19. "This is what's really going on with Australian coal exports", *Australian Financial Review*, Michael Smith, 28 March 2019. https://www.afr.com/world/asia/this-is-what-s-really-going-on-with-australian-coal-exports-20190323-p516w4

20. "Suspicion falls on China after cyber attack on Australian Parliament — and it's not surprising", *ABC News*, Michael Vincent, 9 February 2019. https://www.abc.net.au/news/2019-02-08/australian-parliament-cyber-security-breach-blame-on-china/10795010

CHAPTER 11 • The long game

1. "Coronavirus Australia: Scott Morrison pressures WHO as China re-opens wet markets", Ben Packham, *The Australian*, 14 April 2020. https://www.theaustralian.com.au/nation/politics/coronavirus-scott-morrison-pressures-who-as-china-reopens-wet-markets/news-story/f9e7034b4893bbfe72fc949481775d85

2. "World Health Organization and China's response to the Covid-19 pandemic", Interview on ABC *Insiders* with Foreign Affairs minister Senator Marise Payne, 19 April 2020. https://www.foreignminister.gov.au/minister/marise-payne/transcript/interview-david-speers-abc-insiders

3. "China bristles at Australia's call for investigation into coronavirus origin", Paul Karp and Helen Davidson, *The Guardian*, 29 April 2020. https://www.theguardian.com/world/2020/apr/29/australia-defends-plan-to-investigate-china-over-covid-19-outbreak-as-row-deepens

4. "Changes to foreign investment framework", Treasurer Frydenberg's Media Release, 29 March 2020. https://ministers.treasury.gov.au/ministers/josh-frydenberg-2018/media-releases/changes-foreign-investment-framework

5. "China consumer backlash looms over Morrison's coronavirus probe", Andrew Tillett, *Australian Financial Review*, 26 April 2020. https://www.afr.com/politics/federal/china-consumer-backlash-looms-over-morrison-s-coronavirus-probe-20200423-p54mpl

6. "Tensions with Beijing escalate after Chinese embassy leaks private DFAT exchange", *news.com.au*, 29 April 2020. https://www.news.com.au/national/tensions-with-beijing-escalate-after-chinese-embassy-leaks-private-dfat-exchange/video/99dbe48cceb02da74484de54a476fb3c

7. Prime Minister's Press Conference, Canberra, 29 April 2020. https://www.pm.gov.au/media/press-conference-australian-parliament-house-act-290420

8. "Coronavirus: Trump grilled on use of term 'Chinese virus'", *BBC*, 18 March 2020. https://www.bbc.com/news/av/world-us-canada-51953315
9. "Barley, a problem: China threatens Australia with tariffs ", *Sky News*, 11 March 2020. https://www.skynews.com.au/world-news/barley-a-problem-china-threatens-australia-with-tariffs/video/cab3d91ca76cfb673992c519dec67ad. "'This is payback': China threatens to hit Australia with tariffs amid souring relations", Gavin Fernando and Colin Brinsden, *news.com.au*, 12 May 2020. https://www.news.com.au/finance/economy/australian-economy/this-is-payback-china-threatens-to-hit-australia-with-tariffs-amid-souring-relations/news-story/de42bad31405dae5d41bde3a1938d5b8
10. "Coronavirus: 'Trade war' fears as China suspends meat imports from four Australian abattoirs", Gavin Fernando, *news.com.au*, 12 May 2020. https://www.news.com.au/finance/economy/australian-economy/coronavirus-china-suspends-meat-imports-from-four-australian-abattoirs-amid-rising-tensions/news-story/9cc28264688dc1fe26725295b3e9eed9
11. "Understanding how China's tariff on Australian barley exports will affect the agricultural sector", Australian Department of Agriculture, Liangyue Cao and Jared Greenville. https://www.awe.gov.au/abares/research-topics/trade/understanding-chinas-tariff-on-australian-barley
12. "China turns to stranded Australian coal to combat power crunch -trade", Chen Aizhu, *Reuters*, 6 October 2021. https://www.reuters.com/world/asia-pacific/china-turns-stranded-australian-coal-combat-power-crunch-trade-2021-10-05/
13. "Covid-19 Response", 73rd World health Assembly Resolution WHA73.1, 19 May 2020. https://apps.who.int/gb/ebwha/pdf_files/WHA73/A73_R1-en.pdf
14. "China doubles down on travel warning against Australia as universities feel the pain", Kelly Burke, 7News, 9 June 2020. https://7news.com.au/politics/world-politics/china-doubles-down-on-travel-warning-against-australia-as-universities-feel-the-pain-c-1087444

CHAPTER 12 • It's the economy, stupid

1. Prime Minister's Press Conference, Canberra, 20 March 2020, op. cit.
2. "The Great Lockdown", IMF World Economic Outlook, April 2020: https://www.imf.org/en/Publications/WEO/Issues/2020/04/14/weo-april-2020
3. Treasurer's Ministerial Statement on the Economy, 12 May 2020. https://ministers.treasury.gov.au/ministers/josh-frydenberg-2018/speeches/ministerial-statement-economy-parliament-house-canberra
4. "One year of COVID-19: Aussie jobs, business and the economy", ABS, 17 March 2021 https://www.abs.gov.au/articles/one-year-covid-19-aussie-jobs-business-and-economy
5. Treasurer's Ministerial Statement on the Economy, 12 May 2020, op. cit.
6. "Covid-19", Ministerial Statement to House of Representatives by Health Minister Hunt, 13 May 2020. https://www.aph.gov.au/Parliamentary_Business/Hansard/Hansard_Display?bid=chamber/hansardr/809dc477-581d-4161-a8ca-c741a051ff95/&sid=0150
7. "Coronavirus: Victorians confused by PM's promise of an 'early mark' from Australia's lockdown", Alex Turner-Cohen, *news.com.au*, 2 May 2020. https://www.news.com.au/world/coronavirus/australia/coronavirus-lockdown-victorians-confused-by-pm-scott-morrisons-promise-of-an-early-mark/news-story/b71e444ff88f3f7e7203a151a669e6dc
8. Prime Minister's Media Statement, 8 May 2020 https://www.pm.gov.au/media/update-coronavirus-measures-08may20
9. "Newspoll: Support for PM soars, but Coalition flatlines", Simon Benson, *The Australian*, 26 April 2020. https://www.theaustralian.com.au/nation/politics/newspoll-morrisons-approval-ratings-soar-as-parties-deadlocked/news-story/437e53c44aeb20de354ed1fa46cffc4e
10. "Coronavirus Australia: suicide's toll far higher than virus", Simon Benson, *The Australian*, 7 May 2020. https://www.theaustralian.com.au/nation/suicides-toll-far-higher-than-coronavirus/news-story/25a686904b67bdedbdcd544b1cab7f96
11. Prime Minister's Media Conference 14 May 2020. https://www.pm.gov.au/media/press-conference-australian-parliament-house-act-14may20
12. ABS, "Labour Force, Australia" 17 February 2022 https://www.abs.gov.au/statistics/labour/employment-and-unemployment/labour-force-australia/latest-release#employment

13. "'Significant error': Treasury reveals much lower JobKeeper use", Shane Wright, *Sydney Morning Herald*, 22 May 2020. https://www.smh.com.au/politics/federal/significant-error-treasury-reveals-much-lower-jobkeeper-use-20200522-p54vkl.html
14. *WorkPac Pty Ltd v Rossato* (2020) 278 FCR 179. The case went on appeal to the High Court, which, on 4 August 2021, overturned the Federal Court's decision: *WorkPac Pty Ltd v Rossato* [2021] HCA 23, before Kiefel CJ, Gageler, Keane, Gordon, Edelman, Steward, Gleeson JJ.

CHAPTER 13 • The road to recovery

1. "Australia 'in recession', worse to come in June: Treasurer", Matthew Cranston, *Australian Financial Review*, 3 June 2020. https://www.afr.com/policy/economy/economy-contracts-0-3pc-as-first-recession-in-29-years-looms-20200602-p54ytl
2. "This is the recession we knew we were in, but we might already be on the way out of it", Michael Janda, *ABC News*, 4 June 2020. https://www.abc.net.au/news/2020-06-04/recession-we-knew-we-were-in/1231954. "Australia 'in recession', worse to come in June: Treasurer" *AFR*, Matthew Cranston, op.cit.
3. Ibid, Cranston.
4. *Australia in the World Crisis, 1929-1933*, Douglas Copland. Cambridge University Press 1934.
5. Ibid, Part II, p. 28.
6. Ibid, p. 73.
7. *Joseph Lyons: The People's Prime Minister*, Anne Henderson. NewSouth Press. 2011.
8. *The Forgotten Man: A New History of the Great Depression*, Amity Schlaes. HarperCollins. New York. 2008.
9. Copland, op. cit, p. 10.

CHAPTER 14 • We are all federalists now

1. Maiden Speech by Scott Morrison to House of Representatives, 14 September 2008, Hansard p. 348, at 350. https://parlinfo.aph.gov.au/parlInfo/search/display/display.w3p;adv=yes;orderBy=customrank;page=0;query=morrison%20Date%3A14%2F02%2F2F2008;rec=4;resCount=Default
2. Prime Minister's Press Conference, Canberra, 29 May 2020. https://www.pm.gov.au/media/press-conference-australian-parliament-house-act-29may20
3. "Secrecy laws don't apply to national cabinet: judge", *Australian Financial Review*, Ronald Mizen, 5 August 2021. https://www.afr.com/politics/federal/secrecy-laws-don-t-apply-to-national-cabinet-judge-20210805-p58g9n
4. "Public Health Emergency declared in Tasmania", *Mercury*, Kasey Wilkins, 17 March 2020. https://www.themercury.com.au/news/coronavirus/tasmanian-public-health-emergency-set-to-be-declared-this-afternoon/news-story/942f68315bf5f1bb6f725c982fe192b9
5. NT Government, "Securing the borders to protect Territorians", 21 March 2020. https://industry.nt.gov.au/news/2020/march/business-update-securing-the-borders-to-protect-territorians
6. SA Premier's Media Release, "South Australia's borders to close", 22 March 2020. https://www.premier.sa.gov.au/news/media-releases/news/south-australias-borders-to-close
7. WA Premier's Media Statement, "New border controls to help protect Western Australia", 22 March 2020. https://www.mediastatements.wa.gov.au/Pages/McGowan/2020/03/New-border-controls-to-help-protect-Western-Australia.aspx
8. Queensland Premier's Media Statement, "Border control slows virus spread", 24 March 2020. https://statements.qld.gov.au/statements/89585
9. NSW Government, "NSW and Victorian border closures", 7 July 2020. https://www.nsw.gov.au/news/nsw-and-victorian-border-closures
10. Queensland Premier's Media Statement, op.cit.
11. "Scott Morrison says border closures have some 'heartbreaking' consequences", Latika Bourke, *Sydney Morning Herald*, 28 August 2020. https://www.smh.com.au/politics/federal/scott-morrison-says-border-closures-have-some-heartbreaking-consequences-20200827-p55q2m.html
12. "Queensland Premier Annastacia Palaszczuk to create border exemption unit", Sarah Elks and Geoff Chambers, *The Australian*, 31 August 2020. https://www.theaustralian.com.au/nation/politics/show-compassion-frydenberg-slams-cruel-border-closures/news-story/cbfb2b34ae15bbad2a914a49b6edfccb

13. "Annastacia Palaszczuk wins government in Queensland, making history", Kate McKenna and Lily Nothling, *ABC News*, 1 November 2020. https://www.abc.net.au/news/2020-11-01/qld-state-election-labor-wins-annastacia-palaszczuk-elected/12834982

14. "WA to open almost all intrastate borders", *AAP*, 25 May 2020 https://www.9news.com.au/national/wa-to-open-almost-all-intrastate-borders/d55066e5-c499-48b2-84b0-a5ae99aafb72

15. "Clive Palmer launches high court challenge to Queensland coronavirus border closure", Ben Smee, *Guardian*, 28 May 2020. https://www.theguardian.com/australia-news/2020/may/28/clive-palmer-launches-high-court-challenge-to-queensland-coronavirus-border-closure

16. "Commonwealth withdraws from Clive Palmer border case, Prime Minister's letter to WA Premier reveals", James Carmody, *ABC News*, 2 August 2020. https://www.abc.net.au/news/2020-08-02/government-removes-support-for-clive-palmers-push-to-open-border/12515948

17. *Palmer v Western Australia* [2021] HCA 5, before Kiefel CJ, Gageler, Keane, Gordon, Edelman JJ, 24 February 2021. "High Court says WA's decision to close borders due to COVID-19 was justified", *9 News*, 24 February 2021. https://www.9news.com.au/national/wa-premier-mark-mcgowan-says-clive-palmer-will-have-to-pay-the-state-after-high-court-border-challenge/fc81ff8f-c490-4595-8afe-6d052181adf1

18. "Covid-19 vaccine: Feds could do with shot of leadership on border issue". Professor George Williams, *The Australian*, 24 May 2021. https://www.theaustralian.com.au/commentary/covid19-vaccine-feds-could-do-with-shot-of-leadership-on-border-issue/news-story/48339ac349f7dbb5fa3571d2a1ed7735

19. "Labor's small-target platform risks large voter indifference", Geoff Chambers, *The Australian*, 31 March 2021. https://www.theaustralian.com.au/nation/politics/labors-smalltarget-platform-risks-large-voter-indifference/news-story/1bd5445839b1622c31e26392f4d3eb67

CHAPTER 15 • 'Xi's Chernobyl moment'

1. "China's National Security Law for Hong Kong: Issues for Congress", US Congressional Research Service, 3 August 2020. https://crsreports.congress.gov/product/pdf/R/R46473

2. Prime Minister's Press Conference, Canberra, 19 June 2020. https://www.pm.gov.au/media/press-conference-australian-parliament-house-act-20. "Australian Government and businesses hit by massive cyber attack from 'sophisticated, state-based actor'", Frank Chung, *news.com.au*, 19 June 2020. https://www.9news.com.au/technology/online/hacking/australian-government-and-private-sector-reportedly-hit-by-massive-cyber-attack/news-story/b570a8ab68574f42f553fc901fa7d1e9.

3. "Australia announces $10 billion plan to bolster cyber security in response to China threat", 29 March 2022, *news.com.au*. https://www.news.com.au/finance/economy/federal-budget/australia-announces-10-billion-plan-to-bolster-cyber-security-in-response-to-china-threat/news-story/09914c1c4235625375ab5fad1d4ab2de.

4. "China passes sweeping Hong Kong national security law," Helen Regan, *CNN*, 30 June 2020. https://edition.cnn.com/2020/06/29/china/hong-kong-national-security-law-passed-intl-hnk/index.html. "China's National Security Law for Hong Kong: Issues for Congress", US Congressional Research Service, op.cit.

5. "'We will simply disconnect': Mike Pompeo and the Australian TV appearance that caused a diplomatic storm", Daniel Hurst, *The Guardian*, 25 May 2020. https://www.theguardian.com/us-news/2020/may/25/we-will-simply-disconnect-mike-pompeo-and-the-australian-tv-appearance-that-caused-a-diplomatic-storm.

6. "Australian Prime Minister and State Premier Battle Over Joining China's BRI", Kalinga Seneviratne, *InDepthNews*, 2 June 2020. https://www.indepthnews.info/index.php/the-world/asia-pacific/3586-australian-prime-minister-and-state-premier-battle-over-joining-china-s-bri.

7. Australia warns citizens of 'arbitrary detention' risk in China, 7 July 2020, Reuters, https://www.reuters.com/article/uk-china-australia-idUKKBN2480K. "Hong Kong lashes Scott Morrison on extraditions", Glenda Korporaal and Richard Ferguson, *The Australian*, 10 July 2020. https://www.theaustralian.com.au/nation/politics/hong-kong-lashes-scott-morrison-on-extraditions/news-story/f614a3b1949e91efef14340cbdda69b6

8. "'If you make China the enemy, China will be the enemy': Beijing's fresh threat to Australia", Jonathan Kearsley, Eryk Bagshaw and Anthony Galloway, *Sydney Morning Herald*, 18 November 2020. https://www.smh.com.au/world/asia/if-you-

make-china-the-enemy-china-will-be-the-enemy-beijing-s-fresh-threat-to-australia-20201118-p56fqs.html

The 14 grievances were:

i. foreign investment decisions, with acquisitions blocked on opaque national security grounds in contravention of ChAFTA/since 2018, more than 10 Chinese investment projects have been rejected by Australia citing ambiguous and unfounded 'national security concerns' and putting restrictions in areas like infrastructure, agriculture and animal husbandry.

ii. the decision banning Huawei Technologies and ZTE from the 5G network, over unfounded national security concerns, doing the bidding of the US by lobbying other countries

iii. foreign interference legislation, viewed as targeting China and in the absence of any evidence.

iv. politicization and stigmatization of the normal exchanges and cooperation between China and Australia and creating barriers and imposing restrictions, including the revoke of visas for Chinese scholars.

v. call for an international independent inquiry into the COVID-19 virus, acted as a political manipulation echoing the US attack on China

vi. the incessant wanton interference in China's Xinjiang, Hong Kong and Taiwan affairs; spearheading the crusade against China in certain multilateral forums

vii. the first non littoral country to make a statement on the South China Sea to the United Nations

viii. siding with the US' anti-China campaign and spreading disinformation imported from the US around China's efforts of containing COVID-19.

ix. the latest legislation to scrutinize agreements with a foreign government targeting towards China and aiming to torpedo the Victorian participation in B&R

x. provided funding to anti-China think tank for spreading untrue reports, peddling lies around Xinjiang and so-called China infiltration aimed at manipulating public opinion against China

xi. the early dawn search and reckless seizure of Chinese journalists' homes and properties without any charges and giving any explanations

xii. thinly veiled allegations against China on cyber attacks without any evidence

xiii. outrageous condemnation of the governing party of China by MPs and racist attacks against Chinese or Asian people.

xiv. an unfriendly or antagonistic report on China by media, poisoning the atmosphere of bilateral relations

9. "Why China's infamous '14 grievances' list was a 'massive own goal'", Jonathan Kearsley, 9 News, 23 June 2021. https://www.9news.com.au/national/china-list-of-grievances-australia-backfired-on-beijing/0c67e39e-733b-45e3-bd67-d1d91c6b2467

10. "Afghanistan Inquiry Report", Inspector-General of the Australian Defence Force, 10 November 2020. https://afghanistaninquiry.defence.gov.au/

11. Prime Minister's Virtual Press Conference, 30 November 2020. https://www.pm.gov.au/media/virtual-press-conference-2

12. "Independent evaluation of global COVID-19 response announced", WHO, 9 July 2020. https://www.who.int/news/item/09-07-2020-independent-evaluation-of-global-covid-19-response-announced

13. "WHO's work in health emergencies", WHO Report of the Review Committee on the Functioning of the International Health Regulations (2005) during the COVID-19 Response, 5 May 2021. https://apps.who.int/gb/ebwha/pdf_files/WHA74/A74_9Add1-en.pdf

14. "WHO-convened global study of origins of SARS-CoV-2: China Part. Joint WHO-China study: 14 January - 10 February 2021", 30 March 2021. P.9 https://www.who.int/publications/i/item/who-convened-global-study-of-origins-of-sars-cov-2-china-part

15. "What We Know About the Origins of Covid-19", Drew Hinshaw, Jeremy Page and Betsy McKay, Wall Street Journal, 23 July 2021. https://www.wsj.com/articles/what-we-know-about-the-origins-of-covid-19-11624699801

16. Statement by President Joe Biden on the Investigation into the Origins of COVID-19, 26 May 2021. https://www.whitehouse.gov/briefing-room/statements-releases/2021/05/26/statement-by-president-joe-biden-on-the-investigation-into-the-origins-of-covid-19/

17. "The Wuhan Lab Leak Question: A Disused Chinese Mine Takes Center Stage", Jeremy Page, Betsy McKay and Drew Hinshaw, Wall Street Journal, 24 May 2021. https://www.wsj.com/articles/wuhan-lab-leak-question-chinese-mine-covid-pandemic-11621871125?page=1

18. "What We Know About the Origins of Covid-19", *Wall Street Journal*, op.ci19.
19. Final Report of the Independent Panel for Pandemic Preparedness and Response: "COVID-19: Make it the Last Pandemic", 12 May 2021. https://theindependentpanel.org/mainreport/
20. Ibid, p. 21.
21. Ibid, p. 4.

CHAPTER 16 • Re-enter the Quad

1. "Trump mobilizes US military to end unprecedented riots", *New York Post*, 1 June 2020. https://nypost.com/2020/06/01/president-trump-mobilizing-us-military-to-end-george-floyd-riots/
2. "Police in D.C. make arrests after sweeping peaceful protesters from park with gas, shoving", Tom Jackman, Rebecca Tan, Rachel Chason, Hannah Natanson, Perry Stein and Michael E. Miller, *Washington Post*, 1 June 2020. https://www.washingtonpost.com/dc-md-va/2020/06/01/dc-protest-george-floyd-white-house/
3. "Trump says it's 'common sense' to include Russia in G7", Reuters, 4 June 2020. https://www.reuters.com/article/us-g7-summit-trump-idUSKBN23A285
4. "Malaysia Airlines MH17: The Australian victims", *ABC News*, 22 September 2016. https://www.abc.net.au/news/2014-07-18/malaysia-airlines-mh17-australian-victims/5607188?nw=0&r=HtmlFragment
5. Prime Minister's Address, "Launch of the 2020 Defence Strategic Update", 1 July 2020. https://www.pm.gov.au/media/address-launch-2020-defence-strategic-update
6. "Lethal' capability in PM's \$270bn defence plan", Simon Benson, *The Australian*, 30 June 2020. https://www.theaustralian.com.au/nation/politics/pm-shoulders-arms-to-china-in-10year-270bn-plan/news-story/1d130db628bde59abd6a02726bb94327
7. Prime Minister's Address, "Launch of the 2020 Defence Strategic Update", op. cit.
8. Prime Minister's Speech, Chicago Council on Global Affairs, 23 September 2019. https://www.pm.gov.au/media/chicago-council-global-affairs
9. Prime Minister's Lowy Lecture, "In our Interest", 3 October 2019. https://www.pm.gov.au/media/speech-lowy-lecture-our-interest

CHAPTER 17 • The second wave

1. "'May be impossible' to trace contacts of Black Lives Matter protester with COVID-19", Paul Sakkal and Michael Fowler, *The Age*, 11 June 2020. https://www.theage.com.au/national/victoria/attendee-at-black-lives-matter-protest-in-melbourne-contracts-covid-19-20200611-p551jq.html
2. "How Victoria went from zero daily cases to the worst day on record", Jordan Hayne, *ABC News*, 10 July 2020. https://www.abc.net.au/news/2020-07-10/coronavirus-cases-victoria-numbers/12444034
3. "The culpability stare down with Daniel Andrews the PM refuses to cop", Simon Benson, *The Australian*, 12 August 2020. https://www.theaustralian.com.au/commentary/coronavirus-australia-the-culpability-stare-down-with-daniel-andrews-the-pm-refuses-to-cop/news-story/76ca9f605956c78f6a537d27a83e7091
4. Victorian Premier Media Release, "Judicial Inquiry into Hotel Quarantine Program", 2 July 2020. https://www.premier.vic.gov.au/sites/default/files/2020-07/200702-Judicial-Inquiry-Into-Hotel-Quarantine-Program.pdf
5. "Victoria emergency management commissioner backs Daniel Andrews' controversial ADF claims", Anthony Piovesan, *news.com.au*, 12 August 2020. https://www.news.com.au/travel/travel-updates/health-safety/victoria-emergency-management-commissioner-backs-daniel-andrews-controversial-adf-claims/news-story/aadd60bd70f7b70179b80ad9fc29afa4
6. Defence Minister Senator Linda Reynolds' Media Release, "ADF Support to Victoria", 11 August 2020. https://www.minister.defence.gov.au/minister/lreynolds/statements/adf-support-victoria
7. "COVID-19 Hotel Quarantine Inquiry Final Report and Recommendations", tabled 21 December 2020. https://www.parliament.vic.gov.au/council/tabled-documents/search-tabled-documents/details/3/10188?fromForm1. "Victorian hotel quarantine inquiry report unable to determine who made private security decision", Richard Willingham and Dan Harrison, *ABC News*, 21 December 2020. https://www.abc.net.au/news/2020-12-21/final-victorian-hotel-quarantine-inquiry-report-released/130028882
8. "COVID-19 Hotel Quarantine Inquiry Final Report and Recommendations", op. cit. Vol 1, p.202.

9. "Victoria reimposes coronavirus stage 3 lockdown on metropolitan Melbourne and Mitchell Shire after record rise in cases", *ABC News*, 7 July 2020. https://www.abc.net.au/news/2020-07-07/victoria-reimposes-lockdown-as-coronavirus-cases-rise/12429990

10. Doorstop Interview with Greg Hunt, Minister for Health, Melbourne, 15 July 2020. https://www.health.gov.au/ministers/the-hon-greg-hunt-mp/media/doorstop-interview-in-melbourne-0. Operation Covid-19 Assist, https://www.defence.gov.au/operations/opcovid19-assist

11. "As NSW opens to Australians stuck overseas, could more have been done to bring people home?" Josh Nicholas, *The Gurdian*, 15 October 2021 https://www.theguardian.com/australia-news/datablog/2021/oct/15/as-nsw-opens-to-australians-stuck-overseas-could-more-have-been-done-to-bring-people-home

12. COVAX, https://www.who.int/initiatives/act-accelerator/covax. CEPI, https://cepi.net/

13. Prime Minister's Media Statement, 10 July 2020. https://www.pm.gov.au/media/national-cabinet

14. Prime Minister's Media Statement, 23 October 2020. https://www.pm.gov.au/media/national-cabinet-1. "Final Report of the National Review of Hotel Quarantine," 23 October 2020. https://www.pm.gov.au/sites/default/files/media/final-report-national-review-of-hotel-quarantine_0.pdf

15. "Coronavirus (COVID-19) at a glance – 30 July 2020", Australian Department of Health, https://www.health.gov.au/resources/publications/coronavirus-covid-19-at-a-glance-30-july-2020

16. Media Release by Prime Minister, Minister for Health, Minister for Aged Care and Senior Australians, Minister for Youth and Sport, '$2.4 billion health plan to fight COVID-19', 11 March 2020. https://www.pm.gov.au/media/24-billion-health-plan-fight-covid-19

CHAPTER 18 • Aged care in crisis

1. "Army medics sent into Victoria's coronavirus-stricken aged care facilities amid staff shortages", *SBS News*, 29 July 2020. https://www.sbs.com.au/news/army-medics-sent-into-victoria-s-coronavirus-stricken-aged-care-facilities-amid-staff-shortages/79aaba8c-fcbb-44f1-a389-bc510d41411d

2. "Coronavirus: just two nurses on for 110 aged, says ADF", Olivia Caisley, *The Australian*, 17 September 2020. https://www.theaustralian.com.au/nation/defence/coronavirus-just-two-nurses-on-for-110-aged-says-adf/news-story/e246ad737b65c8071bb1595a5c558ad5

3. "Report into St Basil's and Epping Gardens COVID-19 outbreaks highlights failures", Clay Lucas and Rachel Clun, *Sydney Morning Herald*, 21 December 2020. https://www.smh.com.au/politics/federal/report-into-st-basil-s-and-epping-gardens-covid-19-outbreaks-highlights-failures-20201221-p56pcw.html

4. "COVID-19 outbreaks in Australian residential aged care facilities – National snapshot. Aged care COVID-19 data as at 18 September 2020", Australian Department of Health. https://www.health.gov.au/sites/default/files/documents/2020/09/covid-19-outbreaks-in-australian-residential-aged-care-facilities-18-september-2020-covid-19-outbreaks-in-australian-residential-aged-care-facilities-18-september-2020_0.pdf

5. "St Basil's Home for the Aged, Victoria" Statement from Ms Janet Anderson PSM, Aged Care Quality and Safety Commissioner, 27 July 2020. https://www.agedcarequality.gov.au/news/media/st-basils-home-aged-victoria-statement-ms-janet-anderson-psm-aged-care-quality-and-safety-commissioner

6. "Andrews' admission in Victoria aged care debacle: 'Wouldn't let my mum there'" Samantha Maiden, *news.com.au*, 28 July 2020. https://www.news.com.au/lifestyle/health/health-problems/andrews-admission-in-victoria-aged-care-debacle-wouldnt-let-my-mum-there/news-story/3b8e44b2dc58a99a680c45e9589fbc40

7. Transcript, Doorstop interview with Health Minister Hunt, Melbourne, 25 July 2020. https://www.health.gov.au/ministers/the-hon-greg-hunt-mp/media/doorstop-interview-in-melbourne-on-25-july-2020-0

8. "Australian first – aged care hub network rolled out in record time' Department of Health media release, 24 August 2020. https://www.health.gov.au/news/australian-first-aged-care-hub-network-rolled-out-in-record-time

9. "Review of Dorothy Henderson Lodge (DHL) COVID-19 Outbreak", Department of Health, Lyn Gilbert, 14 April 2020. https://www.health.gov.au/sites/default/files/documents/2020/08/coronavirus-covid-19-review-of-dorothy-

henderson-lodge-covid-19-outbreak-review-of-dorothy-henderson-lodge-covid-19-outbreak.pdf

10. "Newmarch House COVID-19 Outbreak [April-June 2020] Independent Review, Final Report', Department of Health, 20 August 2020, Professor Lyn Gilbert AO and Adjunct Professor Alan Lilly. https://www.health.gov.au/sites/default/files/documents/2020/08/coronavirus-covid-19-newmarch-house-covid-19-outbreak-independent-review-newmarch-house-covid-19-outbreak-independent-review-final-report.pdf

11. Ibid, p.2.

12. "Coronavirus (COVID-19) at a glance – 12 November 2020", Australian Department of Health. https://www.health.gov.au/sites/default/files/documents/2020/11/coronavirus-covid-19-at-a-glance-12-november-2020_0.pdf

13. "Royal Commission into Aged Care Quality and Safety Final Report", Tony Pagone QC and Lynelle Briggs AO, Vol. 1, p. 82. Report presented on 26 February 2021 and tabled 1 March 2021. https://agedcare.royalcommission.gov.au/publications/final-report

14. "GPs sound alarm over aged-care flu standards", Matt Woodley, 9 July 2019, *NewsGP*, published by the Royal Australian College of General Practitioners. https://www1.racgp.org.au/newsgp/clinical/gps-sound-alarm-over-aged-care-flu-standards

CHAPTER 19 • The way out

1. Treasurer Frydenberg, National Press Club speech Q&A, National Press Club, 24 July 2020. https://ministers.treasury.gov.au/ministers/josh-frydenberg-2018/transcripts/national-press-club-speech-qa-national-press-club-0

2. Treasurer Frydenberg, Interview with David Speers, ABC TV *Insiders*, 26 July 2020. https://ministers.treasury.gov.au/ministers/josh-frydenberg-2018/transcripts/interview-david-speers-insiders-abc-1

3. "One year of COVID-19: Aussie jobs, business and the economy - A timeline of significant COVID-19 events and statistical and economic insights over the last year", Australian Bureau of Statistics, 17 March 2021. https://www.abs.gov.au/articles/one-year-covid-19-aussie-jobs-business-and-economy

4. Prime Minister's Press Conference, Canberra, 12 March 2020, announcing JobSeeker: https://www.pm.gov.au/media/press-conference-parliament-house-4. Prime Minister's Media Release, "$130 billion JobKeeper payment to keep Australians in a job", 30 March 2020. https://www.pm.gov.au/media/130-billion-jobkeeper-payment-keep-australians-job.

5. Prime Minister's Media Release 'Morrison Government Commits Record $9B to Social Security Safety Net', 23 February 2021. https://www.pm.gov.au/media/morrison-government-commits-record-9b-social-security-safety-net.

6. 'Record debt 'is price of saving jobs, economy', says Mathias Cormann', Patrick Commins, *The Australian* 23 July 2020. https://www.theaustralian.com.au/nation/politics/record-debt-is-price-of-saving-jobs-economy-says-mathias-cormann/news-story/fc39eebddcb2e2a0a15043619f382a3a.

7. Media Release by Prime Minister, Minister for Employment, Skills, Small and Family Business, "JobTrainer skills package for economic recovery and growth", 16 July 2020. https://www.pm.gov.au/media/jobtrainer-skills-package-economic-recovery-and-growth.

8. "Unemployment passes two-decade high as job applicants 'inundate' employers", Michael Janda and Phillip Lasker, *ABC News*, 16 July 2020. https://www.abc.net.au/news/2020-07-16/unemployment-jobs-coronavirus-june-2020-abs/12460890.

9. Joint media release Treasurer Frydenberg with Finance Minister Cormann, "Economic and Fiscal Update", 23 July 2020. https://ministers.treasury.gov.au/ministers/josh-frydenberg-2018/media-releases/economic-and-fiscal-update

10. Hansard, House of Representatives, Motions, Treasurer Frydenberg, "Victoria: Covid-19", 27 October 2020. https://www.aph.gov.au/Parliamentary_Business/Hansard/Hansard_Display?bid=chamber/hansardr/c6887b2d-28f7-4f5e-b0bc-3c389ed767b9/&sid=0068. "Frydenberg praises 'magnificent' Victorians, slams Andrews government", *Sky News*, 27 October 2020. https://www.skynews.com.au/australia-news/politics/frydenberg-praises-magnificent-victorians-slams-andrews-government/video/73551db10e3064df86bd33eb30cfd615

11. Statement by Philip Lowe, Governor, Reserve Bank of Australia: "Monetary Policy Decision", 3 November 2020. https://www.rba.gov.au/media-releases/2020/mr-20-28.html

CHAPTER 20 • The race for a cure

1. "Greg Hunt wins inaugural Best Minister in the World award at Dubai summit", *ABC News*, 10 February 2016. He was Environment minister at the time. https://www.abc.net.au/news/2016-02-10/greg-hunt-best-minister-in-the-world-government-summit/7154244
2. "EU gives itself power to block coronavirus vaccine shipments to Australia", *ABC News* 30 January 2020. https://www.abc.net.au/news/2021-01-30/european-union-eu-coronavirus-vaccine-shipments-australia/13105718
3. "More than 700,000 AstraZeneca doses secretly flown to Australia from Britain", Bevan Shields, *Sydney Morning Herald*, 8 April 2021. https://www.smh.com.au/world/europe/more-than-700-000-astrazeneca-doses-secretly-flown-to-australia-from-britain-20210407-p57hcl.html
4. 'The vaccination programme done safely, done properly, which is what we're doing here in Australia. It's not a race. It's not a competition.' Prime Minister's Doorstop Interview - Sydney Domestic Airport, NSW, 11 March 2021. https://www.pm.gov.au/media/doorstop-sydney-domestic-airport-nsw
5. "How a secretive Pentagon agency seeded the ground for a rapid coronavirus cure", Paul Sonne, *Washington Post*, 30 July 2020. https://www.washingtonpost.com/national-security/how-a-secretive-pentagon-agency-seeded-the-ground-for-a-rapid-coronavirus-cure/2020/07/30/ad1853c4-c778-11ea-a9d3-74640f25b953_story.html
6. WHO Covid-19 Solidarity Therapeutics Trial, WHO Director-General's opening remarks at media briefing, 18 March 2020.
7. "Trump announces potential 'game changer' on drugs to treat novel coronavirus, but FDA says more study is needed", Stephanie Ebbs, *ABC News*, 20 March 2020. https://abcnews.go.com/Politics/trump-announces-potential-game-changer-drugs-treat-covid19/story?id=69693560
8. "WHO temporarily halts trial of hydroxychloroquine over safety concerns", David K. Li, *NBC News*, 26 May 2020. https://www.nbcnews.com/news/world/who-temporarily-halts-trial-hydroxychloroquine-over-safety-concerns-n1214341
9. "Draft landscape of COVID-19 candidate vaccines", WHO, 20 April 2020. https://www.who.int/blueprint/priority-diseases/key-action/novel-coronavirus-landscape-ncov.pdf
10. WHO Director-General's opening remarks on COVID-19 at media briefing, 8 April 2020. https://www.who.int/director-general/speeches/detail/who-director-general-s-opening-remarks-at-the-media-briefing-on-covid-19--8-april-2020
11. "Solidarity Therapeutics Trial produces conclusive evidence on the effectiveness of repurposed drugs for COVID-19 in record time", WHO, 15 October 2020. https://www.who.int/item/15-10-2020-solidarity-therapeutics-trial-produces-conclusive-evidence-on-the-effectiveness-of-repurposed-drugs-for-covid-19-in-record-time
12. "COVID-19 vaccine rollout update", Australian Health Department, 2 March 2022 https://www.health.gov.au/sites/default/files/documents/2022/03/covid-19-vaccine-rollout-update-2-march-2022.pdf
13. Prime Minister's interview on *Today* show, Channel 9, 24 July 2021. https://www.pm.gov.au/media/interview-allison-langdon-and-karl-stefanovic-today-show
14. "Understanding mRNA COVID-19 Vaccines", CDC Centers for Disease Control and Prevention. https://www.cdc.gov/coronavirus/2019-ncov/vaccines/different-vaccines/mrna.html
15. Health Minister Hunt Media Release, "$2 million for vital coronavirus research", 25 February 2020. https://www.health.gov.au/ministers/the-hon-greg-hunt-mp/media/2-million-for-vital-coronavirus-research
16. Release by CEPI, "The University of Queensland, CEPI and CSL partner to advance development and manufacture of COVID-19 vaccine candidate", 5 June 2020. https://cepi.net/news_cepi/the-university-of-queensland-cepi-and-csl-partner-to-advance-development-and-manufacture-of-covid-19-vaccine-candidate-2/
17. Release by CSL, "CSL to manufacture and supply University of Queensland and Oxford University vaccine candidates for Australia", 6 September 2020. https://www.csl.com/news/2020/20200907-csl-to-manufacture-and-supply-uq-and-ou-vaccine-candidates-for-australia
18. Health Minister's Media Release: "Budget 2020-21: Record health and aged care investment under Australia's COVID-19 pandemic plan" 6 October 2020. https://www.health.gov.au/ministers/the-hon-greg-hunt-mp/media/budget-2020-21-record-health-and-aged-care-investment-under-australias-covid-19-pandemic-plan

19. Health Minister's Media Release: "Australia secures a further 50 million doses of COVID-19 vaccine", 5 November 2020. https://www.health.gov.au/ministers/the-hon-greg-hunt-mp/media/australia-secures-a-further-50-million-doses-of-covid-19-vaccine

20. University of Queensland Release, "Update on UQ COVID-19 vaccine", 11 December 2020. https://www.uq.edu.au/news/article/2020/12/update-uq-covid-19-vaccine

21. Prime Minister's Press Conference, 11 December 2020. https://www.pm.gov.au/media/press-conference-australian-parliament-house-11

22. AstraZeneca Release, "AstraZeneca's COVID-19 vaccine authorised for emergency supply in the UK", 30 December 2020. https://www.astrazeneca.com/media-centre/press-releases/2020/astrazenecas-covid-19-vaccine-authorised-in-uk.html

23. Media Release by Prime Minister and Health Minister, "First Pfizer Vaccine Doses Arrive in Australia", 15 February 2021. https://www.pm.gov.au/media/first-pfizer-vaccine-doses-arrive-australia

24. Media Release by Prime Minister and Health Minister, "300,000 AstraZeneca Vaccine Doses Arrive in Australia", 28 February 2021. https://www.pm.gov.au/media/300000-astrazeneca-vaccine-doses-arrive-australia

25. Prime Minister's Press Conference, Canberra, 7 April 2021. https://www.pm.gov.au/media/press-conference-australian-parliament-house-act-070421

26. "China 'vax-mail' to swap jabs for access", Geoff Chambers and Ben Packham, *The Australian*, 24 March 2021. https://www.theaustralian.com.au/nation/politics/china-vaxmail-to-swap-jabs-for-access/news-story/21478d2f8c907fab9efabde82f4c4e5a

27. "Millions in Brazil thrown back into poverty as pandemic aid dries up", Jamie McGeever, *Reuters*, 27 March 2021. https://www.reuters.com/article/us-brazil-economy-poverty-idUSKBN2BI2OE

28. "Brazil Needs Vaccines. China Is Benefiting." Ernesto Londoño and Leticia Casado, *New York Times*, 15 March 2021. https://www.nytimes.com/2021/03/15/world/americas/brazil-vaccine-china.html

29. Prime Minister's Press Conference, Singapore, 11 June 2021. https://www.pm.gov.au/media/press-conference-istana-singapore

CHAPTER 21 • How Delta killed Covid-zero

1. "Where did Australia's first cases of the Covid Delta variant come from and how infectious is it?", Josh Taylor, *The Guardian*, 6 June 2021. https://www.theguardian.com/australia-news/2021/jun/04/where-did-australias-first-cases-of-the-delta-variant-come-from-and-how-infectious-is-it

2. "WHO classifies India variant as being of global concern', Stephanie Nebehay and Emma Farge, *Reuters*, 10 May 2021. https://www.reuters.com/business/healthcare-pharmaceuticals/who-designates-india-variant-being-global-concern-2021-05-10
   "Living Evidence – SARS-CoV-2 variants", NSW Agency for Clinical Innovation, COVID-19 Critical Intelligence Unit. https://aci.health.nsw.gov.au/covid-19/critical-intelligence-unit/sars-cov-2-variants.

3. "Framework for National Reopening" November 2020. https://www.pm.gov.au/sites/default/files/media/framework-national-reopening-nov-2020.pdf.

4. "Young staffer Brittany Higgins says she was raped at Parliament House", Samantha Maiden, *news.com.au*, 15 February 2021. https://www.news.com.au/national/politics/parliament-house-rocked-by-brittany-higgins-alleged-rape/news-story/fb02a5e95767ac306c51894fe2d63635. "Brittany Higgins breaks down on The Project speaking about alleged rape at Parliament House", Samantha Maiden and Ben Graham, 15 February 2021. https://www.news.com.au/national/politics/brittany-higgins-breaks-down-on-the-project-speaking-about-alleged-rape-at-parliament-house/news-story/3c54d90a75f5255ed8f531ee7f200626

5. "Scott Morrison, senators and AFP told of historical rape allegation against Cabinet Minister", Louise Milligan, *ABC News/ Four Corners*, 26 February 2021. https://www.abc.net.au/news/2021-02-26/pm-senators-afp-told-historical-rape-allegation-cabinet-minister/13197248.

6. "Bursting the Canberra Bubble", *ABC Four Corners*, 8 March 2021 https://www.abc.net.au/4corners/bursting-the-canberra-bubble/13227810.

7. "Disbelief over Scott Morrison's comments on the women's March 4 Justice", Ally Foster and Charis Chang, *news.com.au*, 15 March 2021. https://www.news.com.au/national/breaking-news/live-breaking-news-investigation-after-toddler-found-in-toilet-with-stranger-at-aquatic-centre/live-coverage/21fb4fe982624a99939f764e44646406.

8. "Reynolds facing lawsuit over 'lying cow' jibe on Higgins", Tom Dusevic, Rosie Lewis and Sharri Markson, *Weekend Australian*, 4 March 2021. https://www.

theaustralian.com.au/nation/politics/defence-minister-linda-reynolds-openly-called-brittany-higgins-a-lying-cow/news-story/eca38d5e36b8ecb6458fa33e89462d91

9. "Christian Porter takes 'appropriate action' by quitting as minister, Scott Morrison says", Amy Remeikis, *The Guardian*, 19 September 2021. https://www.theguardian.com/australia-news/2021/sep/19/christian-porter-takes-appropriate-action-by-quitting-as-minister-scott-morrison-says

10. "India Covid crisis: US tells citizens to leave the country", *BBC News*, 29 April 2021. https://www.bbc.com/news/world-asia-india-56932513

11. Health Minister's Media release, "Travel arrangements to be strengthened for people who have been in India", 30 April 2021. https://www.health.gov.au/ministers/the-hon-greg-hunt-mp/media/travel-arrangements-to-be-strengthened-for-people-who-have-been-in-india

12. "Joint Leaders Statement on AUKUS", Prime Ministers Morrison and Johnson, President Biden, 16 September 2021. https://www.pm.gov.au/media/joint-leaders-statement-aukus https://www.whitehouse.gov/briefing-room/statements-releases/2021/09/15/joint-leaders-statement-on-aukus/

13. "G7: Scott Morrison has historic talks with Biden, Johnson; leaders set to back PM's call on WHO powers", Geoff Chambers, *The Australian*, 13 June 2021. https://www.theaustralian.com.au/nation/politics/scott-morrison-holds-historic-meeting-with-us-president-joe-biden-uk-prime-minister-boris-johnson-at-g7-summit/news-story/7261bf0b48f086f342c073c02f830da5.

14. "'If you make China the enemy, China will be the enemy': Beijing's fresh threat to Australia", Jonathan Kearsley, Eryk Bagshaw and Anthony Galloway, *Sydney Morning Herald*, 18 November 2020. Op. cit.

15. Prime Minister's Press Conference, OECD Headquarters, Paris, 16 June 2021. https://www.pm.gov.au/media/press-conference-oecd-headquarters-france

16. "Scott Morrison's secret G7 side trip revealed", Samantha Maiden, *news.com.au*, 21 June 2021. https://www.news.com.au/finance/work/leaders/scott-morrisons-secret-g7-side-trip-revealed/news-story/e7b877726b59d22cad0eabf378043a7b

17. "ATAGI statement on revised recommendations on the use of COVID-19 Vaccine AstraZeneca", Australian Health Department, 17 June 2021. https://www.health.gov.au/news/atagi-statement-on-revised-recommendations-on-the-use-of-covid-19-vaccine-astrazeneca-17-june-2021

18. "ATAGI statement on AstraZeneca vaccine in response to new vaccine safety concerns", Australian Health Department, 8 April 2021. https://www.health.gov.au/news/atagi-statement-on-astrazeneca-vaccine-in-response-to-new-vaccine-safety-concerns

19. "Queensland's Chief Health Officer rejects Prime Minister's comments on AstraZeneca's COVID-19 vaccine for under-40s", Stephanie Zillman, *ABC News*, 30 June 2021. https://www.abc.net.au/news/2021-06-30/qld-cho-rejects-morrisons-astrazeneca-comments-covid-vaccine/100256022

CHAPTER 22 • The Delta wave

1. "CCTV captures 'scarily fleeting' encounter that resulted in Bondi COVID-19 cluster growing", Kathleen Calderwood, *ABC News*, 22 June 2021. https://www.abc.net.au/news/2021-06-22/covid19-cctv-footage-worrying-nsw-health-authorities/100231832

2. "The Woman who Saved Australia", Phillip Coorey, *Australian Financial Review Magazine*, 30 April 2021.

3. "Melbourne reopens as world's most locked-down city eases pandemic restrictions", Sonali Paul and Melanie Burton, *Reuters*, 22 October 2021. https://www.reuters.com/world/asia-pacific/melbourne-reopens-worlds-most-locked-down-city-eases-pandemic-restrictions-2021-10-21/

4. Sally McManus, @sallymcmanus, Twitter, 13 May 2021.

5. "Strollout chosen as Macquarie dictionary's 2021 word of the year", Stephanie Convery, *The Guardian*, 30 November 2021. https://www.theguardian.com/australia-news/2021/nov/30/strollout-chosen-as-macquarie-dictionarys-2021-word-of-the-year

6. Prime Minister's Press Conference, 21 April 2021. https://www.pm.gov.au/media/press-conference-berkeley-vale-nsw

7. Joint media release by Health Minister Hunt and Industry, Science and Technology Minister Porter, "Australia to develop onshore mRNA manufacturing", 21 May 2021. https://www.minister.industry.gov.au/ministers/porter/media-releases/australia-develop-onshore-mrna-manufacturing

8. National Plan to transition Australia's National COVID-19 Response, 30 July 2021: https://www.pm.gov.au/sites/default/files/media/national-plan-to-transition-australias-national-covid-19-response-30-july-2021.pdf
9. Prime Minister's Press Conference, Canberra, 30 July 2021: https://www.pm.gov.au/media/press-conference-canberra-act-9
10. Doherty Institute Modelling Report for National Cabinet, 3 August 2021. https://www.doherty.edu.au/news-events/news/doherty-institute-modelling-report-for-national-cabinet
11. Joint Statement by Queensland Premier Palaszczuk and Health Minister D'Ath, "Pause on interstate hotspot arrivals", 25 August 2021: https://statements.qld.gov.au/statements/93039
12. "Sealing states from the rest of the nation ruins lives, jobs", Editorial, *The Australian*, 30 August 2021. https://www.theaustralian.com.au/commentary/editorials/sealing-states-from-rest-of-the-nation-ruins-lives-jobs/news-story/341c894d3e4dcb5018dcb9e5e206e9f6
13. Statement by Dr Philip Lowe, Governor, RBA, "Monetary Policy Decision," #2021-19, 7 September 2021, https://www.rba.gov.au/media-releases/2021/mr-21-19.html
14. For example, "Peter Dutton hasn't missed opportunity to 'slam Queensland government' for lockdowns", *The Weekend Australian*, 4 April 2021. https://www.theaustralian.com.au/news/peter-dutton-hasnt-missed-opportunity-to-slam-queensland-government-for-lockdowns/video/4fc66781d8dd542ceaa8dcd8fd089532

CHAPTER 23 • A new world (dis)order

1. "Joint Leaders Statement on AUKUS", Prime Ministers Morrison and Johnson, President Biden, 16 September 2021. Op. cit., chapter 21.
2. "AUKUS alliance: Turning point for Australia", Paul Kelly, *The Australian*, 16 September 2021. https://www.theaustralian.com.au/nation/politics/aukus-alliance-turning-point-for-australia/news-story/f6e2cd9ef462b00e7817730b2f3eec4f
3. "Australian submarines to be built in Adelaide after French company DCNS wins $50 billion contract", Anna Henderson, *ABC News*, 26 April 2016. https://www.abc.net.au/news/2016-04-26/pm-announces-france-has-won-submarine-contract/7357462?nw=0&r=HtmlFragment
4. "Christopher Pyne confident 'we will reconcile with France'", *Sky News* 17 October 2021: https://www-skynews-com-au.cdn.ampproject.org/c/s/www.skynews.com.au/australia-news/defence-and-foreign-affairs/christopher-pyne-confident-we-will-reconcile-with-france/news-story/3f3722a254faf1362ed52c0a1fc7d183?amp
5. "Australia considered buying nuclear submarines from France before ditching deal, Peter Dutton says", Tory Shepherd, *The Guardian*, 17 September 2021. https://www.theguardian.com/australia-news/2021/sep/17/australia-considered-buying-nuclear-submarines-from-france-before-ditching-deal-peter-dutton-says
6. "Defence looking at alternatives to French submarines in case $90 billion program falters" Andrew Greene, *ABC News*, 2 June 2021: https://www.abc.net.au/news/2021-06-02/defence-contingency-planning-french-submarine-program-germans/100184644
7. Ibid.
8. "Integrated deterrence in the Indo-Pacific: Advancing the Australia-United States alliance", Jane Hardy, Assistant Secretary, Department of Foreign Affairs and Trade, US Studies Centre, 15 October 2021. https://www.ussc.edu.au/analysis/integrated-deterrence-in-the-indo-pacific-advancing-the-australia-united-states-alliance?utm_medium=email&utm_campaign=NEW%20RESEARCH%20%20Australia%20a%20key%20player%20in%20Bidens%20Indo-Pacific%20deterrence%20strategy&utm_content=NEW%20RESEARCH%20%20Australia%20a%20key%20player%20in%20Bidens%20Indo-Pacific%20deterrence%20strategy+CID_62e27c3b79eb50800865f72c52cbe537&utm_source=USSC%20Campaign%20Monitor&utm_term=Integrated%20Deterrence%20in%20the%20Indo%20Pacific%20Advancing%20the%20Australia-United%20States%20Alliance
9. "France Ending Nuclear Tests That Caused Broad Protests", Craig R. Whitney, *The New York Times*, 30 January 1996. https://www.nytimes.com/1996/01/30/world/france-ending-nuclear-tests-that-caused-broad-protests.html
10. 2017 Foreign Policy White Paper, "Opportunity Security Strength", November 2017, page 43. https://www.dfat.gov.au/publications/minisite/2017-foreign-policy-white-paper/fpwhitepaper/foreign-policy-white-paper.html

11. "Scott Morrison unveils Government plans to reassert Australia's influence in South-East Asia", Stephen Dziedzic, *ABC News*, 14 November 2020. https://www.abc.net.au/news/2020-11-14/australia-canberra-new-aid-south-east-asia-scott-morrison/12883088

12. "Scott Morrison declares AUKUS defence agreement to be a 'forever partnership' with UK, US", Dominica Funnell, *Sky News*, 16 September 2021. https://www.skynews.com.au/australia-news/politics/watch-live-scott-morrison-to-address-the-nation/news-story/01db3b063cd35789612164cfdbfa9d87

13. Anthony Albanese's Press Conference, Sydney, "Discussing the AUKUS alliance, national security and more", 16 September 2021. https://anthonyalbanese.com.au/media-centre/sydney-press-conference-16-sept-2021

14. "'China has changed': Albanese pushes back at Keating's criticism of Labor and AUKUS", Daniel Hurst, *The Guardian*, 11 November 2021. https://www.theguardian.com/australia-news/2021/nov/11/china-has-changed-albanese-pushes-back-at-keatings-criticism-of-labor-and-aukus

15. UN Climate Change Conference UK 2021, 31 October – 12 November 2021, Glasgow. https://ukcop26.org/

16. "Australia's nuclear submarine deal fundamentally changes our relationship with the world", Laura Tingle, *ABC News*, 18 September 2021. https://www.abc.net.au/news/2021-09-18/australia-nuclear-submarine-deal-aukus-change-relationship-world/100471990

17. "Statement on the phone call between President Emmanuel Macron and Prime Minister Scott Morrison", Official website of the President of France, 28 October 2021. https://www.elysee.fr/en/emmanuel-macron/2021/10/28/statement-on-the-phone-call-between-president-emmanuel-macron-and-prime-minister-scott-morrison

18. "Morrison and Macron speak for first time since AUKUS fallout", Courtney Gold, *news.com.au*, 29 October 2021. https://www.news.com.au/finance/work/leaders/morrison-and-macron-speak-for-first-time-since-aukus-fallout/news-story/3a2b49bc6a297bccc7fc112eecdfc4ad

19. "'Clumsy': Biden's swipe at Australia's handling of French subs deal", Adam Creighton and Geoff Chambers, *The Australian*, 30 October 2021. https://www.theaustralian.com.au/nation/defence/clumsy-bidens-swipe-at-australias-handing-of-french-subs-deal/news-story/caff39085f85c00778dcb335e4e493ad

20. "Australians Aghast as Joe Biden Calls Prime Minister 'That Fella Down Under'", Brendan Cole, *Newsweek*, 16 September 2021. https://www.newsweek.com/joe-biden-scott-morrison-australia-aukus-down-under-fella-1629680

21. "French President Emmanuel Macron accuses Australian Prime Minister Scott Morrison of lying about submarine contract", Andrew Probyn and Matthew Doran, *ABC News*, 1 November 2021. https://www.abc.net.au/news/2021-11-01/french-macron-accuses-morrison-of-lying-submarine-contract/100584196

22. "Scott Morrison sinks Emmanuel Macron's subs contract 'lie'", Geoff Chambers, *The Australian*, 2 November 2021. https://www.theaustralian.com.au/nation/defence/i-dont-think-i-know-emmanuel-macron-accuses-scott-morrison-of-lying-over-submarine-deal/news-story/55052c44c8918f68573fed2ed0572950

23. Prime Minister's Press Conference, Glasgow, 1 November 2021. https://www.pm.gov.au/media/press-conference-glasgow-scotland

24. "Former prime ministers must be better than this", editorial, *The Australian*, 3 November 2021. https://www.theaustralian.com.au/commentary/editorials/former-prime-ministers-must-be-better-than-this/news-story/99a5e447a0e295ed3b0b6aad50b822a

CHAPTER 25 • Omicron's curse

1. Media Statement by the Prime Minister, Minister for Foreign Affairs, Minister for Home Affairs, Minister for Education and Youth, Minister for Women, "Further steps to reopen Australia and secure our economic recovery", 22 November 2021. https://www.pm.gov.au/media/further-steps-reopen-australia-and-secure-our-economic-recovery

2. Media statement by Prime Minister, Deputy Prime Minister, Minister for Infrastructure, Minister for Infrastructure, Transport and Regional Development, Minister for Foreign Affairs, Minister for Women, Minister for Health and Aged Care, Minister for Home Affairs, "Pause to further easing of border restrictions", 29 November 2021. https://www.pm.gov.au/media/pause-further-easing-border-restrictions

3. "Time to come home, says Greg Hunt", Adeshola Ore and Max Maddison, *The Australian*, 2 December 2021. https://www.theaustralian.com.au/nation/politics/time-to-come-home-says-greg-hunt/news-story/67e5ed81c5b00887854da6199c2eb5b9

4. Health Minister's Media Statement, "Human biosecurity period extended until 17 February 2022", 10 December 2021. https://www.health.gov.au/ministers/the-hon-greg-hunt-mp/media/human-biosecurity-period-extended#:~:text=10%20 December%202021-,The%20human%20biosecurity%20emergency%20period%20 under%20the%20Biosecurity%20Act%202015,continue%20until%2017%20 February%202022.

5. Prime Minister's speech to the Sydney Institute, Star City, Pyrmont, 13 December 2021. https://www.pm.gov.au/media/remarks-sydney-institute-dinner

6. "mRNA vaccines to be made in Australia", Media Release by Prime Minister, Minister for Finance, Minister for Industry, Energy and Emissions Reduction, Minister for Health and Aged Care, 14 December 2021. https://www.pm.gov.au/ media/mrna-vaccines-be-made-australia. "Partnership secures Australian-made mRNA vaccines", Media Release by Prime Minister, Minister for Finance, Minister for Health and Aged Care, Minister for Industry, Minister for Industry, Energy and Emissions Reduction, 24 March 2022. https://www.pm.gov.au/media/partnership-secures-australian-made-mrna-vaccines.

7. "State border changes: what you need to know", mypolice Queensland, 10 December 2021. https://mypolice.qld.gov.au/news/2021/12/10/state-border-changes-what-you-need-to-know/.

8. "All passengers on two flights to Queensland sent into COVID isolation", 14 December 2021, *news.com.au*. https://www.news.com.au/national/ all-passengers-on-two-flights-to-queensland-sent-into-covid-isolation/ video/43180bd24bc2549622b8325ff520045e

9. Prime Minister's interview with Spencer Howson, *Radio 4BC*, 15 December 2021. https://www.pm.gov.au/media/interview-spencer-howson-4bc

10. "Covid flight passengers to be released after Queensland slammed for isolation rule", Samantha Maiden and Natalie Brown, *news.com. au*, 16 December 2021. https://www.news.com.au/travel/travel-updates/ whats-the-point-queensland-slammed-over-flight-isolation-rule/news-story/24dba75bbe7dc99107170d3a5a578148

11. "Test positivity rates soar as nation records record high daily cases", *The Guardian*, 29 December 2021. https://www.theguardian.com/australia-news/live/2021/dec/29/ australia-covid-news-live-case-numbers-nsw-vic-qld-morrison-vaccines-omicron-testing-delays

12. "Novak Djokovic Is Refused Entry Into Australia Over Vaccine Exemption", Matthew Futterman, *New York Times*, 5 January 2022. https://www.nytimes. com/2022/01/05/sports/tennis/novak-djokovic-australia-visa.html

13. "Djokovic flies out of Australia after losing court appeal", Sudipto Ganguly, Sonali Paul and Loren Elliott, *Reuters*, 16 January 2022. https://www.reuters.com/ lifestyle/sports/detained-djokovic-fight-australian-deportation-court-2022-01-14/

14. Prime Minister's speech to National Press Club, 1 February 2022. https://www. pm.gov.au/media/address-national-press-club-0

15. Prime Minister's Q&A at National Press Club, 1 February 2022. https://www. pm.gov.au/media/questions-and-answers-national-press-club-canberra-act

CHAPTER 26 • New threats emerge

1. Coronavirus (Covid-19) case numbers and statistics, Australian Dept of Health, https://www.health.gov.au/health-alerts/covid-19/case-numbers-and-statistics

2. "WA border opening date is March 3, as Mark McGowan announces new COVID restrictions", James Carmody and David Weber, *ABC News*, 18 February 2022. https://www.abc.net.au/news/2022-02-18/mark-mcgowan-announces-wa-border-update/100843126

3. Prime Minister's Press Conference, 24 February 2022. https://www.pm.gov.au/ media/press-conference-sydney-nsw-11

4. Prime Minister's Media Statement, 1 March 2022. https://www.pm.gov.au/media/ media-statement-7

5. "Bill Gates: 'If every country does what Australia did,' the world could prevent the next pandemic", Megan Sauer, *CNBC*, 24 February 2022. https://www.cnbc. com/2022/02/24/bill-gates-australia-covid-blueprint-could-help-prevent-next-pandemic.html

INDEX

ABOUT THE AUTHORS

SIMON BENSON

Simon Benson is the political editor and former national affairs editor at *The Australian*. Prior to that he was the national political editor for the *Daily Telegraph*. He has reported on state and federal politics for 18 years. He is the author of the bestselling 2010 political book *Betrayal: The Underbelly of Australian Labor*. Benson was awarded the Peter Hunt Eureka Prize for environmental journalism in 2001.

GEOFF CHAMBERS

Geoff Chambers is chief political correspondent at *The Australian*. He was previously *The Australian's* Canberra bureau chief and Queensland bureau chief, news editor at the *Daily* and *Sunday Telegraph*s and head of news at his hometown newspaper, the *Gold Coast Bulletin*. Chambers has worked in the Canberra, New South Wales and Queensland press galleries and covered major stories, elections and budgets across the country and overseas.